MEMOIR OF KEITHIE'S NUMBER SEVENTEEN

BY
STACEY WILLIAMS

GERRY & LORRAINE CASSIDY

LIVE ACCORDING TO YOUR RULES
AND THE WORLD WILL ADJUST.
NEVER ALLOW THE WORLD TO TAME
YOUR GREATNESS. LIVE OUT LOUD!

S. WILLIAMS
2022

This book is dedicated to my late father Keith Albert Williams who I would like to thank for always believing in me.

CONTENTS

INTRODUCTION

Memoir of Keithie's Number Seventeen is a collection of blog posts which tells the real life story of a teenage Jamaican mother. The story spans from age sixteen to thirty two.

The story was captured in the form of blog posts to make reading easier & not daunting for persons who aren't avid readers.

The blog posts will take you through the journey of love, lies, deception, betrayal, survival & breakthroughs. The story will also give you insight as to the potential end result once you choose to never give up & always believe that anything is possible.

HOW IT STARTED

WHO IS S.A.W?!

Stacey A Williams is the 6th child for her mom (washbelly) & the 17th child for her dad (almost washbelly). She has always striven for excellence from an early age. First in her class all through prep/primary school and no less than top ten throughout high school. She was driven by her circumstances to succeed. She was born & raised in the inner city community of Southside. She resided there until she was 13 years of age at which time she went to reside with her other maternal siblings at her grandmother's house in Vineyard Town. The move came as a result of the separation of her parents, a change that was very hard for her to cope with, but she did. Who is she now? A Banker, a self love enthusiast, a proud single mother to an amazing son & just an all round lover of life. Let us take a look into her life journey.

LIFE AT 34

So in my introduction I mentioned being shipped off to my grandmother's house to live. Let us pick up this post from there. 34 was my grandmother's gate number. Nobody ever says they are going to grandma, the talk was always "we are going to 34". What was it like living at 34? Picture it Jamaica 1998(in my Sophia from Golden Girls voice), a seven bedroom house occupied by three generations and filled to capacity. It was hard to have a moment to yourself, the house was always buzzing. There were at least twenty occupants. Imagine having twenty different personalities under one roof, you know there were bound to be clashes and clashes there were. But outside of the occasional clashes that would result in our neighbour across the street, whom we referred to as the "area leader" summoning the police to come & check us for disturbing the residential neighbourhood, we had a lot of good times which contributed to my life in a positive way.

My first cooking lessons started in the summer of 98 when the adults would leave money for my cousin and I to "run boat" so their dinner would be waiting when they got home. My cousin was 5 years my senior. The first time we attempted to make stew peas we ended up having to pass it off as peas soup. Go figure! We were also charged with the job of babysitting our younger nieces & nephews. Big mistake! One wrong move and they were in punishment. We had to show them who was boss. I was always the one handing out the punishment. I was feared and I loved it!

Another feature was the Friday games night. I learned very early that gambling was not my thing. Whenever I lost at bingo or cards, I would always cry for them to give me my money back. Next lesson learned early, losing was not in my DNA, so my aim was always to win at anything I attempted.

Then there were the Sundays when we would be given the coconut brush & the genie floor polish, I'm sure y'all know what was up. O how we hated our neighbours who had electric polishers, them standing tall & gliding it on their verandahs while we were on all four. When the left hand got tired, the brush was switched to the right. When the knees got numb you tried finding some kind of cushion, usually a piece of padded cloth. But after all this torture, you felt proud of your handy work when you saw how shine the floor was. Next lesson learned, the value of hard work.

Now as the last child for my mom, I think my older brothers saw me as their very own Cinderella. Man I couldn't catch a break! On Sundays in addition to washing my school uniforms, I also had to wash my brother's work uniform & undergarments. Man, your girl had to launder his big white Hanes briefs & I was not amused. With every scrup scrup (if you know you know), I would always say to myself "mi cah wait fi big & lef out yah". They told me that they were helping to mold me for adulthood. Look at the irony, washing machines are now our bestfriends. So all my scrups scrups were in vain. If I was ironing my uniforms, I had to iron their work clothes as well (sidenote I hate ironing now). It must be because of the childhood trauma surrounding this activity because if I dare put in a double seam, I wouldn't hear the end of it. Sometimes I put in the double & triple seams on purpose because I wanted to lose the job. That didn't work! Instead I got constant on the job training to improve my skills.

Overall I would say my life at 34 was great! So many experiences had, so many lessons learned, so many memories made & values instilled. 34 taught us all to live life to the fullest & to make the most of everyday. It also taught us that life was never about our start but more about our finish, so never give up. So I close by saying no matter what, NEVER GIVE UP.

Big Man She Want She Nuh Want Nuh Likkle Youth

Recently my friends & I had a moment of introspection. We were trying to understand why we opted to date & eventually settle with older men in our teenage years. The general feedback was that the decision was based on our situation at the time which would have featured some kind of lack whether financial or otherwise. One of my friends who shall remain nameless exclaimed that she didn't lack anything, according to her & I quote "me did jus fool & nuff". If you know my friends this should be easy for you to figure out.

During my high school life I could never identify with school boys my age. Their immaturity was stifling! I can't forget how quickly the news circulated among the young people at my church when my then boyfriend gave me my first chups. That boy got a piece of my tongue shortly after & it wasn't because the chups got upgraded to a french. I could not believe that he had made our chups a topic of discussion among his little friends. The school boys that came thereafter were no different, they were all packaged in immaturity and had a big "chat nuff" bow.

But what made me so much more mature than these males in my age group? Blame it on 34! Outside of my two young nephews, I was the youngest teenager living at 34. So imagine being surrounded by numerous grown folks, listening to grown folks conversation, fassing in grown folks business (yes my brothers & cousins had a lot of different female visitors, & two of my female cousins I at one point thought were producers or operated a studio, because most of their male visitors were entertainers). I was always in the know, nuttn nah pass mi. So by my estimation my mature nature was as a result of the living environment to which I was exposed.

Why an older man though? My honest answer to this question would be my circumstances at the time. You see whilst living at 34 I depended on my older maternal siblings & maternal uncles for support. My parents by this time were not working. Now you should all know how it goes when you have to depend on other people, one wrong move and that help can be gone. My help was gone with the wind at one point during high school & the reasons behind same were hilarious.

My first "cut off" came as a result of my brother dating a girl that the family didn't approve of because she was dating our cousin previously. So because we didn't welcome her with open arms, we all got disowned. There goes my weekly lunch money! My maternal sisters along with my other maternal brother tried filling the gap when they could. Shortly after this "cut off", my sister with whom I shared a room got pregnant. God help me! My other brother now thought it necessary for me to leave 34 & move in with him because my sister being pregnant had suddenly become a bad influence on me & I was somehow going to catch the baby virus. When I thought about moving to live with him & possibly having to wash those big white Hanes briefs again, my response was "mi nah go!" So my refusal to move house resulted in my assistance from this brother also being "cut off". So the struggle was on. My mother then started cooking & selling soup on Saturdays to try and generate an income to at least be able to assist in providing my weekly lunch money.

So it wasn't surprising that the first male that came along and dangled his cash in front my eyes without me even having to ask, I welcomed with open arms. I was lured by the comfort that his presence would now represent. After all, who doesn't like comfort? Comfort was my new bestfriend. I lacked nothing! My school fee was being paid, lunch money readily available & in my teenage mind, life was GREAT! What I failed to recognise in all this was how I was being groomed by this gentleman, that was the furthest thing from my mind. I also wasn't thinking about what would happen when he was ready to collect on his investment.

Looking back I can clearly see how my circumstances lead me down a certain path. However, I would never blame anyone for the choices I made, I stand by them and take full responsibility. This post is not by any means intended to paint a victim of circumstances picture, but rather just to encourage you my readers to ensure you do all you can for your children that way the person dangling the nice big rainbow candy in the streets is not appealing to them.

RETURN ON INVESTMENT (ROI)

We make certain investment moves for the expected returns. Sometimes the gains aren't what we expected them to be, sometimes they exceed our expectations & other times events like Covid result in an even more significant decline.

Similarly, I was somehow seen as an investment, something I learned years later when I attempted to exit the unhealthy situation. So yes I had now finished school, got my 9 CXCs & was now wondering what next? Many of my friends decided on 6th form & so I myself also applied.

I however knew that there was a strong possibility that I wouldn't be in Jamaica to attend 6th form because Christopher had plans for me to join him in sunny England where he was now residing. He had previously discussed his plan with me & had also outlined the benefit. He said there was nothing in Jamaica & I would be open to more opportunities in England. He went on further to say that there was also a shortage of nurses presently & they were paying for people to go to nursing school to bridge that gap. So my education would pretty much be free had I chosen to go in this field.

It all sounded like a very good plan & offer although I had no interest whatsoever in nursing. I can't even take an injection without having some kind of anxiety attack much less to go & administer one. But this was the year 2001, everybody & dem puss & dog did wah reach a foreign. So whatever the plan was I was going to work with it.

I remember the next move was for him to have a discussion with my mom about the plan. It was sold from the angle of doing what was best for me & giving me a future that her & my dad were not financially capable of. It was about not letting my potential go to waste. It was about helping me so that I in turn could help them (my parents). The song sounded very good! The melody was sweet.

After the conversation, my mother was pretty much in agreement. She knew however that nothing could be said to anyone about the plan just in case there was any opposition. There was one individual though with whom she shared it & he immediately objected. But was his objection coming from a place of genuine concern or did he have his own motives?

You see a couple months prior my sisters & I along with Christopher who was visiting at the time, all went clubbing with this same family friend who might I add was my big sister's high school crush while she was at Alpha & he was at STGC. So yea, we all went out & everyone had a good time.

A short while later he somehow saw it necessary to give me a review & also make me an offer. He started by telling me that prior to Christopher's departure he had seen him out with another female. He went on further to say that Christopher & I were nothing alike & as such it didn't make sense pursuing anything with him. The two comparisons he made was the fact that I was tall & Christopher was short, & Christopher was dark skinned & I was light skinned. Now even if I wanted to take him seriously I really couldn't after this statement. He went on further to say should I decide to stay & not leave for England, he would pay my way through 6th form & provide any other support I may need.

So you see I wasn't surprised when he expressed to my mom that he wasn't in agreement with the England move because clearly he too was trying to make an investment with hopes of collecting his returns in the near future. My mother on the other hand didn't have the insight that I had. She thought all that he was saying was because he had my best interest at heart.

So here it was there was a nice new big lollipop being dangled in front of me. Whilst it is very appealing & curiosity would push you to try & find out what it was like, I had already chosen another with which I had become familiar, knew its taste & the fact that it wasn't sweet right through. There were definitely some bitter & sour patches but the reality was that I knew it & so was not willing to take the risk attached to choosing a new one in fear that its taste could be even worse than the one I was already eating.

So it was settled! With my ticket bought & the same family friend escorting my mom & I to the airport, I was off to sunny England. England didn't disappoint at all. The drama started on day one.

LIFE IN ENGLAND

ARE WE THERE YET???

So after bidding my mother adieu, it was now time to navigate my way through the airport. This was the first time I was travelling. All prior trips to the airport was to go up to the waving gallery to see people off. I remember following the crowd, typical Jamaican behaviour when you're not too sure where to go. I remember being pulled over to the side by an officer who asked to see my passport & ticket, same was provided. She glanced through the documents & then asked me to follow her. I started wondering what the hell was going on.

I was then taken into this room. She went on to ask whether I was carrying anything on me. By this time I was even more confused, so I asked anything like what. She went on to say any illegal substances that a third party might have asked me to transport. I was now confused to the tenth power but I managed to reply with a very strong NO. She then went on to say that they would have to search me. So I went on to question what exactly would they be searching as I had no hand luggage. Next thing I heard was drop your pants. Now my sisters will tell you that they have never seen me without clothes because I am always hiding. Now here we have this stranger commanding me to drop my pants. I guess it was either comply or be denied access to the flight & so I dropped my pants as requested.

Once I did this she started patting my vagina. O wow, what a piece a madness was the thought that was going through my head. Then when she said stoop, I was like you got to be kidding me. Apparently by stooping she would be able to see any bulging. I remember stooping & she gave out what is that as if she had struck gold. She proceeded to touch my vagina again. Then she went oh you are wearing a pantyliner, yes ma'am I am. Then she touched again what is this puffing up? Miss that is all just my vagina, yes it has a little meat. I was finally given the all clear to go on my merry way.

So I was now seated on my flight awaiting departure. I ended up with a middle seat sandwiched between two gentlemen who didn't allow my ears to eat grass. As soon as one finished a conversation the other started. Even when I pretended to be asleep, as soon as I opened my eyes I was greeted with a big smile from the one to my left who somehow opted to watch me sleep & comment on how peaceful I looked. I felt as though I slept a million times & was still yet to reach my destination. The last time I opened my eyes & saw all these chimneys made out of red brick, I remember thinking to myself "Then a England this weh people a kill up demself fi go."

One of my row mates encouraged me to do a sprint when I came off the plane. So I asked him why? He said the immigration lines get very long & after they have admitted a certain amount of visitors they tend to turn back the rest. I was grateful for the heads up but I knew for a fact that this girl would not be running anywhere, not with my knock knees. I exited the aircraft & the gentleman was right. I saw people sprinting. Some were empty handed & others with rum & suitcase & a host of other things. I remember seeing one person fall but quickly got up & started running again. As for me, I was walking briskly & the fact that I opted to walk meant my row mate that was seated to my left decided to walk as well.

We got to the hall & the lines were indeed very long but they moved quickly. I noticed most persons were being sent to the side to sit on a bench. I was like oh okay those must be the people who have gotten through. So in my mind I needed to be sent to the bench. It wasn't until I got closer & could hear the conversations that I realised that the persons being sent to the bench are those who have been denied entry & would be sent back home on a flight later that day. Once I came to this realisation I was like God please nuh mek mi end up over di bench. It was now my turn to be questioned by the immigration officer. This was the longest two minutes of my life but eventually it was over, my passport was stamped & I was allowed entry.

It was now time to head outside to meet Christopher who was waiting for me at the airport. As I walked towards to the exit, I heard someone say "Excuse me miss." As I looked around I saw a police officer. You see my passport (the big blue book) was sticking out of the little bag I was carrying & so he was able to clearly Identify that I wasn't one of theirs. As he came closer he asked to see my passport. I provided him with same & once he saw the entry stamp he sent me on my way. I started wondering how could I have gotten this far if I wasn't allowed entry?! But I guess stranger things have happened & nothing is impossible.

So finally I was outside & the cold breeze bax mi hard & mi seh Jesus mi neva ready fi dah part here. I remember spotting Christopher & his in law who had accompanied him. We headed to the parking lot but not before I was warned that a old car run the place a England. So I was like then you leave Jamaica come a England come drive old car?! There it was! A red Fiat Uno I remember laughing to myself & thinking life here is definitely going to be interesting.

It seem as though that thought came too quickly because the next thing I knew the gentleman was getting a call from his wife from whom he had said he was separated. When he said hello I could hear her at the top of her voice "You think mi wouldn't find out seh yuh buy ticket fi di f*&$ing gal & bring har come yah?!" She then went on to say that his family had told her that I would be getting there sometime that day. He went on to say that he was driving & ended the call. The entire drive from the airport she called non-stop. I started wondering what the hell was going on? I didn't sign up for this? This wasn't the life I was promised, neither was it the picture that was painted to my mother & it got even more interesting.

HIDE & SEEK

So I had finally arrived at my new abode in West Norwood in London England. The house was a shared house & two of the other occupants were Christopher's brother & his girlfriend. The room I would occupy was one that you could have described as an attic room. If you stood in the bed you could easily have touched the ceiling. Not to mention the fact that you had to bend to get to one section of the room based on how it was shaped as the chimney was on the side of the house where my room was. It was an eye opener to say the least. The furniture was very ancient, the wallpaper was very ancient & the television was very ancient. I kept wondering how was this a first world country & why was Jamaica considered third world but yes I know the measurement for this was not based on the furnishings we had back home.

Now remember that Christopher's wife had been calling the phone non-stop. So clearly he had a fire to put out. So after I was dropped off I was told that he was going to get me some food & would soon be back. He returned hours later. He provided me with a phone so I could contact my mom to let her know that I had arrived safely. So now it was bedtime & trust me I was exhausted from the flight. So in the dead silence of the night I kept hearing a sound but I couldn't figure out what it was. It wasn't until I saw Christopher jumping up & acting crazy that I realised that clearly something was going on. So the sound I was hearing was the doorbell. Then I heard his brother's girlfriend Simone calling out his name from downstairs & saying "This is the same thing I was telling you that I didn't want here." Next thing I knew I was being told to get dressed & I saw him lifting up my suitcase & taking it out the room. Then I heard "Come with me." So I was still clueless as to what exactly was happening but nevertheless I was following the directives given. Next thing I knew Christopher was asking Simone to have me stay in her room with her for a little. She was not amused & kept saying I told you I didn't want this drama here AGAIN. The word again stood out to me.

So now I was in the room with Simone & I could hear a female's voice saying yuh think yuh smart, weh she deh. So it was now becoming clear that it was his wife that was outside ringing the doorbell & that she had clearly come in search of me. We could hear the arguing & then the arguing turned into fighting & when it became too much Simone went outside & told the wife she had to leave. She told her that they should take whatever issue they had elsewhere as they were disturbing her sleep & she had work in the morning. So they both left the house & clearly went to finish fighting at the wife's house as the next time I saw Christopher he had a fractured finger from being hit by her with a broomstick.

In the morning Simone explained to me that Christopher had moved back in with his wife & so him suddenly coming to sleep back at her house despite him having a room there, would raise suspicion. She then went on further to explain that prior to me coming, there was another female that he had staying there who the wife also found out about & it caused a problem. So now her AGAIN reference started to make sense.

She said she had told him she didn't want back anyone from Jamaica in the house based on some of the things that happened whilst the other female was staying there but he assured her that I was different. My heart was racing and was in a stiff competition with my brain. I started thinking to myself was this all a mistake. Christopher told me nothing but lies! Nothing is as it was made out to be. By this time I felt hurt & disappointed & had now decided that I am going to spend the one month that was stamped in my passport & then return to Jamaica. I was not ready for all the excitement that was now presenting itself & neither was I ready to be arguing with anyone over a man who misrepresented himself to me.

ON MY OWN

I eventually got a call from Christopher at which time I was told that he would be coming by shortly. I asked him what was I to do for food until he got here. As you can imagine by this time I was starving. He quickly said there should be some money in the room & I should just walk down the road & all the shops were there. Now this was my first day in a foreign country & I was being sent out on my own. I was reassured that it was a straight road, typical Jamaican direction. I was a little scared but if I was going to eat that day I had to put on my big girl panties & head on out.

So I followed the directions & eventually found the shops. The damn coins gave me hell when it came to paying but I was good with the paper notes. This was like a learning on the job internship. I eventually got what I needed & headed back in. Christopher would appear later.

As I had mentioned before he was now modelling a fractured finger. I queried what the hell was really going on as this wasn't what I signed up for. He went on to say that everything was good because the fact that his wife didn't find me at the location she is now of the view that his family got their information wrong. So I went on to ask at what point had he reconciled with his wife & why wasn't I made aware of this. He tried to convince me that it wasn't a reconciliation but was more about him getting his papers sorted out. His exact words were "When yuh hand ina lion mouth you afi tek time tek it out." I went on to ask why was I brought here if you knew your situation wasn't stable, his reply to which was because he missed me so much. I literally raised my eyebrow as I typed the previous line just like I did when it was said. Then he said & if I left you too long in Jamaica, I knew it would just have been a matter of time before you moved on. So the reality was that none of what was being done was in my best interest but rather in his!

I called my mom in his presence & told her about the drama & the fact that I was pretty much going to be dumped in a house with strangers while Christopher plays house with his wife. It was nothing like the dream we were sold & so I told her I was just going to stay the month & return home. He quickly took the phone & started going on about me throwing away my future because of people. He went on to say that he had sorted out the situation & there would be no problems going forward & that I just needed to focus on school. My mother, I guess knowing she didn't have the wherewithal to support me, encouraged me to just ignore the lady & focus on what I wanted to achieve.

So I asked Christopher what next? When was I going to register for school? It was mid September & most schools had already started. I was now being told that the nursing program was no longer free for international students & the cost was now £5000. I really wasn't interested in nursing anyway was my reply, that was your choice, not mine. So he queried what is it that I wanted to do & I confirmed my A Levels. So I was told that come the next day I was to meet someone at the train station down the road & they will escort me to the college to register because he had work. When I asked who I was meeting I was told his wife's brother Doug. Like WHAT THE HELL??? So my question was "Him nah go tell him sista seh mi deh yah?" His reply to which was no as he was not like that & they were cool.

So once again I was on my own trying to manoeuvre life in this strange place with little or no guidance. I wasn't even told I needed to purchase a pass to get on the trains. I was just told which train to get & from which station. It wasn't until I was kicked off the train at one leg of the journey for not having a ticket that I even knew I needed one. When I called Christopher to tell him what had happened he somehow found it funny & went on to say that most people didn't buy tickets once there were no barriers at the station. I really didn't want to be most people.

So three trains later & I was finally at the college. I registered for my A Levels & was told that as an international student the cost would have been £4000. I knew there was no way Christopher was going to pay this money but you see if my visa was to be extended, I had to enroll in school.

I completed my first day in England, not doing touristy things like I would have imagined but instead trying to figure out a life that I thought was already planned out & was just awaiting my arrival. I guess my expectations were a little too high. I quickly recognised that I was somewhat on my own despite the promises made.

So I got home & was in the kitchen fixing something to eat when Simone walked in & said "Suh a you did a write di letter dem & a send picture & mek war a bruk every minute." Had I had food in my mouth at the time I can guarantee you I would have choked.

STORY COME TO BUMP

What are you talking about? What letters? What pictures? She went on to say the ones you sent while you were in Jamaica. She said a lot of times his wife got hold of them & world war 3 got started. I was royally confused & in my confused state went on further to ask how did she get them because as far as I knew they lived separately & I was sending them to his address. She quickly said, oh you didn't know Sophia was living here at one point? Remember by this time I was just at day three enuh & the old houses just a tumble dung & lick mi.

So after I got myself together I replied & confirmed that I had no idea his wife lived there. So she said most mornings he would leave out early for work before the mailman came & so anything that came with his name on it, the wife would take possession of it. So she said she would read & then in the evening they argued.

Now you see the web that he weaved? He couldn't tell me not to write because then I would know something was up so his best option was to seek the assistance of Simone to try & collect his mail before the wife does. She described it as a rat race to see who could collect the mail first.

Simone didn't want to come out directly & tell me to run but indirectly I got the feeling she was trying to give me a heads up. I didn't take anything she was sharing as her trying to be malicious but rather her just trying to help in painting the picture of what the reality of the situation was so I can quickly remove the fairy tale one that was sold to me.

She went on further to say that after the wife moved out, Christopher later brought another girl from Jamaica who was staying there. She further explained that that also came with some drama as Sophia eventually found out. She went on to call the girl's name & asked whether I knew her. I couldn't help but laugh because I remember being in Jamaica & being told about that girl by his family & he denied any involvement. I couldn't put much merit on what his family said at the time because they thrived off drama & creating it, but here it was being revealed that it was all true.

Again I started singing my one tune, mi a go spend my month & go back a my yard! Seriously, weh mi a do wid so much man problem at the tender age of sixteen? To say I was hurt by all this new information would be an understatement. Then when I thought I had heard it all, Simone adds on the part that I wasn't the only one sending letters. Then she said I'm sure if you search in that room some should still be there.

She didn't need to tell me twice! I went & turned the place upside down.

SEEK & YOU SHALL FIND

The search was on. I emptied every drawer on every piece of furniture. First thing I found was a few of my pictures that I had sent in letters I wrote. I found one picture of me where half of my body had been torn off. I didn't even need to guess what happened to it, it clearly went through the world war 3 that Simone had mentioned.

I kept searching for the letters that I heard about but so far my search was coming up empty. I found a lot of female clothing but not the letters. So there was one place left to look, the closet. It had no drawers & from the outside seemed to only have space for hanging but when I opened it, it had a little shelf & what did I find to the back of that shelf, a bag with a lot of papers.

I emptied the bag & alas letters, pictures, postcards & they weren't all from me. The two letters that stood out to me was one from his sister's friend who worked with a travel service & the other from a nursing student who lived at 44 remember now I lived at 34. He had always maintained that they were both just his friends but the content of the letters said otherwise.

The travel agent who might I add was the person who booked my ticket to leave, started out her letter by firstly stating her disapproval of his affiliation with me. She highlighted the fact that I was young & it didn't look good him being over ten years my senior. She also made reference to the fact that she was reliably informed that he had been sending his mother's money to me to drop off & that too didn't look good. Put it this way the letter was all about me, & everything concerning me didn't look good to her.

I felt so important! Imagine someone wrote a letter, went to the post office to mail it & waited anxiously for at least two weeks for it to be delivered just to speak about ME. I was getting bored hearing about her disapproval of me & then there it was her very own application being submitted for the position she assumed I had.

As for the nursing student, he had clearly made her an offer to visit England. He had also told her about the same nursing program that he had introduced to me. So her letter was in response to the offer that he had made. She confirmed her interest & also made mention of the fact that she missed him. She encouraged him to make the arrangements & she would be ready. Is a big rat race did a gwan! Everybody did a get invitation from Christopher fi reach a England!

I wasn't even confirmed in the position as yet & travel agent was vying for it. But you know what the biggest problem was? The money I was perceived to be managing. Everybody wanted that role. Apparently my youthful innocence landed me the job. The others could not be trusted.

I didn't even make it known that I had found these letters. I instead just started preparing myself mentally for college which I would have been starting in a few days. I kept reminding myself that I came to better myself & that had to be my main focus. Besides, even if I was to have confronted Christopher he would have just lied, so it really made no sense.

AND THEN

The next couple of weeks went smoothly. I had started college & was getting adjusted. School in England was a totally different environment from the one I was accustomed to. Christopher's brother in law Doug who also attended the same college showed me the ropes & welcomed me in his little circle of friends. His friends were fascinated by the fact that I was Jamaican but somehow didn't match the image they had in their heads of what Jamaicans looked like.

I remember one saying that they thought only black people were in Jamaica, so I replied by saying but I am black. He quickly said no he was referring to complexion, like dark skinned. I told him all shades were present in Jamaica including his. He then went on to ask if I smoked weed. When I replied by saying no, he said nah you're not Jamaican, all Jamaicans smoke weed. Umm no we don't was my response to that. It was shocking the image that they had in their minds of us. It was like the only thing we did in Jamaica was smoke weed, party & curse bombocloth.

They were also interested in the latest dance moves. Now unuh know me love dance already! So circle form round mi & mi a showoff. I think signal di plane & blazè did a gwan dem time & strawberry which my mother always said was an old dance called mash potato & they revamped it.

My classes were going well. Mi did feel well bright! I was studying Chemistry, Math, ICT & Sociology. My chemistry professors loved me because I was always ahead of the class, big up to Dr. Matthews, my chemistry teacher in high school.

I remember getting my reports & copying them & mailing them to my mom so she could see that I was putting in the work to accomplish what I had set out to.

So my routine was pretty much the same for the next couple of weeks & everything was going well without any problems until that evening in November. I saw a call coming in from a blocked number. I answered the phone only to hear "Bitch you think you a come a England come get weh mi fi get?" I quickly recognised that it was Christopher's wife Sophia & so I hung up the phone. She kept calling back & I didn't answer.

You might be wondering how she got my phone number. She went through the gentleman's phone & called every number in his call log that she couldn't identify until she struck gold. You see all the numbers stored in Christopher's phonebook were codes, no names. But she was on a mission & wouldn't give up until she found what she was looking for.

She was as much a victim as I was & if there was anybody to be blamed it would be Christopher because he had no business bringing me there if he knew he was working out things with her. So I was not going to argue with her because had I been in her shoe, I would have been hurt about the situation as well.

But some people just never know when to stop! She called me on a few other occasions & I did the very same thing, hang up as soon as I heard her voice. She sent me some very disrespectful messages & I didn't reply. I kept telling myself that I just needed to focus on why I was there & to achieve something out of the situation.

The fact that I opted not to answer her, I think she thought I was a walk over & so she kept pushing & pushing. She clearly didn't know that 34 afforded me lessons in cursing & "dunning a gal."

It was clear that unless I stood up for myself, she was never going to stop & clearly there was nothing that Christopher could do because remember fi him hand ina lion mouth. I wasn't afraid to go back to my yard but clearly he was! So once again she come & decide fi press mi button only this time I didn't hear her voice & hang up, mi give it to har! Dun har like a gun!

PACK YOUR BAGS

So after standing up for myself & defending myself, Sophia threw Christopher out of their house.

When he arrived at my house all hell broke loose. He kept asking why did I have to answer her, why I couldn't just continue ignoring her. He also reminded me of the fact that his status in the country was dependent on her & that if that gets messed up for him, then I too would be affected. He repeated his favourite saying "When yuh hand ina lion mouth tek time tek it out." So I asked him why couldn't he have told her to leave me alone, there was no response.

For the next couple of days he would leave work & then proceed to his wife's house under guise that he was visiting his son but really he was testing the waters to see whether she would allow him to move back in. Eventually he got the green light & was gone again.

He apparently reassured Sophia that me being in England had nothing to do with him. He told her that my family sent for me & I was living with them in North London. If this wasn't bad enough I was also asked to participate in the lie. He told her that she could call me to confirm the validity of his story & guess what she did. I went along with the storyline & told her that that was the reason for me lashing out at her because I wasn't a problem to her but she was somehow becoming a problem to me. This conversation smoothed things over & she was back in her corner & I in mine.

But there was another surprise brewing. You see I had always had an irregular menstrual cycle. I would go anywhere between 1 & 3 months without having a period & that was normal for me. It was now the middle of the third month & still nothing yet but I was feeling all the pre-menstrual symptoms so I took that as reassurance that it would appear soon.

The funny thing was that everytime I brought up the topic, Christopher would say yuh pregnant but I dismissed him & the thought. Pregnant at sixteen was not in my plans & especially not now when everything was going wrong & there was a strong possibility that I would be returning home.

The end of December was approaching & still no sign of my period. I started losing my appetite, looked very pale & would sleep sometimes for an entire day. The nearer it came to December 31st the more anxious I became. I even purposely fell off my bed twice because I kept saying if anything was there, it had to go.

A new day & a new year had dawned, 2002 & my period was still a no show. By this time I had spoken with Simone about the situation. She agreed to follow me to the pharmacy to purchase a pregnancy test, I guess it was time to know my fate.

When we got to the pharmacy I remember being so numb that I couldn't ask for the test. I remember Simone saying "Yuh cah shy fi order pregnancy test when you a have sex enuh." I think she was trying to loosen me up but it wasn't working.

We got home & it was time for the moment of truth. I had spoken to Christopher prior & had advised him of the plan of action so he too was waiting to hear the verdict although he had already given his.

When those two lines appeared on the test kit, I bawled like a baby. I felt disappointed in myself & like I had let down so many people. I felt like my life was ruined.

MORNING AFTER

I had cried myself to sleep. I didn't even know that it was morning until the sunlight started coming through the window. As soon as I got up the first thing I did was to revisit the pregnancy test & the screen somehow only had one line now & not two. I started wondering whether I had gotten a false positive & was in luck. I remember starting to feel happy & upbeat.

I went downstairs to Simone & was telling her about the new discovery. She recommended visiting the neighbourhood GP to be sure. The doctor's office was two doors down from where we lived & so I got ready & walked down.

So once again I was waiting to hear my fate. The nurse came back in & said yes you are pregnant. When I asked how far long she said four months as she had counted from my last period in September. I explained to her that I didn't have a regular cycle but she said in the scheme of things this didn't matter. I was once again in a lull. She went on to add that my options were somewhat limited based on how far long I was believed to be. This was like her throwing more salt in the wound.

I walked back home & once Simone saw the look on my face she knew exactly what the verdict was. She went on to ask whether I had spoken to Christopher & I told her not yet but I would be doing so shortly. She encouraged me with the words that everything was going to be okay.

I called Christopher, by this time I was bawling again. Once he heard the brokenness in my voice he knew the verdict. One thing I knew for sure was the fact that he didn't sound surprised any at all & I kept wondering if all this was a part of the twisted plot. Anyway, once I opened my mouth & said I hadn't decided what I was going to do as yet because I cannot go back to Jamaica with a child, he paused. He then went on to ask whether I was saying what he thought I was saying & if I was thinking about an abortion. Remember now the nurse already ruled that out as an option for me but I decided to play along. So I asked what if this was the better option for me?! The gentleman made it crystal clear, he didn't mince words. He said should I opt to go that route, I would be on my own. He said I would need to make alternate living arrangements & support myself until my passport was returned & I can leave the country. He also made it clear that when that time came I would also need to source a ticket as he wouldn't be purchasing one. So in other words it was either I kept the child or get cut off in a foreign country where I had no family & only one friend from high school who was in no better position than myself.

Based on the options presented it was a no brainer, I had to keep the child. So it was time to start bracing myself for the changes to come. How was I going to break this news to my parents, my family, my friends? I knew everyone had high hopes & expectations for me. How would I convince them that this situation was not going to suddenly make me a failure? How would I get them to continue believing in me? This was all very hard to take in & accept.

MY NEW REALITY

So for the next couple of weeks it was all about getting prepared for the changes to come. I continued going to college but some days I felt so sick that I couldn't make the journey. I didn't have morning sickness or any vomiting but I had dizzy spells coupled with cold sweat which would result in me feeling faintish. Whenever the feeling came on I had to quickly find somewhere to sit down or to lay down.

I later received a package from the GP with details of clinics that I could register for antenatal care. You see in England pregnant teenagers were separated from adults. We had our own antenatal clinics & midwives assigned to us. Based on where I lived the clinic I was to register with was in an area called Dulwich. I wasn't familiar with the place but you already know I was on my own & as such I would have to find it.

It was still early days & so I told myself I had time. I was more concerned about telling my family the news. I remember telling a few of my friends & they were all supportive, I wasn't judged & that made me feel just a little better about everything. The greatest thing was there was no baby bump showing so unless I told you, you wouldn't know.

It was now February & for some reason Christopher started staying at my house. It was all very unexpected. I couldn't put my finger on why he was there but I figured there must have been some argument & he was once again thrown out of his wife's house. He didn't mention what happened & to be honest I didn't ask seeing that I had my own crap dealing with.

One night I was in the room watching TV when I suddenly heard this big uproar. I recognised Simone's voice & I heard his so I realised that they were arguing. I opened the room door & stood right by it to hear what was going on. I heard Simone saying she was sick & tired of him & all the problems he had been causing since they rented him the room. I was now confused because I didn't know of an issue since being there. Then she made mention of him bringing me there & she having to feed me sometimes because he didn't buy grocery. I felt so embarrassed when she said this but she spoke no lie. Now the thing with Christopher is that he was one who went toe to toe with you in an argument. So I could hear him telling her that she was acting as though she was better than him & a people shit she deh a England a clean. This took the argument to another level to the point where Simone drew a meat chopper & ran after him & the other housemate Jude had to hold her back.

What I still couldn't figure out was what was the cause of all this?! How did it move from a quiet evening to all this drama? Well you see what had happened was this young white school girl Michelle came to the house with her parents.

Her parents asked to have a meeting with Christopher to discuss his affiliation with their daughter & to get his side of the story before they called the police to report him. Now the other housemate Jude was a social worker. She was in the kitchen & heard what Michelle's parents were accusing Christopher of. She in turn went to Simone to complain to say this can't be happening in the house that she was living in based on the nature of her job. So this was just one complain too many & so Simone blew a fuse.

So I was there in the room clueless to the fact that these people were accusing him of being involved with their young daughter. Apparently the girl was his wife's little sister's friend from school. She would bring them to the house after school in the days & sometimes they would babysit his son who was about 4 years old at the time. It seem as though at some point he started hooking up with Michelle & this is what caused the problem. This is what also resulted in him being thrown out because Michelle's parents went to the wife's house first.

During the argument with Simone I heard when she asked him to leave by the end of the month. In reality it wouldn't be him leaving it was me who would now need to find somewhere to go. So he came & stormed in the room & said Simone & Jude disrespected him & he wanted nothing more to do with them & he was going to have to find somewhere for me to go.

When I thought all was now calm, Christopher started cursing me asking why was I eating Simone's food for her to use it & curse him. So I asked him if he had bought food for me to eat?! His grocery provision for me was never consistent. He made me feel like I was a burden. You would never have thought that he was the one who sent for me based on his behaviour.

Now remember he denied everything that Michelle's parents accused him of. Well that same night while he showered a text message came in from her & she said "they bought it, everything is good now, love you". So clearly they had planned out their story prior to the meeting.

WHERE TO GO?

So for the next couple of weeks there was constant talk about finding somewhere for me to live. Now renting a house in England was not the easiest thing to do. Some places required background checks, some required details of your job & income & all required a hefty deposit. Now if Christopher was not buying me grocery on a regular basis, do you really think he was going to do all this to rent me a place? I don't think so.

I had recently learned that a friend of mine that lived a few houses down from 34 was also in England with his girlfriend. Christopher was also aware of this & so it didn't come as a surprise when he suggested that I ask to stay with them for a little, while he tries to find me a new place. I asked & they didn't hesitate.

Now for the first couple of weeks I felt like I had been dumped. Remember now I didn't have a job & Christopher gave me no money to keep me afloat. So once again I had become someone else's problem & responsibility. I started pressing & asking him for money because my friend with whom I was staying was also struggling to stay afloat & was in no position to take care of me.

When he eventually agreed to give me some money, I was told that I had to visit the location that he was working at for the day to collect same. So by the time I got that money I would have to put aside money to pay back my friend who would have given me the money to pay my fare to get to Christopher.

As time went by I started feeling as though I was non-existent to him. There was little to no interest in me or my wellbeing & I was no longer hearing any talks about a place being rented for me. As a matter of fact I hardly heard from the gentleman. Sometimes if I didn't try reaching out, days & weeks would go by & I wouldn't hear from him.

I remember one night I started spotting & went to the emergency room. When I contacted Christopher all he said was he didn't think it was anything serious but I should let him know the outcome. I was expecting to hear him say that he was coming, but I guess that was wishful thinking. My friend's girlfriend & I spent the entire night at the emergency room. I wasn't given the all clear to leave until after 6am the following morning. Our next worry now was the fact that our one day bus passes had now expired & we had no money to pay our fares. So we decided to chance it with the recently expired pass, not like we had much of a choice as it was either chance it or walk, but thankfully we made it home on the bus without incident.

I contacted Christopher & told him I needed to get some pre-natal vitamins that were recommended along with some folic acid. Once again if I was to get the money I had to find him at whichever location he was working for the day. You would never believe that this man owned a vehicle.

This living arrangement continued for approximately three months. Looking back now I can only imagine how inconvenienced my friend must have felt. You see the flat was a one bedroom flat. He gave his girlfriend & I the bed to sleep on while he slept on the floor. But I must have been cock blocking as they would say but even if I was, I was never shown any bad face & I was never made to feel like I was a burden or problem.

I remember the first time in my life I experienced hunger was while living at this flat. In all my time in Jamaica I had never not had anything to eat, no matter how small it was there was always something to stop a gap. I remember Kermit & I being at the flat & both of us looking at each other. I was previously instructed not to eat nuts as it was believed the unborn child could develop an allergy but some ital nuts was the only thing that was in the house & so we started munching on that. Luckily his brother came to our rescue. He went on the road & was able to do an odd job & got paid. He took the money to the chicken shop & bought us all the £2 chicken specials. When we got that food it felt as though we were having an expensive meal.

Simone reached out to me to see how everything was going. She told me that the gentleman wasn't seeking anywhere to rent & that he would still come by her house occasionally. She also told me that he was taking someone there who she believed to be the same young white girl Michelle. She said they kept moving like phantoms so whenever she tried to see who it was, she either missed them or saw the back of the person. She went on to say that if it wasn't working out at my friend then I should come back.

Eventhough she told me this, when I spoke to Christopher about moving back he was shutting it down initially. He only agreed when he had no choice because Kermit had to give up the flat because the owner wanted it for their use. Even when it came time for me to move back, I had to sort out my own transportation. The excuse this time was that he had work & wasn't able to assist with the move. Every day suggested was not good for him. Eventually it was Jude who assisted in relocating me back to West Norwood.

So I was back at my old house, this would have been May of 2002. Christopher showed up & paid up the rent monies he owed while I was away & we saw this gesture as an indication that he would be doing better going forward. Boy were we wrong!

FEMALE STALKER

So I moved back & it was like I never left. I continued going to college & tried keeping up despite everything else that was going on. I remember going over my mental notes from my first GP visit & recalling when the nurse said my due date would have been August 30, 2002. Based on my maths I started thinking that I wasn't as far along as I was told initially. I wasn't going to make a fuss, as that ship had now sailed & so I just had to deal.

The next couple of weeks went smoothly & without any major episodes. The gentleman even took me grocery shopping & I started thinking wow God must have spoken to him. But do you remember while growing up when they use to tell you that all good things must come to an end? They were right.

One morning as I headed out to make my way to the train station I heard a horn tooting. When I looked back I realised it was the gentleman's wife Sophia. Now remember I had only recently moved back to the house, so why did she find it necessary to park on the side road & stake out the house now? Why didn't she do it before? Unless she was & just didn't make any progress, but today she bingoed.

Anyway, as she pulled up beside me she rolled down the window & said "yuh neva know mi woulda find you?" so I asked her if I was lost. So she went on to say if this was the North London that I claimed I lived. Now all she was talking I continued walking because you know everything in England runs on time & I wasn't about to miss my train.

So she continued driving beside me talking all kinds of crap & I ignored her. Then she went "mi hear seh yuh pregnant, suh who is the father?" At this time I replied to her & said GUH ASK YUH HUSBAND & walked across the road & into the train station.

Next thing I knew I saw the gentleman calling my phone asking me what was the problem. So I told him to ask his wife who had a stake out outside the house. He went on to say that she sent him a message to say that she was going to run me over with her car. So I asked him then why didn't she? At the end of the day that would be her giving her freedom away. He further added that she was at the house "mashing up" the place & apparently packing his things to once again throw him out. I don't know if all this was suppose to evoke some kind of response out of me. To date I had not gone out of my way to make trouble for the lady, I stayed in my lane & corner. She was always the aggressor & so she doesn't get to play the victim role to me. I might have seen her as a victim initially based on Christopher's actions, but now she was just being a b!@ch.

When I got home from college I was telling Simone about the incident & even she was confused. She couldn't understand why she kept trying to come in my way when all I've been doing since I arrived in England was to avoid her. I remember Simone saying "Wait a she own England?!"

Anyway, later that night we heard the doorbell. Everybody was saying they weren't expecting anyone. When Simone went downstairs there was an envelope that had been dropped through the mail flap with my name on it. So she took it upstairs to me & asked whether I was expecting anything. I started laughing & proceeded to ask her if she eva see mailman a work a night. There was no doubt in my mind that the package came from Sophia.

When I opened the envelope there was a handwritten letter in all CAPS telling me that I could have Christopher & a host of other rubbish, the details of which I can't recall at this time. What I do recall though is that enclosed in the envelope was a credit card that was joint with Christopher & her wedding ring. Laughing spoil the night! Like was this lady for real? What was the point of all this?

I knew she might have been hurting but all this was just ridiculous. I could understand if I was calling her phone & trying to make trouble or I was being a nuisance to her but I wasn't. She just wasn't satisfied that I was in the same country as her, I should have been left in Jamaica where I belonged. This clearly was her biggest problem.

I kept looking at the ring & thinking to myself then a weh she gi mi dah popcorn ring yah fah, weh she expect mi fi do wid it? And just like that I got the best idea ever! I am going to pawn this shit! I remember previously passing a pawn shop down the road close to my train station. So I decided to visit them on my way home from college the following day.

Next day just as planned I visited the pawn shop with the rings. The owner weighed them & said they didn't weigh much & the stone didn't seem to be a diamond but rather a cubic zirconia. I was just waiting to hear how much I was getting as I had no interest in the details. Alas he said I could give you £70 for these & I quickly said I will take it. It wasn't even about the money, I was just sick & tired of the lady & her bullshit.

So now I was £70 richer thanks to wifey. I can't recall everything I did with the money but one thing I know for sure was that it was put to good use. I am almost certain I bought some baby stuff from the Argos catalogue with it. As for her credit card, I wasn't going to fall for that trap. I was smarter than that. I knew usage of that would put me in problems.

Couple weeks went by & the next thing I knew Christopher was now asking me for the rings & so I told him I pawned them. The look on his face when I said it was priceless. He then went on to ask why would I do that?! So I explained to him that they were given to me & I didn't want them to wear so I did the next best thing. So when he asked me about going back for them I told him the pick up date had passed. I suggested to him that he could probably go to the shop & see if he could buy them back. I was told all the swear words in the book but at this point I really didn't care.

Couple days later when I thought all this ring excitement was over, I would receive a call from Sophia. She said she was told that I had pawned her rings & she wanted her half of the money. I laughed so hard when I heard her request & proceeded to hang up my phone. By this time I made a pledge to myself to ignore the lady because clearly she was either fully mad or getting there.

I guess ignoring her wasn't enough because shortly after I received a call from the police. Guess what the call was about?

SOMEONE PLEASE CALL 999

Throughout this entire ordeal I have tried as best as possible to avoid Sophia, so how is it I was now being contacted by the police to answer to an allegation of harassment?! I explained to the police that I didn't know what harassment the lady was referring to but I do have evidence of her harassing me & I was asked to visit the police station with same.

So it was time to visit the South Norwood Police Station to clear my name. I took along with me the letter that I had just received. I remember watching them bag the letter in an evidence bag, at which point I started thinking that all this madness could never be that serious but in England it was. I also handed over my mobile phone for them to read the numerous messages I had gotten from the lady. At the end of the investigation they placed a call to the lady in my presence at which time they informed her that based on the evidence I had presented it was obvious that she was the one harassing me. She was given a warning and was asked to refrain from making any further contact with me.

I left the police station & made my way home but not before getting a call from Christopher asking why I went to the police station to report her & accusing me of constantly trying to cause problems. I had to dress him down properly & let him know that SHE was the one who reported me & all I did was to pay a visit to clear my name. I believe that because his status in the country was dependent on her, no matter what she did she was never going to be blamed. It was always somebody else's fault.

I got home & was updating Simone about the day's drama. Even she couldn't believe the new lengths that Sophia had gone to. She once again encouraged me to just continue focusing on school. You see Simone had started looking out for me & would even tell people that I was her adopted daughter. We developed a good relationship. Most days when she had work I would cook dinner for both of us & when she was off she would do the same. I don't think Christopher was pleased with the connection because he recognised that she was also helping to slowly open my eyes to who he really was & the fact that I deserved better.

It was now time for me to have my 5 month check & scan. I remember seeing the nurse laying out six vials in front of me. When I asked what they were for & she said blood, my heart started racing. I had a terrible fear of needles. One thing I've learned over the years though is the fact that I apparently have good veins, one prick & the river flows. So in no time I was told I could open my eyes which were tightly closed. I also did my second scan on the same day. I saw the baby sucking its thumb & at the end I was told that I would have been having a boy.

Thinking back I think ideally I wanted a girl so when I was told boy I asked them to double check & yes they were indeed correct. I remember heading back home & sharing the news with Simone. I was skeptical about calling Christopher because he was still in his feelings about the police report situation.

Eventually I had the conversation & Christopher's reaction was not very encouraging. His whole attitude was like it was neither here nor there. When I started the discussion about wanting to start buying up stuff for the baby it was quickly shot down with a "baby nuh need nuttn til dem born." I was dumbstruck! I quickly asked him what he meant? The gentleman said "baby a wear clothes ina belly?" So I asked him if we were going to wait until I went into labour to go shopping for the necessities?! I received no reply.

One thing that was becoming clearer by the minute was the fact that I was definitely on my own with this child. I was sharing the conversation with Simone & she made me an offer. She worked night shifts on Thursdays & Fridays & some Saturdays. She proposed for me to look after her son whenever she worked nights, & I would take him to school on Friday mornings. She agreed to pay me £30. It was a no brainer, I had to accept the offer. How else was I going to be able to start make preparations for this child?

BABYSITTER ON DUTY

It was now time to start my new babysitting gig. The little boy would have been about 6 or 7 years old at the time. I pretty much had to get him ready for bed in the nights & make his breakfast, get him ready & take him to school the following morning.

I remember getting paid after the first week & immediately going to Argos to purchase baby clothes. I was able to get some onesies, monkey suits & receivers. The following week I went back again & purchased a storage chest for the baby's clothes. This went on for the next couple of weeks. I was the happiest person on Saturday mornings when I got that little money. It might not have sounded like a lot but for me it felt like millions. I would constantly be on the look out for sales & specials. I remember when Superdrug Pharmacy advertised their special on Avent feeding bottles I was the first person there the next morning stocking up.

The gentleman was still yet to make a move in regards to assisting with making preparations for the birth but nevertheless I continued to do what I could with the little I was now getting. I don't know why I still had such great expectations where Christopher was concerned, when he was also once again defaulting on the monthly rent. If he wasn't paying the rent or buying me grocery did I really expect him to be active in preparing for the birth of this child? It was evident that I was in denial & understandably so. You see I had witnessed the lengths he went to for his first child, playing the role of the doting dad, meeting all his son's needs. I actually considered him to be a good father based on everything I witnessed, so what was different now? You would think that the gentleman wanted this child based on the ultimatum I was given when I first discovered that I was pregnant but maybe what he really wanted was to just somehow "trap" me.

Later that week I was called back to the hospital to collect my results from my blood work which I would now need to take with me to my antenatal classes. Once again this was another hurdle that I would be going over on my own.

I started the classes & I felt comfortable based on the fact that all the attendees were teenage moms. It played an integral role in getting us ready for the journey of motherhood. I was relieved to know that we were not going to have to be in the same space with adults. I remember hearing stories of how badly pregnant teenagers were treated at the Victoria Jubilee Hospital in Jamaica. As to whether there was any truth to the stories I don't know but the stories were enough to leave me scared. I didn't want to have to deal with being judged which is one of the many things that comes with being a teenage mom.

I eventually made friends with some of the other teenage moms but one in particular & I became very close because we realised that we lived in close proximity to each other. Natasha & I would meet up & attend our classes & partner up for any activity that required a partner as we both had absent baby fathers. The fact that we were somewhat in a similar situation made me feel a little better about my ordeal.

I was coming up to my seventh month of pregnancy & I was still yet to tell my family about it. I kept trying to work out when would be the right time but the more I thought about it, no time felt right. I also didn't want to worry my mother with details of the life I was now living, so it was just easier pretending that everything was great.

After a conversation with Simone, she encouraged me to tell my family about the pregnancy. She discussed with me all the uncertainties that came with being pregnant & the fact that she wouldn't want for anything to go wrong that would result in her having to give my family news about something that they had no knowledge of & so she encouraged me to tell them the truth.

Later that evening I went to the corner store, bought a phonecard & finally made the call.

THE BIG REVEAL

So I finally made the call. I remember speaking to my sister Annmarie first & telling her. I also expressed to her my fear of telling our mom her reply to which was "Yuh nuh yuh own big woman now, leave school & deh pon yuh own, weh yuh fraid a?" With that being said I asked her to get my mom to come to the phone.

My mom came to the phone & I did the whole chit chat thing before dropping the bomb. I told her I was now seven months pregnant & was due in August. I paused & waited for her to start shouting or cursing but instead I heard her ask whether I knew the sex. I told her that it was a boy after which she went on to say old people usually say your womb is blessed if your first child is a boy. She went on to ask whether I was sick & I confirmed that I wasn't. I felt like a burden had been lifted off me just being able to discuss the pregnancy with her. As to all the drama that was taking place with Christopher & his wife, that was better left unsaid.

The next couple of weeks were uneventful, thank God. I continued doing my babysitting gig & preparing for the baby. College was also coming to a close as I had already sat my final exams. I would now need to determine my next move as Christopher didn't pay my tuition in full so I wouldn't be able re-register at the same college for year two of my A levels. I would have to look into attending a new college to once again be able to get my visa extended. The other issue was the fact that I had to be in school fulltime. How was this going to work with a newborn? I didn't have the answers but I guess I would figure it out as I went along just like everything else.

The rent had once again backed up & Simone had mentioned to me that the landlady was furious. She said if she had the money she would have paid it because she hated the embarrassment. Simone had recently hurt her back at work while lifting a patient & so her work hours were reduced & she also had to be taking a lot of time off work. She said everyday Christopher would promise her to come with the money but was always a no show. She went on to say that she didn't have a choice but to tell him that if he didn't come with the funds by the weekend, then they would have to put me out the house.

The fact that I could do nothing to help my situation was so frustrating. Once again my fate was in the gentleman's hand & I wasn't hopeful based on his track record. I remember calling him & asking about the rent his reply to which was that they should wait. I reiterated the fact that I would be "put out" of the house to which he replied that I was pregnant & they could get into problems with the law should they do that. This was in no way comforting to me.

This was the fastest I've ever seen the weekend arrive. It's as if it was anxious to see me out on the streets. Despite the threat made to the gentleman, he was still a no show. I remember Simone calling him & cursing him & telling him how wicked he was. I remember her saying to him "Imagine mi tell u seh wi a go put out Stacey wid har belly & not even that nuh mek yuh budge." It got so bad that even Simone's brother decided to call him as well.

I remember hearing Simone's brother cursing the gentleman about the stress he was causing his sister & the fact that he was ready to "do him somn" for his sister. The argument escalated very quickly & the next thing I knew there was talk about where they were going to meet to fight it out. I remember hearing him saying to Christopher "Yah gwan like you a bad man enuh but bet seh mi knock you out." No matter how Simone tried calming him down it didn't work. He was ready to go kick ass in honour of her. We were eventually able to get him to recognise that Christopher wasn't worth getting into trouble for.

Once everything had calmed down, it finally hit home, the fact that despite being told that I would be going on the streets with his unborn child, Christopher still didn't show up. Once again I was reminded that he cared zero about my wellbeing & that of his child. At the end of the day he had a roof over his head & clearly that's all that mattered to him.

IT'S TIME

So I didn't get thrown out on the streets but Simone had made it clear to Christopher that until he sorted out the monies owed he was not welcomed at the house. I'm sure this was music to his ears. He would surely use it as an excuse as to why I would get no help from him.

I remember for the next couple of weeks I was hooked on tuna. I was eating tuna with literally anything. This was a change from spinach, cow foot & strawberry nesquik which were my prior cravings.

Simone had planned on leaving for a week to spend time at her mom's house. I remember her giving me my cab fare to get to the hospital just in case I went into labour when she wasn't there. She also ensured my bag was packed & everything was ready for me to grab & go.

It was Tuesday August 27, 2002. Once again I made my tuna this time with sweetcorn & pasta for my dinner. I ate & proceeded to watch TV. There was a program coming on at 10pm that I wanted to watch but I felt myself falling asleep & so I went ahead & set my phone alarm. The alarm went off & I got up & watched the program. Whilst watching it though I had bad indigestion & heartburn. I went to the kitchen & had a glass of milk & this gave me a little relief.

I finished watching the program & decided to go back to bed. I fell asleep but at approximately 1:30am I was awaken by contractions. I got the clock & started timing to see how far apart they were. I remember calling my assigned midwife who told me that it was early days & it wasn't time for me to go to the hospital as yet. She recommended that I take a warm bath & some paracetamol.

I repeated this action on two other occasions as advised by my midwife. I remember the third time I went to soak in the bath, I couldn't get out. I kept trying to get up without success. I eventually had to turn on my side, hanged on to the side of the bath, got on all fours & tried climbing out the bath.

During this time I had messaged both Simone & Christopher to update them on what was happening. I asked Christopher whether he would have been able to take me to the hospital his reply to which was that I was to let him know when I was ready. As for Simone, she didn't have a car & so she would have to wait until public transportation started operating before she could leave her mom's house.

I remember calling back my midwife at about 6am & telling her I needed to go to the hospital. She advised against this & told me to await her arrival to do a home visit to see how dilated I was after which she would determine whether I was ready to go to the hospital or not.

I waited until about 6:30am but she was still a no show. I remember messaging Christopher & telling him I was ready to go to the hospital to which he replied that he was on his way. Simone was also on the bus making her way to me.

So guess who got to me first? Simone of course! We called the cab & made our way to the hospital. While on my way I had informed my midwife that I had left home & she agreed to meet me at the hospital. We didn't see or hear from Christopher.

We arrived at the hospital at 7am, they took me to the ward & got me set up at about 7:30am & I gave birth at 8:20am. My midwife was a no show for the delivery. She arrived while I was getting my stitches. I remember myself shouting at her for being late & telling me to stay home despite me telling her I needed to leave for the hospital. The gas & air aka laughing gas made me a hot mess. I remember yelling "Noooooooooo" when Simone told me that the baby looked like Christopher, a statement she quickly retracted once they had placed the baby under the heat & his complexion & features started coming in.

Once the laughing gas had started wearing off, I quickly recognised that Christopher was a no show & through it all it was Simone that was by my side. She quickly told me how I almost tore off her clothes during labour. It was the joke of the day. I remember her calling Christopher & telling him that the baby was born & asking him to take me some food to which he agreed. We waited patiently & he was still a no show. She had to leave to get me something to eat & return.

Christopher would eventually call her back to say he was on his way but even after this call he was still a no show. I was told that I would have been admitted to the hospital for a few days to ensure that the baby was feeding properly & to also facilitate me being monitored. You know everything in my life comes with some kind of excitement, & my new mom experience was no different. The new excitement was the fact that my breasts had no milk. The part that felt like punishment was the fact that I was told that I still had to have the baby suck the empty breast to stimulate it & bring the milk down. This felt like I was being tortured. It hurt like crazy.

Day one had ended but there was still no sign of the baby daddy. He called me in the night though to say he was checking to see if everything was alright. Oh my, how sweet. Day two in the hospital & the only person I saw was Simone & our other housemate Jude, Christopher was still a no show. I spoke with the doctors & they informed me that I would possibly have been discharged the following day eventhough I still had no breast milk. They had started the baby on formula & the feeding was going well & so they were comfortable with sending me home.

Once again I received a call from the baby daddy, no visit, asking how everything was going. I told him that I would possibly be discharged from the hospital the following day. Once again he said I was to just let him know when I was ready & he would pick us up.

It was Friday August 30, 2002 & the doctors confirmed that I would be released later that day. I sent a message to Christopher advising him of same. Once again I was told to just let him know when I was ready. My friend Kermit & his girlfriend Kaydiane came by the hospital to pay me a visit. They were there with me until I was officially discharged. I contacted Christopher & he told me he was on his way. This could have been from about 3:30pm. When we saw it coming up to almost 6pm & there was still no sign of him, Kaydiane offered to pay for a cab & accompany me home.

Once I got home I was greeted by Simone who was furious. She could not believe that the gentleman didn't show up. The other problem that we had now was the fact that we needed to buy formula as there was still no milk in my breasts & the hospital only gave me a few bottles of formula to take home. Simone called the gentleman & began cursing him out. He reckon he got tied up sorting out some business & this was the reason for him not showing up. She told him that the baby needed formula ASAP & he agreed to get it. I know I didn't have to tell y'all that he didn't show up with it either.

Simone had to call her brother & ask him to run to the supermarket to pick up the formula. That's how I got milk for the baby that night. The father was a no show & continued to be missing in action for the next two weeks.

My friend Natasha that I had met through the antenatal classes, was the one who started supplying me with milk. You see she got tokens from the government for free formula for her baby who was born six days prior to mine but her daughter didn't drink formula, she was strictly breastfed. So Natasha would give me all the formulas she got for my son. This was a blessing in disguise because as y'all can clearly see Christopher had already planned on being an absent father.

MISSING IN ACTION

Milk finally started spraying from my breasts the Saturday morning. It was like I had struck gold. After all the combing & lettuce leaf & cabbage leaf remedies I was told to administer it would have been very disappointing if the milk didn't show.

I was visited almost everyday by nurses who checked on the baby & myself. After a while I got tired of being poked to see whether my womb was contracting. I also had no appetite & was told that I had to force myself to eat based on the fact that I was breastfeeding.

The first couple of days were hard. I got little to no sleep, my nipples seemed as though they were falling off & I was still having constipation issues. Some days I would just sit & cry as I felt so overwhelmed. I missed home & the help I knew I would have gotten if I had my family around.

I remember Simone's brother telling me that he felt my pain as he knew I was between a rock & a hard place. He went on to ask whether I would accept some gently worn baby clothing from him. His son was a little under one year old at the time. I told him I would gladly accept. After all I still needed a lot of things.

Christopher was still a no show but kept on calling & messaging asking how the baby was doing as if he cared. The last call I got I was so annoyed I told him to stop calling my phone because baby cah talk pon phone.

Simone had called him & told him that the baby needed a cot to sleep in. He went on to complain about me being disrespectful & as such he wouldn't be giving me his money. She told him to give it to her then so she can do what was necessary for the child. He eventually transferred £100 to her for her to get the cot & a push chair. In all this he was still yet to see his son.

Approximately two weeks later who would show up, the father of the year. He had paid up some of the outstanding rent monies & so was able to comfortably make his debut. The first thing he did when he saw the baby was to criticise the clothing he was wearing. I remember telling him that the baby had to wear secondhand clothing because he didn't buy any. I reminded him of his statement that the baby didn't need anything until he was born. I told him that it had been two weeks since his birth & I was still yet to receive anything from him for the child.

I don't think he liked the fact that I was now speaking up & challenging him. I think he preferred the naive version of me. His visits over the next couple of weeks were very few. It was almost like the child wasn't his.

Simone & I started discussing my plans for school. She made it clear that fulltime school was not going to be possible based on everything that was going on. She went on to say that she wanted to try & see if she could submit an application for an extension of stay for me as my guardian seeing that I was under the age of eighteen.

I had the discussion with my mom & had asked her to get a lawyer to draft a document naming Simone as my legal guardian in England. She got the documents prepared & sent them to us via courier. I later went on to enroll at Lambeth College for a part time course. We were able to put all the documentation together, sent off the application & hoped for the best.

We didn't tell Christopher anything about the plan & so I kept asking him what was going to be done about my visa renewal. Each time I would ask I got the run round & so I knew he didn't plan on doing anything.

I remember having my six weeks doctor visit. The baby was doing good & was flourishing. As a teenage mom you had to agree to go on some form of contraceptive at your six weeks consultation & so I agreed to the pill, a decision I never regretted.

I started sending out job applications but the common response was that they regret to advise that I wasn't successful at this time. Some employers would call you in to do their entry tests in most cases math & english & still respond with the famous unsuccessful line. Had I not had confidence in my math & english, I would have started believing that I was failing the tests & this was the cause for me being unsuccessful. I think the fact that I had no work experience played a major role in me being constantly denied any job opportunities.

It was time to register the baby & Simone agreed to accompany me to the registrars office. We had informed Christopher of the date & time & he had promised to meet us there but as was the norm with everything else we waited until we could wait no more & he was still a no show. You were not able to add the father's name if they weren't present & so the child was registered & his name left off the certificate.

Having now been given a legal document stating she was my guardian, Simone decided to make contact with the benefits office to see whether she could claim the child benefit for my son. I think the payment at the time was £10 per week. She made the query & was given the go ahead. So I started getting that £40 or £50 monthly to help me out with the child because help from the father was pretty much on a when he felt like basis, it wasn't consistent.

Everything was going well for a while when one day out of the blue Christopher said he is going to claim the child benefit for the baby. I had to now let him know it was already being done to prevent any duplications & problems. He was mad that we had done this behind his back & had not consulted him prior to doing it. He went on to say that the child was his so he should be the one making the benefit claim. It was hilarious how selective he was about when he chose to be a father.

When we thought this was a done deal, the benefits office contacted Simone & said they had received an application for child benefit from someone who identified themself as the child's father. They went on to say that if the father was in the picture then his claim would override hers as he was blood. Once they eventually made the switch in claimant, I no longer received the money. The gentleman held on to it.

OOPS WE GOT TRICKED!

For the next couple of weeks the gentleman kept pressing us to make another appointment to go to the registrars office to add his name to the birth certificate.

His reasoning was that it was his intention to submit an application for citizenship for my son. He went on to say that once the baby got his stay then mine would be automatic. For once it really seemed as though he was trying to do something beneficial for both myself & the child.

Based on what was presented, I didn't delay. The appointment was made & he actually showed up this time. He even picked us up! This all seemed too good to be true.

You know that I got conned right? His urgent need for his name to be added to the birth certificate had nothing to do with wanting to help me & the baby, it was more about wanting to help himself. You see he submitted the child benefit application but he was not named on the birth certificate as the father so he needed his name added for this purpose. So they had placed his application on hold pending submission of the birth certificate.

When I did my research I learned that the only way he could have filed for citizenship for the child was if we were married. You see England had a law which stated that any child born after 2001 would automatically get its citizenship from its mother. Previously they would have gotten citizenship from their father. England differs from America in this regard. Children born in England doesn't automatically acquire British citizenship. So basically whatever citizenship I had, the child had.

I was once again sending out job applications. This time I was called in for an interview for a job as a steward. I really didn't know what the job entailed but the fact that I didn't get a decline letter made me happy.

When I arrived at the location for the interview I realised it was a mass recruitment. The conference room was filled with people. Once again I was given the usual math & english tests. After this was completed they had an immediate selection process & guess what I made the cut. Over the next three days I would have to report to their headquarters for training.

So what did this steward job entail? I would be working at football matches. If you watch football, do you recall seeing people on the pitch & in the stands in these high visibility vests & jackets who are apparently deployed to maintain order? Well yes that would now be me!

I remember going to my first Fulham match. When I arrived at the stadium we were briefed on where we would be deployed along with other important information about how to proceed in the event of an emergency among other things. When the schedule was uploaded I saw that I was assigned to the gate. My deployment started from 9am & ended at 4pm with only two breaks in between. This felt like the longest day of my life & really didn't feel like a job I wanted to do but I had a child to take care of & so I had to do what was necessary.

The company to which I was employed had contracts with Millwall, Fulham, Queens Park Rangers, Crystal Palace & Brentford football clubs so at any point in time I could be assigned to work at any of these club matches. Thankfully my son wasn't a "bawly bawly" baby & so people were willing to babysit for me so that I could work. Babysitters cost an arm & a leg in England so I was grateful for the help. Some days Simone or our other housemate Jude would babysit for me, some days it was my friend Natasha that I had met at antenatal classes & other times it was Simone's brother who babysat for me.

I think at this time I was earning about £3.50 an hour. So on Average I was getting a little under £25 per event. In the scheme of things we all know this wasn't a lot of money but some money was better than no money at all. I would eventually meet a Jamaican supervisor at one of the matches. Once he realised that I was from "yard" he started looking out for me. Any additional shifts that I could get he would put me down for it. He also started deploying me in the stands so I wouldn't have to stand at the gates for hours in the cold. That cold was like punishment. Not even the jacket that the company provided could save you some days. I really appreciated him looking out for me. We soon became good friends & would oftentimes discuss our many woes & try to support & encourage each other in anyway we could. He too was trying to stay afloat by working & sending himself to school to facilitate the renewal of his student visa. He had hopes of finding a British woman to marry him & solve all his problems.

Although I was doing this job, I never stopped job hunting. I would receive an invitation for an interview with a retail chain a few months later. Once again working in retail wasn't my desired job but I was in survival mode.

A NEW DAY HAS DAWNED

It was time for my interview. I was so nervous & this was very evident to the interviewer who encouraged me to just relax. He started the interview like we were two friends having a conversation then he went on to ask about my work experience. I explained to him that I had none in sales. I also explained to him that this was one of the main reasons I had been denied jobs previously. He went on to say "Well if you never get employed how will you gain experience? I am going to give you the opportunity to gain experience that will help to build your CV(resume)." And just like that I was hired.

I started working on a part-time basis. The location I was employed to work was not yet opened & so I floated between stores. Most days I was deployed to the front of the store to greet the customers as they walked in & see whether I could help with their shopping. If you know me then you would know this was not my personality. It was so hard at first but over time it became a little easier. Some days I was deployed at the entrance, some days I was deployed at the fitting room to check people in when they were going to fit clothing & some days I would be deployed to cash.

I started getting the hang of things very quickly & started enjoying the job. I remember getting my first paycheck a couple days before my son's first birthday. I was so excited by the fact that I would now have been able to at least purchase something for his birthday.

August 28th, 2003, It was my baby's first birthday & as per usual his father was a no show. You see earlier that day instead of calling to discuss doing something for his son, even if it was to just buy a cake, he instead called with some sex argument & because I wasn't speaking his language he didn't bother turning up. He didn't show but my son still had a good first birthday. You see Simone's brother had picked up the baby & I during the day & took us to Baby Gap to go shopping as a birthday treat.

He also took us to McDonald's which was every kids favourite place & lastly he took us to Sainsbury's to purchase a birthday cake.

Once I got home we all gathered, sang happy birthday & cut cake. I felt a sense of accomplishment watching my son enjoy the moment & the toys that I was able to purchase for him.

Whilst I was now able to try & cover rent, there was still all this back money owed which I would never be able to cover. Looking back now I can't believe the gentleman thought it hard to pay £170 in rent for me when he was earning in excess of £1000 per fortnight from the CCTV security job he was doing at the time.

I continued to do what I could with what I was earning. I remember finally being able to buy myself a good jacket, all along I didn't have one of those. I had been wearing layers of clothing along with the padded vest the gentleman had given to me when I arrived.

Christmas was approaching & Simone had planned on travelling to America to spend the holidays there with family. This meant that my son & I would have been alone for the holidays. Based on Christopher's track record I really didn't expect him to show up for Christmas especially when he didn't even show up for the baby's birthday. So my friend from high school Deon, & I decided to have our very own Christmas celebration.

We had decided on cooking lamb, chicken, mac & cheese, rice & peas & the works. We also decided on baking a fruit cake which would have been a first for both of us but nevertheless we decided to experiment. We also bought our beverage of choice for the celebration, bacardi breezer.

Our first attempt at a cake wasn't bad. The cake actually tasted very good on the day it was baked but by the next day it was kind of hard. Being the novices that we were we didn't know that we were supposed to have left some of the red label wine to throw on the cake after. We found a work around though. We just microwaved the cake when we were ready to eat to get it back soft.

All in all we had a good Christmas. We made the most of what we had which probably wouldn't seem like much to many but to us it was a lot.

It would have been a new year, 2004 & my 19th birthday in a couple days. Birthdays had just become another day to me. Christopher had never taken the time to do anything for me & so I really didn't expect this to change now.

I remember Simone & my other housemate Jude coming together & purchasing a cake & a little gift to celebrate my birthday. I was very grateful. Christopher on the other hand was more caught up with accusing me of being involved with Simone's brother. The accusations came about all because the guy was decent enough to try & help me out when he could. Instead of using this fact as a wake up call for him to do better as a father, he instead used it to cause an argument to provide himself with one more reason not to play his role.

I started picking up additional shifts at work which came in very handy. One day after finishing my shift, I checked my phone & saw some missed calls from a blocked number. I figured whoever it was they would call back & they certainly did.

I answered the phone to hear the gentleman's wife Sophia asking if I thought me & my bastard pickney was going to get status in England. I had to remind her that her child was conceived in more sin than mine because she got pregnant while both her & Christopher claimed they were big Christians, very active & serving in the church but were fornicating. I'm sure she didn't know that I knew all this. I also had to remind her that the sham wedding that they had was to save face because she was already pregnant outside of wedlock. When I started reading her file including the part about the man she was sleeping with in the storeroom at work while she claimed she was married, she got dumb. I told her if my child was a bastard then she was a b@$ch. Next thing I knew she hung up.

She then went to war with the gentleman because she now realised that he has had discussions with me about her just as how he was having discussions with her about me. That man had no sense of loyalty. He just did whatever he needed to to constantly put us up against each other. I don't think Sophia recognised exactly what he was doing because she kept falling for the bait. Once again he called with his hand in lion mouth line & I told him that neither him nor her were doing anything for my child & I so my hand was in no mouth.

SICK BABY ON BOARD

I would eventually relocate to share house with my cousin Tiffany. She was having a hard time keeping up with her rent & bills & both of us coming together would have cut our individual expenses in half. There was also the issue of the back rent at my current residence which I was in no position to address & so I made the difficult decision to move house. I would definitely miss Simone but I had to do what was in the best interest of myself & my child.

Once I had moved house I didn't inform the gentleman right away as to where I was living. My son's babysitter lived in the same house as his niece & so when he felt like it he would go there to see him. It was agreed that he would pay the babysitter which he did for the most part because his niece held him accountable. On the odd occasion though I would arrive to pick up my son & got held hostage because he didn't visit to pay the babysitter. It is sad to say that she had already gained knowledge of his dirty ways & so she knew that had I left with the child, he wouldn't be coming to pay her. It would have just been one excuse after another. So I had to sit there & wait until he came by with the money before I was allowed to leave. The babysitter was Jamaican so you know she nah joke bout har money.

Couple months had passed & the gentleman still had no knowledge of where I was living. It wasn't until my son fell ill & was admitted to hospital that the information was shared. Surprisingly he showed up at the hospital this time & took me home to pack a bag & took me back to the hospital.

As I'm writing, I am now wondering whether he showed up only because he was curious to find out where I was now living because for the next couple of days while my son was hospitalised he didn't visit not even once. I remember even when my son got discharged my cousin & I had to take the bus home because as per usual he committed to picking us up but didn't show.

Now as parents you know how stressed out we get when our children are not well. So you know it was not the time for Sophia to be calling me about some stupid bullshit.

I saw the blocked call coming in & I immediately thought about her & so I didn't answer. I kept sending the call to voicemail. So she decided to leave me a long ass message accusing me of coming to her house & stealing a phone. You know what was funny the gentleman gave me the phone because mine had stopped working. Also, he took the phone to me at the babysitter's house, I didn't go to her house.

My cousin was so upset. I remember her saying "No man dah gyal yah brite, she see yuh look like thief?" Anyway, my cousin was praying for her to call back because we had decided to fix har business.

She was so predictable! She was never going to stop calling until she got to tell me whatever it is that was on her mind. I don't think she was prepared for what would greet her this time. She called back & as soon as I answered she asked if I wasn't going to return her phone before she calls the police, before I could say anything my cousin grabbed the phone & said " Big pu#$y Sophia, weh yuh nuh leave mi cousin alone?! From she come yah you a tek set pon har tru you think she nuh have nobody but mi deh yah fi yuh! Stop call har a ask bout fu@&in# phone weh yuh man tek & gi har, she neva thief nuttn from yuh & a nuh fi har fault mek di man a bun yuh!" She was at a loss for words & had no choice but to hang up.

You see while I felt guilty about the fact that Christopher not only wronged me but also her, so I was sometimes understanding of her antics, my cousin on the other hand couldn't care less whether she was wronged or not. Her thinking was if you call to make trouble, you are going to get back trouble.

She later reported to her husband that my cousin & I ganged her. So I asked him if it was possible to gang people through the phone? I asked him why did he give me a phone that belonged to her his reply to which was that phone wasn't hers & she just saw that it was no longer in the house & automatically assumed that he had given it to me & so she decided to call & accuse me of stealing it. After hearing this I no longer felt bad about how my cousin dealt with her.

I don't know if it was the hospital situation that had frightened Christopher but the next thing I knew he had agreed to start doing the grocery shopping. So I would pay my rent & bills & he would now be not only paying the babysitter but also buying grocery monthly. Should I get excited? Maybe not, as I just might jinx it!

PLENTY OF FISH

So the gentleman lived up to his commitment to purchase grocery monthly. As for the babysitter, he hardly had to pay her. The house that I had moved in with my cousin was occupied by 5 other females all Jamaicans. Everyone had their own little struggle & so we all came together & helped each other however we could. So each person would babysit my son on their days off & so I didn't need a babysitter most of the time.

Two of the females were hairdressers, O how I longed to have my hair done professionally. Previously it was Simone who would try to relax & wash my hair. Hairdressers in England were very expensive & many didn't have a clue about how to do black people's hair. I knew my housemates needed the money, we all needed money but they knew I didn't have it to pay & so they did my hair for free & they made no fuss about this. I remember on some occasions once their bosses weren't at work, I would get to have the salon experience. You wouldn't begin to understand how privileged I felt & this was all because I knew that ordinarily this wasn't an experience I could have otherwise afforded.

Now I had locked shop on the gentleman. If this terminology is new to you it simply means that I was withholding sex. Maybe this was the reason I started getting the groceries or maybe the groceries was his statement to say he had changed.

I remember meeting this nice white guy called Tony. He was a teacher & an athlete. The only thing that freaked me out about Tony was his tongue & eyebrow piercings, I really didn't care much for those. I met him at the store & he just kept on coming by everyday until I decided to go out for drinks with him.

I remember getting dressed in a mini denim jeans skirt & a mesh black, white & red zip front long sleeve top & my heels. I remember the excitement in the house after I got dressed. By this time I was saying to myself it's time to move on & leave Christopher & his wife alone.

Tony came to pick me up from my house & we went to a pub in Croydon to have a meal & drinks. Once I got into his car, I reached into my purse, took out my scissors & said to him in my Jamaican accent "Nuh bada think you can try nuh funny business wid me, mi will stab yuh!" The poor guy's face went bright pink but nevertheless he assured me that he wasn't one of those guys. We had a good night out never to be repeated. Why? Because after all my tough talk, the first sign of Christopher pretending to love & care about me resulted in me going right back to him & in his web of lies.

The gentleman came with his sorry story & like I told Tony, he is my child's father & so I felt the need to give it another shot with him. So just like that I had sent Tony on his merry way. But by now y'all would know that my life had a way of constantly showing me up as a yamhead, & it decided to do so once again.

One day I got a phonecall from Christopher's niece asking me if I didn't hear that Michelle was pregnant, so I said no. She went on to say that she had just seen her on the bus very heavily pregnant & when she mentioned to her that she wasn't aware of the fact that she was expecting, she replied to say "So your uncle didn't tell you?" I could not believe what I was hearing. So his niece went on to say yes mi love she seh a fi him pickney. Now it was by all means possible that this child was indeed his as we all knew about him & her sneaking around. Remember I had seen text messages between them previously but not only that I had caught her at his house as well.

One day I went to pick up my son after work & the babysitter said she wasn't paid so you know the drill, I had to sit & wait. I kept calling him & he kept saying he would be there shortly. His niece passed the remark to say that he was clearly busy with his white schoolaz. So I asked her what she was talking about. She went on to say that he drove pass her earlier with Michelle in the front of the car. He didn't live far from the babysitter so I told them I would soon be back.

I decided to walk around to his house. He lived in an apartment building so you had to be let into the building. I buzzed his door number & he picked up the intercom. I could hear the surprise in his voice asking me what I was doing there. I told him I came to collect the babysitter's money. All of this conversation was taking place through the intercom. He went on to say that I should go & he would drop the money off. So I told him no I wasn't leaving without the money because I am being told that I can't take home my child until the money was paid. As luck would have it someone was exiting the building & so I was able to get in. As I walked in I saw Michelle with her shoe in her hand being sent up on the other floor to hide.

I was so enraged that I ran into his apartment, ran to his kitchen, grabbed a knife & ran off him. He started screaming to his son to call the police & at this point I remembered my child & so I told him to just hand over the money so I could leave.

As I was waiting to get the money, Michelle came back in his apartment & I heard him chasing her out like a dog, telling her she was fu@%ing stupid all because he wanted her to go hide & she refused to. He threw her bag & whatever else she had in the apartment through his living room window. Please bear in mind that this was the same apartment where his wife lived, she was just at work. I collected my money & left.

While walking back to the babysitter I heard someone calling my name, it was Michelle. Clearly she knew about me as well. She was crying to say how horrible Christopher was & that he was a bastard & a host of other things. I just kept on walking because she really didn't know the anger that was boiling inside of me & it was by no means for her. I was angry with myself! Like why the hell did I decide to get back with this man?!

I got to the babysitter, paid her & left but not before the gentleman's niece deciding to laugh about the madness that just took place. You see he called her to ask if she was the one who told me that Michelle was at his house. I couldn't get home fast enough. I needed to just go & buss a bawl & get it out my system.

BACK TO THE DRAWING BOARD

After learning about Michelle's pregnancy, it was time to go back to the drawing board & re-visit my prior decision to get back with Christopher. I felt so embarrassed I couldn't even find the courage to reach out back to Tony.

So it was time to go fishing again to see what I could drag in this time. Most evenings after work I would go by Tiffany's workplace to wait on her to get off work so we could go home together. So one evening while I was there waiting she introduced me to her manager. He seemed like an okay guy, British with Jamaican parents.

I don't remember clearly at what point we exchanged numbers but we did & we would communicate. I just needed to keep myself distracted so I didn't feel the need to buy into Christopher's lies once again. We hung out on a few occasions & eventually started hooking up. We were both clear on the fact that the situation would be going nowhere as he lived at home with his babymother at the time, & as for me I really didn't know who or what I wanted.

I remember being at work one Sunday & getting a call through the switchboard, it was Christopher. The first thing I heard was "Yuh neva know mi woulda find out bout you & di man weh yuh cousin set you up pon?" So I asked him what was he on about. He went on to say that he had made contact with one of our former housemates & after promising her financial assistance, she pretty much told him everything that took place in our flat. So I asked him why would anything I do be of any concern to him when he had Michelle pregnant & had now started seeing another young white girl Mary. He went on to say that he was done with me & some other madness which I didn't really hear as I was so confused by his reaction.

While making my way home that evening I must have gotten about a million text messages where I was called every name under the sun. I was told once again that it was over & I replied to this particular message to say okay, no problem. Being the mamma man he was he also called my cousin's boss trying to curse the man & telling him to leave me alone. My cousin's boss told him not to call his phone with any drama, he was not on that. He also told him if he felt as though I was with another man, he should check himself to see why I found it necessary.

I got home & started telling my cousin everything that was going on. When I walked in, the family members of our former housemate were there as we had gotten in touch with them to come & remove her belongings from the apartment. She had done a disappearing act on us as soon as her rent became due. All efforts to make contact with her proved futile. They too were trying to make contact with her without success & so they agreed to visit to see how much stuff was there to be removed & to determine whether they would have been able to remove them on her behalf.

While we were there speaking to the ladies we heard the doorbell. My cousin went to get the door. She looked through the peephole & saw that it was Christopher. With everything that I told her that was happening I don't know why she decided to let him in, but she did. One minute I'm standing in the hallway having a conversation with the ladies & the next thing I knew I was grabbed by my neck & was being dragged into my room which was at the end of the hallway.

My cousin started shouting for him to let me go & started jumping on him to try & get him off me. By the time she eased him off & asked him what the hell he was doing, he replied to say why she didn't ask me what I was doing when she was giving me man. I don't know who told me to open my mouth & utter the fact that not only does he have a wife but a babymother in the making plus another woman, so I was within my right to do as I wish. Before I could finish the statement I was punched in my stomach. He kept saying "a bighood man yuh want?" Clearly this was something else that our former housemate had fed him. As you all know women talk, so she gave him every bit of detail from our conversations.

Once I overcame the shock of being hit, I picked up the phone & dialed 999. I remember him pulling the phone out the wall & running out the house. Once I had plugged the phone back in, it was already ringing. The police was calling back. I told them what had happened & they asked me whether he was still at the house & I told them no. They asked me to describe the vehicle he was driving & I did. They used the CCTV cameras to locate him, blocked his vehicle & arrested him. I remember my cousin saying to me "Stacey a yuh babyfather, nuh mek dem lock him up." I was very short in my response to her & all I had to say was "my father neva lick me yet, suh mi nah tek no man lick."

The next morning on my way to work I saw his car parked up on the sidewalk. He didn't get very far before being arrested. The one thing I appreciated with England was how serious they took domestic disputes & domestic violence. Hours before he was released I got a call from the police asking whether I felt safe or if I required a restraining order. They also went on to ask whether I wanted to take out a protective order to restrict him from being able to see my son. Listening to all this, the measures sounded very extreme. Him spending the night in jail was enough for me.

Christopher clearly didn't know where my head was at & what would be my next move & so as soon as he was released he made his way to my house to "smooth" things over. It was during this visit that I would hear a conversation between him & our former housemate who we had not been able to contact but he somehow could. She pretty much called to see whether the information she had provided had done its intended damage. I don't think she was amused when she asked him if he was around me & he replied yes. She quickly ended the call.

I continued to get calls from the police asking whether I had decided to press charges against Christopher but once again I told them that I didn't wish to pursue the matter any further. It was after all this excitement that I was given the first engagement ring. Don't ask me why the hell I took it! After all, the man was still married so the ring was clearly some poppyshow business, but guess what I was the biggest poppyshow.

MY NAME IS STACEY & I AM A MAN CLOWN

So I took the popcorn ring. Not only did I take it but I felt so proud & overjoyed that I even took pictures & posted them on then social media platform Hi5. Did I stop to think that Christopher would probably never get divorced & I would be engaged forever, NO. The thought never crossed my mind, not even once.

Why did I somehow get so much joy from this ring? Why did I decide to ignore the ever present reality I faced daily? Immaturity maybe? Or maybe it was because from the outset this was the picture I had painted in my mind that Christopher was going to be my husband, we were in for the long haul & he would be my forever. I am so happy that I was this stupid at a young age because being an old man clown wouldn't be cute at all.

Shortly after I was given the ring, I was called by not just one but three women all with a different case that they somehow thought it necessary for me to hear. I guess I was a judge by occupation & didn't even realise it. The first call came from the wife because she somehow just found out that Michelle was pregnant & her husband's name was being called so she saw it fit to share the news with me. The weird thing was she thought that by telling me she was somehow throwing egg on my face, like how stupid is that?! So after she made her speech & I said to her &? She went on to say him nuh want you! So I asked her if he wanted her, seeing that she was his WIFE & he had now fathered not one but two kids while being married to her. I think she recognised how stupid she looked & sounded & so she hung up.

The next call came from the new babymother Michelle, don't ask me how she got my number. Probably the same way I got information many times. You see the gentleman sleeps very sound so it was the easiest thing to break into his phones while he was asleep. Anyway, she called to tell me that she was pregnant & he was denying that it was his child & that he was the only man she was with. So I asked her what was I to do with the information she was giving me. The young miss said ME Stacey Williams mus go talk to him because ME know seh dem did deh because I caught her at his house more than once. God know mi neva wah diss har because I realised that her call was out of desperation so I just hung up on her. You see Christopher had this way of saying he was not the father once kids came in the picture & would start asking the females for a DNA test even when the whole world knew he was with these women.

The final call came from Mary, his wife's sister's best friend. You know what was interesting, Michelle, Mary & his wife's sister Catherine were all friends from school. So they were all brought to his house by his wife's little sister after school during the days where they would hang out & oftentimes babysat his son. Now the fact that he was sexually involved with all of them, this ruined their friendship & the competition was to see which one out of the lot he really wanted to be with. So anyway, back to Mary. She called to tell me to leave her man alone & that she was the one he wanted. Now this shit was funny. You see a few months prior I met this girl up close & personal. How? My son had an appointment & when Christopher came & picked us up she was in the car along with his wife's sister Catherine. He had made mention that she was the sister's friend. Now if you had something to say to me, you saw me in person & had the opportunity to, why didn't you? Anyway, I asked her if she had called his wife to give her the memo as well to leave her man alone, she went silent. You see the wife saw her as her little sister's friend & welcomed her in, even took her to Jamaica with them on holiday & now she was claiming the lady's husband. I wasn't going to waste my time on her because I saw her in person & she couldn't walk in my shoe no day, she wasn't in my league! But I guess we could say that she won the prize because she is still with Christopher to this day! They now have two children together, one of which was conceived during the time he & I were together. He constantly denied that the child was his but we all witnessed the child calling him daddy at some point.

Work was going well. I was selected to go on a training program at the end of which it would be determined whether I would be promoted to the role of senior sales which was similar to a supervisor. I went to the training, did my thing & voila I was promoted. Whilst retail would never have been my career path had I been in Jamaica, I was starting to love it. I loved being in the know re fashion trends & having firsthand information on styling. What was even better was the fact that I got a 50% discount on all items that I bought. I remember hooking up the girls in the household by making purchases for them on my discount.

I remember even shopping for Christopher whenever he was slated to visit Jamaica. I wasn't able to travel as my passport was still with immigration pending a decision on the application that Simone had submitted on my behalf. Shortly thereafter I would receive a registered document from the Home Office stating that the application submitted by Simone was denied on the basis that my parents were still alive & as such a guardian wasn't necessary. They went on further to say that seeing that I had family back in Jamaica it wasn't unreasonable to be asked to return home to said family.

It was like I was hit with a tonne of bricks. My next move was to engage the services of a legal aid lawyer that was referred to me by my friend's girlfriend Kaydiane. I met with the gentleman who might I add was Jamaican. He instructed me to try & enroll back in college & they would resubmit an application for an extension of the student visa. The next couple of days were spent running up & down trying to get everything in place. I must say that the gentleman came through with providing bank statements for himself & his wife & providing a letter to say that they were my sponsors in the country. I knew his wife didn't have a clue that he had copied her passport & other documents & had given same to me but this was one time that I felt no guilt about anything, I was just trying to get myself sorted out.

You see England wasn't the easiest place to survive if you were an illegal immigrant. Their officers could see you anywhere & do a random on the spot name check to determine your immigration status & based on what the check returned you could be detained on the spot & later deported. It was also difficult to work without proper documentation due to the fact that employers could be charged up to £5000 if they are found guilty of employing illegal immigrants. So to avoid all this added stress, I just needed to try as best as possible to get myself in order.

An appeal & new application was submitted for me by the lawyer. Once again it was back to waiting to see the outcome. I remember Simone & others suggesting to Christopher that he should try & look into arranging a business marriage for me which would have probably been the easiest route to me getting documented. He shot down the idea almost immediately & went on to say that most men even after being paid still ask the females for sex as part of the payment package to see the process through. Even when it was suggested that he used one of his friends who he trusted, the answer was still no.

I figure he was just trying to keep me under his thumb & one such way to do that was to keep my immigration status in limbo. But how long did he think he could do this for?

TRAVEL WOES

One of the things that weighed on me heavily was my inability to travel. The fact that I was stuck didn't stop Christopher from living his best life.

Shortly after being given the engagement ring, the gentleman travelled to America with his wife & son. Again I found myself wondering why I took the ring & the more I thought about it the clearer it became that the ring was just given to me to "cool me" & provide some false sense of security.

They say we are to try & look for something positive in every situation, so I guess I should look at the fact that at least he told me about this particular trip to America. You see previously he & his family went to Disneyland Paris & I only found out when I was not able to contact him for days & decided to call his niece. There I was thinking something had happened to the gentleman only to learn that he had gone on a family vacation.

It was very hard not being able to travel to see my family especially when I heard some of what was happening with my parents health wise which they tried to keep from me most of the time & I would only learn of the situations after the fact. I always feared getting bad news & not being able to move. So to be this disturbed by my inability to travel & to constantly have to watch Christopher jet off was even more stressing.

To be honest, he never seemed bothered or concerned by the fact that I was not able to see my family. I guess it was all about being in control. I remember when I learned that I had an older brother in England & my dad told me that he had given him my details to get in touch how excited I was. The minute I was in contact with my brother & he started visiting & coming around, Christopher started to accuse me of putting my family before him. He very rarely slept at my house, most times only after he had been thrown out by his wife but the moment he heard that my brother was coming to spend the weekend with my cousin & I, he started a big argument because apparently he had planned on sleeping over that very same weekend & now I was telling him he couldn't because of my brother & my space constraint. Once again I was accused of putting my family before him & he went on to add that I better hope my family is always there for me. I just couldn't win.

Sad part was the fact that he actually got the opportunity to say to me "seet deh yuh family let yuh dung". You see one Easter he was in Jamaica & I had an emergency & needed some cash. In England it was very difficult to save because of all the bills you had to pay. Light, water, gas, TV license (yes you had to pay to watch your own TV), rent, council tax & your monthly travel card to take you to & from work. I lived pay cheque to pay cheque. So once there was any kind of unforeseen expenses, I would have to ask for help. He had asked his nephew to take the cash to me but that didn't work out. When it didn't, he suggested that I borrow the money from my brother until he returned. The request didn't sound unreasonable to me & so I decided to ask.

I called my brother & had explained the situation to him. His first question was weh yuh babyfada deh? So I explained to him that he was presently in Jamaica but once he returned he would have been reimbursed or if his nephew got to me first, then he would have gotten back the funds even sooner. My BROTHER went on to say that the fact that he had only just known me for a year or so, he doesn't think that I should be asking him for any favours. He went on further to say that we didn't grow together as brother & sister & so favours were off limits. The last thing he said to me was if my babyfather wasn't covering what he was supposed to, then I needed to go & look another man. I was dumbstruck! After I picked my jaw up from the floor, I reminded him that he had daughters & I asked him if he would have told them to go & look a man had it been them asking for help, his reply to which was sure once they are old enough.

When I reiterated what my brother had said to Christopher, he laughed non-stop & said "And a him you did wah put before me? All a tell mi mi cah sleep over cause breda a come spend weekend" & he started laughing again. I was low key embarrassed by the whole situation. I remember telling my dad who was just as surprised by my brother's reaction. I knew my dad wasn't there for him as a child & he might still have been bitter about that, but in the year or so that I had known him, I never saw any indication of ill feelings, we got on very well.

If he had just said no he wasn't able to, I wouldn't have had an issue. My issue was with all the extra hurtful things that were added. That was the last time we spoke. It is now years later & to this day I still haven't tried having any kind of contact with him. Sometimes we have to love some of our relatives from a distance.

NEW BOSS, WHO THAT?

I had now started on my journey of being one of the senior sales representatives for my location. The new title meant that on some days I would be responsible for closing the store. I didn't get opening duties mainly because they were aware that my daily commute to get to work was over 2 hours long. Just to give you an idea, I would get a bus from home to the train station, get a train to another train station where I would then take the underground tube. I would then change at one of the underground stations to get another train called docklands light railway. This train would then take me to the area where the mall was located that I worked but I still had to get a bus to take me from the train station to the mall as it was not in walking distance. Most days I felt exhausted before I even started working but I knew I had to do what was necessary as I had a child to take care of.

In addition to closing the store, I was also now responsible for doing the banking & just pretty much running the day to day operation on days when the managers were off. Have you ever gone to the supermarket or any store for that matter & heard the cashier saying override & you would see someone walking briskly towards them, I was now that someone. I also had the very difficult task of taking decisions on refunds. This was always a nightmare.

You see it was customary for people to purchase clothing, wear them & then feel as though they were entitled to a refund all because the tags were still attached & they had a receipt. Well not on my shift! Sometimes you could smell the perspiration in the clothing along with perfume & cigarette but they still had the nerve to take the clothing back for a refund. I guess nothing tried nothing done.

As part of my duty I also had to helicopter the floors. So one little body overseeing the operation of two floors. I remember my second time closing & everything had gone smoothly throughout the day. It was ten minutes to closing time &

everyone was busy sizing back clothing, straightening shoes etc to get the store ready for opening the following day, when we heard the slide doors open followed by the security tag alarm. Someone had just driven up in front of the store, ran in & grabbed one set of jeans that were at the front, ran back out & sped off in the getaway car that was waiting. Security was very inefficient on that mall, they were never there when you needed them. We radioed them but they weren't even able to spot the vehicle on camera, the culprits were long gone. So now I would have to write a report detailing what occurred for submission to our loss prevention unit.

You see shoplifting wasn't uncommon. You had the persons who did the grab & run, & then you had those who came in the store pretending to be customers. I remember being in the back one day doing stock taking & hearing on the radio that there were some suspicious females in the store. My coworkers had only recently learned that I was Jamaican, all this time they thought I was mixed race British. Once they were armed with this information, they would always summon me whenever Jamaicans came in the store speaking patois so that I could translate. Once they heard the patois they automatically assumed a robbery was being planned.

It was sad to see my people being stigmatized this way but the harsh reality was they made this name for themselves & so the good suffered for the bad. I myself had gone into other retail chains & was constantly followed around by workers & security all because my accent wasn't British.

So yes I was summoned to come on the shop floor because of suspicious Jamaicans that had entered. Anyway, I walked out to go & see who the potential culprits were. When I looked one of the females was someone I attended high school with. She greeted me & was saying she didn't know I was in England & started asking how long I had been there etc. I got straight to the point & said to her "A thief you come in here wid yuh fren fi thief?" I could see the shock on her face but she knew that was definitely her intention. So she went on to say that it was her hustle. I told her to go hustle somewhere else because they suspected her & police was on standby.

You see clutching as it is called was a very prominent job in England. You would believe it was legal based on how serious it was taken. They, the clutchers, left home early like regular working people & returned late. I remember sharing a house with someone in that job sector. What was alarming to me was that this lady was a mature individual in her 50s. I remember her telling my cousin & I that anything we wanted from any of the top stores, we were just to take a picture & show it to her & she would get it for us & we pay her half price. Having worked in retail & knowing the impact of the losses to these businesses, my conscience wouldn't allow me to be one of her clients. We eventually had to give her notice because I swear she was going to beat us off in our own place (the lease was in our names & we rented her a room).

This wouldn't have been the first time my cousin & I had to go through hell with Jamaican housemates. The first one was so bad we moved house in record time, 24hrs! We had to leave before he got released from lockup.

SAY NO TO DRUGS

Some of our original housemates had moved out & so the landlord started showing the property to new prospects. Next thing we knew we had a new housemate, a Jamaican male.

This was the first time we were having to share the space with a male, the house had been all female previously. He seemed to be low key at the start. We hardly saw him & sometimes the only way to know he was there was by the loud music he played.

He eventually moved in his girlfriend. As per usual, my cousin struck up a friendship with her. So whilst her boyfriend didn't speak much to us, she on the other hand would. We noticed however that if the boyfriend was home, then she couldn't speak to us at all.

It wasn't before long that he started abusing her constantly. I remember my cousin asking her why doesn't she go back home to her family to escape the abuse her reply to which was that she loved him. Not only did she love him but she was also terrified of him. She defended him by saying he wasn't always like that. So we asked what had changed? She refused to answer.

You see our room was on the ground floor & was pretty much the front of the house. We could hear anyone coming in & out & we could also see. Her boyfriend was very active throughout the night, going in & out constantly. We came to the conclusion that he was obviously dealing something but as to what we weren't sure.

I remember one night he was beating his girlfriend for hours & when my cousin & I thought it was going on for too long we decided to call the police. Now this was where it all started. When the police arrived his girlfriend told them that it was just a simple argument & she was okay. Like I mentioned previously our room was on the ground floor, they were above us. We could hear her being tossed around & screaming & crying for him to stop but like she said it was just a simple argument so the police left. Once they left she got another beating for letting the "dutty gal dem downstairs" call police on him.

The fact that we had called the police now made us public enemies number one & he forbade her from speaking to us. This didn't stop her from hiding & speaking to us though. After all, she had to because sometimes he left her there without food & we had to help her out. Despite our encouragement to her to go home to her family, she decided to stick with her man.

I can't say for sure what the boyfriend was selling but whatever it was it was very obvious that he was trying it out too. The first thing he started to do was to break all the bulbs in the communal areas in the house. So the kitchen, hallway & bathroom were in darkness. As soon as we would replace the bulbs, he would break them again. We reported the matter to the landlord but he too seemed to have been afraid of him & so nothing was done.

On another occasion he went & doused the bath, which was white, with browning. It was like he poured bottles upon bottles of browning in the bath. It was one shared bathroom & as such we had to clean the mess. We reported the matter to the landlord again & nothing was done.

On Saturday mornings when he knew everyone was home he would start blasting music from as early as 7am. All of this was because we decided to call the police on him for abusing the girl. This erratic behaviour continued for a while.

One Saturday I had to work & my cousin was babysitting my son. He had started playing the loud music before I left. So after I left for work my cousin decided to play her music also, it was going to be a sound clash. He sent his girlfriend to tell my cousin to turn down her music & she declined. It was clear he thought he was the boss of the house.

Once his girlfriend reported that she had declined, he came downstairs to our room door & started arguing. If there was one thing about my cousin, she was not going to walk away, she was going to argue with you. One thing lead to another & knives were drawn, please bear in mind my child was in the midst of this madness.

She went into our room, locked the door & thought everything was over only to hear the door being kicked. He was trying to come in on her to do what, only God knows. She had to use the chest of drawers to brace the door & proceeded to call the police. When he couldn't get into our room, he went into our kitchen cupboards & dumped all of our grocery all over the kitchen. The police came & they arrested him.

I got a call at work & was told all of what was going on. The police asked that both my cousin & I visit the station to give statements about present & past events. I left work & headed to the police station. While we were there we heard a gentleman asking to see our housemate & asking the police what he was being held for. While the police explained we pretended not to be the persons involved.

Once I returned home & saw the damage, I felt mostly hurt by the fact that all of my son's food had been dumped. Like does he know how hard we were working to make ends meet? We reported the matter to the landlord & had explained to him that the police would have been contacting him to confirm whether he wanted to press charges for the damage to his property or not. We were told that because it wasn't our house, we couldn't.

Based on the landlord's reaction, we knew he didn't plan on doing anything & so it came as no surprise when we were called by the police to say that he had refused to press charges & so they would have to release the mad man. The police told us that they didn't think it was safe for us to be in the same house with him going forward & suggested that we try to relocate. They agreed to hold him for another 24hrs to allow us the time to get out.

Where have you ever heard it possible to find somewhere to live in 24hrs?!

YOU HAVE 24HRS

We had to start planning our escape. There was no way we were going to get somewhere to rent in a day. We had called our landlord to ask whether any of his other properties were available, his reply to which was no.

By this time I had already informed Christopher of the drama. I had now called him back to advise him of the fact that I had 24 hours to relocate. Lucky for me his wife was in Jamaica & so the plan was to store my stuff in a shed that they had & to stay at their house until I found a place. I think she was going to be in Jamaica for a month. As for my cousin, she also went to her boyfriend's house.

I have never had to pack so many things in such a short time. Not only did we have to pack but we also had to arrange a moving van & keep in mind that we were going to two different locations so you know it was going to also cost us a lot. I remember by the time the police called us to say the mad man had been released, we had already left.

Over the next couple of weeks we were actively house hunting. After this experience we decided not to share house with any strangers going forward. The plan was to rent an entire house for ourselves. Our female friends that we had lived with prior knew someone who had a flat renting & so they had put in a word for us & we were able to get it.

I really wanted to go back in my own space as it felt very weird being in a house that was filled with pictures of Christopher & his wife. I saw pictures taken at places that I didn't even know that he had gone to. There was a lot of vacations happening that I had no knowledge of.

One night he was in the living room on his computer. How it was set up his back was to the entrance door & so he couldn't see me coming in. When I looked he had a picture up of a little girl which seemed to have been Michelle's baby. After seeing that picture one thing I knew for sure was that the child was mixed race & the father was definitely a black man. I had no doubt that the child was his. I didn't create a scene or made him aware that I had seen the picture because my plan was to go into the computer once he had left for work to read the email that came with the picture.

As soon as he left for work the following evening, he worked night shifts at the time, I went into his AOL account to see what was happening. I found the email which pretty much spoke about him denying being the father of the child. She also reassured him that he was the only man that she had been with. To be honest most young white British girls had very bad reputations, they were very bad or as we would say in Jamaica manny manny. I am not saying this to say that she was lying, I am just sharing my observation for the 5 years I was there. She sent the pictures like she said to show him how much the little girl looked like him. In the email she also made mention of the fact that she had named the child Destiny which I think is self explanatory.

The next thing I came across on the computer was a video which seemed to have been made in his house based on the lilac wall paint in the background but the person in the video was a different white British girl. His face was not in the video but his penis was & I'm very sure it was him. This I definitely confronted him about & he stood there & insulted my intelligence by saying it was a porn video that he had downloaded & that the person in the video wasn't him.

I waited again until he left for work & made some further checks. When I went into his AOL account I realised that he was hooking up with people who he had met in the chatrooms. So the video I found was of one such girl. I found the conversation where they planned their rendezvous as she didn't even live in London. So she travelled to come & collect the penis.

You see I didn't know a lot of what was going on due to the fact that we lived separately so it wasn't until I started staying at his house that my eyes were opened to so much more. Another thing

I came across were prescribed antibiotics. My sister is a pharmacist & I knew for a fact that those capsules were for germs. Now my thing was if it is that you suspect you have some kind of infection don't you know that unless ALL your partners are treated it will just be recurring?! When I asked him about the antibiotics he told me that they were for his sinus infection. Prior to now I had never heard this man speak of having sinus issues. Nevertheless, I listened to his bullshit story & kept quiet because guess what remember I was "kotching" at his place. I used the presence of those pills as a reminder to myself that I needed to go do my checks & to be more careful when it came on to him. I would receive a call a few months later from Mary telling me that I should go check myself for chlamydia because both her & Michelle tested positive & they must have gotten it from him. I remember telling her "Cheers mate but I'm not a part of that party."

The time had come for us to move into our own place. I was so happy to be back in my own space. The flat needed a little work as it had been locked up prior to us moving in but we didn't mind, we just wanted to regain our freedom.

We took our time & did what we needed, to get the place to the point where it felt like home. I remember buying a brand new bed & getting the delivery in boxes. This was my first bed purchase, my other beds came with the houses. At first I told the delivery guy that there seemed to have been a mistake & that I had ordered a bed. He replied by saying that the delivery was indeed a bed. So I asked him why was it in boxes his reply to which was that I would need to fit it up.

But this is serious! Screw up bed?! This was like a culture shock for me. When the closet & chest of drawers were eventually delivered in boxes too I was now over the shock & better prepared. In no time our new flat felt like home & we were back to our regular schedules.

CHANGES CHANGES CHANGES

There was a vacancy that had come up at work for a menswear sales manager. They decided to have me act in the post. I enjoyed dressing the men that entered the store. They would just provide details of the event they would be attending & I would put some looks together for them.

Another responsibility I had was to merchandise the floor to ensure the best sellers were promoted & were very visible. It was after being assigned to the menswear department that I became very close with a colleague called Victoria. Prior to now we had just been cordial with each other, but didn't speak much. The fact that we were now working on the same floor meant we chatted a lot.

It was from all this chatting that I learned that she had kids with a rastafarian who she later married. He wasn't Jamaican but was from another caribbean island. I also learned that weed was her best friend & she made no apologies, she was proud of her weed smoking. I would later meet her family one evening when they came to pick her up from work. She brought them in & introduced them all to me. Her kids were the sweetest.

What I admired most about her was the level of respect she had for me. Despite the fact that she was a much older person & had been working with the company longer than I was, she had no problem taking directives from me. It made life so much easier. She also didn't try to undermine my authority in anyway. She ran all queries & suggestions by me before moving forward. She was a very genuine person & I appreciated that.

It wasn't long before she had invited me over to her house for dinner. I knew it would have been English cuisine but I had faith in the fact that her husband was caribbean & so the food would have been well seasoned & indeed it was. She fell in love with my son & he loved the company of her two smaller children. Next thing I knew he was being invited over for a sleep over.

You know how we are as parents & so my first reaction was one of apprehension & I kept saying to myself just say no. After a while I thought about it & agreed to have my son go. He had an amazing time & looked forward to going back. I remember my son coming home with bags of clothing where they had taken him shopping. He also came home with toys that her kids had grown out & he somehow fell in love with during his stay. My son soon became a regular at her house & was affectionately called "my likkle twanny" by her.

I was later informed that they had selected someone from outside the company to fill the role of sales manager. I was devastated! I was told that the reason for the decision was the fact that she had prior experience in a similar role. I remember being a complete b@$ch to the girl when she arrived. When she would ask me things I pretended not to know. I kept saying to myself they claim you are more experienced, so you should know it all.

She reported me at one point for insubordination. I explained to the manager that what she was asking me to do was not what was set out in the operations manual & so I declined. If you want to do something outside of policy, do it yourself. Nothing came out of the situation.

One thing that was clear to management though was the fact that we weren't getting along & they totally understood my position because they knew the work that I had put in to get the sales numbers up, & to ensure that we were always featured in the top ten. So this new person was just riding off the wave that I had put in motion.

It came as no surprise when they recommended me for a sales manager post at another location when it became available. I was very happy to be moving & I'm sure my coworker was even happier to see me go. We all fear change but sometimes it isn't so bad.

Victoria & I kept in touch even after I moved to the other store. I was still working in the East London area where she lived & so sometimes she would pop into my store to visit & we would have lunch & catch up. She still took my son on weekends & holidays for sleepovers.

Everything was going well & I was really starting to see a little light at the end of the tunnel. I was now earning more & was better able to meet my monthly expenses. I was also now able to send a little thing for my parents every now & again.

From early on in my life though I realised that if things were going too good for me, trouble would be looming. With this in mind it came as no surprise when I got called into a meeting at work based on an anonymous call that was made to my employer where it was alleged that I was in the country illegally. So who do you think would make such a call?

TROUBLE NEVA SET LIKE RAIN

So I was called in a meeting at which time I was told that I would need to provide a copy of my passport to confirm my eligibility to work in the UK. You see up to the time of the call, the persons at my new location had no Idea I was Jamaican. They all thought I was mixed race British.

I explained to them that my passport was not in my possession but instead was at the Home Office due to a pending application. They queried the visa I had prior to the submission & I confirmed that it was a student visa. Now the problem with a student visa is that it only allows you to work 20 hours per week, my new position required me to work fulltime.

Another thing the anonymous caller alleged was that I was stealing company property & supplying my boyfriend & myself. Now I use to shop for all my friends & the gentleman also because I got a 50% discount. The average jeans in the store went for approximately £45 minimum at the time, so the discount made a big difference. As sales manager I wore plain clothes & so any item of clothing I purchased for myself as uniform was discounted by 75%, so my jeans were sometimes £8, why would I need to steal? It was easy to disprove her claims because details of all purchases made were kept on our files so there were receipts for the men clothing she mentioned.

So by now you should have gathered that it was the gentleman's wife Sophia who had made the call. The sad thing is this wouldn't have been her first attempt at getting someone fired, she did the samething to Michelle. Sadly she was successful in getting her to lose her job.

Michelle was employed to a supermarket part time. What she would do was have Christopher visit her location whenever she was cashing. He would go to her to cash out his goods & she would swipe her employee discount card so his bill would be minimal. The discount card was not intended for the use of friends & family so the fact that she used it was a breach coupled with the fact that she cashed out her boyfriend. Friends & family should be referred to another cashier to make payment. She was immediately fired.

But how did Sophia know all this? Christopher told her! So apparently she kept seeing branded items in her house from this particular supermarket. Over the years they had always shopped at Tesco so she couldn't understand the new found interest in the other supermarket. So when she asked Christopher about it he told her that Michelle worked there & he was getting discounts. She didn't make it seem like it was an issue but clearly she had a plan.

So how do I know all this? She told me! I got a warning call to say that I was next because nobody was going to come to England & get weh she fi get. In my mind it was a silly threat because unlike Michelle, I knew using my discount was legitimate & as far as I was concerned she didn't know where I worked, so she was just trying to get me frightened.

Clearly she knew where I worked but how could she have known? When I called Christopher about what was happening at work, the first thing he said was a must Sophia. So the million dollar question was how did she know where I worked? There was a little umm ummm until I heard that he had apparently visited my house & searched it up looking for my payslip because he was curious to know what I was now earning. After locating the payslip apparently he heard my footsteps & so he pushed the payslip into his pants pocket. He went home & forgot that it was in his pocket. So when his wife searched as she usually does, she found it. I could not believe what I was hearing.

Imagine I went & got myself a job because he failed not only me but my child & now because of him my financial independence was being threatened again. I was so pissed! If you wanted to know how much I was earning, why couldn't you have just asked? Or is it that you think I wouldn't have told you the truth?

Coming out of the meeting I was asked to have my lawyer provide me with a document to confirm that I had an application pending at the Home Office. I visited the lawyer, he prepared the document & I took same into my manager. This settled the dust for a little but I could tell that going forward they would still be hounding me to provide my passport. Every business feared being fined £5000 for employing persons not eligible to work in the UK. So I knew it was just a matter of time before the issue arose again.

Apparently Christopher had confronted his wife about her antics & told her she was pure evil. Sounds like pot cursing kettle to me. He told her she was wrong for trying to stop people's income when she knew they had children to provide for. I don't think she took kindly to what sounded like him defending me & so I would shortly receive a chain of text messages telling me about my parts. I ensured I topped up my phone because the war was going to start.

WAR OF THE TEXTS

So it was the war of the texts, who fah text dem a sting hotter? That's what it came down to. Now remember I didn't trouble this lady, she decided to curse me after her husband confronted her.

Now she went to her little sister Catherine & her brother Doug & made it seem as though I was the one that was troubling her. I guess mi text dem did a lick hot so she called for back up. Remember her brother & I were friends from college, so his text message was pretty much to say that I was to desist from contacting his sister or else. So I asked him or else what? I told him to go & check her phone & see who was contacting who as I could guarantee that I wasn't the one reaching out to her. That was pretty much it from him.

The little sister Catherine who looked like the big sister because of her size, saw it fit to speak about my child. Now no matter how intense the arguments got between Sophia & I, I have NEVER mentioned her son because at the end of the day he is a child & has no business in the adult argument & despite what he was always going to be my son's brother.

Now her sister Catherine decided to tell me that I should spend more time looking after my son & if I didn't notice how thin he was like he was lacking food. She went on further to say that my kid looked malnourished & didn't seem to be healthy & looked sick. She then proceeded to say if I didn't see how her nephew looked healthy & well fed. You know by this time I was seeing straight red & so I read them their file.

I firstly addressed her & told her that the notion that being fat meant being healthy & slim unhealthy made her sound illiterate. I told her she was obese! I told her that as a young girl for her legs to be permanently glued together even when she walked meant she was obese. I told her that she couldn't walk for a minute without being out of breath. I told her to go & check herself in the mirror again & see if her reflection says healthy. I asked her if she could see her toes or even bend to touch them.

I went on further to tell her that she had no business getting involved in an argument that her sister started. She replied by saying she had all right, it's family. So I asked her if her sister wasn't family when she had her best friend sleeping with her husband?! There was a pause. I really couldn't understand her new found sense of loyalty. I mean even when I was staying at Christopher's house previously she saw me there on more than one occasion because I guess her sister left her to keep tabs, & I am sure she never once mentioned to her sister that he had me staying there. So for her to want to attack me now in the name of family was just hypocritical.

Anyway, I decided to address her comments about my child looking malnourished. I once again reminded her that fat doesn't mean healthy. I asked her what contributed to her nephew's weight that she was praising as healthy?
Before she could answer I started listing the items. Morley's chicken & chips, McDonalds, Walkers Crisps & a host of other junk foods. I reminded her that her sister couldn't cook, so a good meal was a scarce commodity in that household. So I told her not to be fooled by my son being slim, he was use to good food & was healthier than her entire family combined.

Now when I thought that was the end of that madness, I didn't know round two was brewing. I was in my room seated at my computer desk when I heard Christopher bursting through the door breathless. He was on top of his voice but to say I heard what he was saying would be a lie. So I asked him what was the issue? He said how dare I disrespect his son & that the wife had forwarded messages to him that I had sent. You know before I answered I started laughing because that's all I could have done at the time.

I proceeded to ask him whether he was shown the trail of messages or was he just sent one? He was still there carrying on as if he was getting into spirit. So I told him that her sister spoke on my child to say he looked ill among other things & I responded accordingly. Apparently I was wrong & I shouldn't have stooped to their level & speak about his son. So I said to him they disrespected your other son, so why aren't you defending that? His reply to which was "him deal wid dem already."

I turned my back & went back to playing my solitaire. The next thing I knew his finger was all up in my face & he was shouting & carrying on. He really came prepared to defend his son's honour. He proceeded to remove the hat he was wearing & started flashing it in my face as he spoke. I remember saying to him on more than one occasion "mine yuh mek the dirty hat lick mi ina mi face." I think me saying this pushed him to ensure that the hat would indeed hit me in the face. I guess he wanted to see what I would do. So when the hat eventually hit me in the face, I jumped up & I boxed him. He pushed me & I pushed him back & in the blink of an eye I was punched in the face.

As I held my eye & asked him "a weh yuh really just do?" I picked up the phone & called 999. As I spoke to the police he held on to my leg in tears, bawling & begging me not to report him. The more information I gave the more he turned on the water works. When he realised I was not going to honour his request, he ran out of the house before the police came.

When the police arrived & was knocking the front door, I decided not to answer in hopes that they would just leave & the whole issue would just die a natural death. But leaving was not in their plan, the knocks got louder & louder & started sounding more like bangs. I eventually opened the door at which time I was told that they were just about to break down the door. So I asked why? Their reply to which was that based on the nature of the call it could be assumed that I was inside & injured & so unable to come to the door. They asked me what had happened & I explained. Despite the fact that I told them it was okay I didn't want to pursue any action, they saw the bruising in my face & so despite me saying it was just an argument, the police man said no you were hit, that's domestic violence. I was asked for the details of the vehicle he had been driving & just like deja vu he was tracked via CCTV cameras & arrested at his house. For the next couple of days I would sport a black eye.

MY NEW FACE ACCESSORY

I had to call in sick to work based on the big black & blue ring that I now had around my eye. I however would need to figure out how to conceal it as I would need to go to work the next day as I was going to be closing the store.

I decided to try using some makeup to cover the bruise but it was so bad that I couldn't get it fully covered without my face looking heavily made up. So I decided to use the story that I was parting a fight between my cousin & her boyfriend & got hit in the process.

I remember walking into work & everyone asking what was wrong with my face. I had to ask if it was that obvious as I thought I had somewhat toned it down with the makeup but I guess not. Anyway, I ran with my story I got hit parting a fight. I was too embarrassed to disclose the truth.

I got home that evening & I called my mom & told her what had happened. She asked for Christopher's number & said she would give him a call because he had now crossed the line. I knew she probably wouldn't have gotten through to him anyway because he possibly was still in lock up.

His wife had sent me a message to say I was wicked because I was somehow wrong to have called the police. I had planned on ignoring the message but when I thought about why he got arrested in the first place & the fact that she created the situation, I had to put things into perspective for her because clearly she was suffering from memory loss.

After I reminded her of the fact that she was to be blamed for everything, she replied by saying I got what I deserved. After I had gotten over the shock of her telling me I deserved to be hit, I told her that the same was true for her husband, he also got what he deserved.

I spoke back with my mom the following day at which time she told me that she had gotten through to the gentleman. This was the only way I would have known that he was released from police custody as he was still not speaking to me. I think he too like his wife blamed me for how the situation ended. Now I was the only person hurt in this ordeal but I was still somehow made out to be the villain.

My mother advised that the gentleman told her that him hitting me was self defense because I was the one who had hit him first. When she told me what he had said my first reaction was to laugh. I then proceeded to explain to her exactly what had happened. Telling my mom was just for venting purposes because I knew there was absolutely nothing that she could have done. She also advised that Christopher disclosed that he was upset with how far I took things as I didn't have to call the police. She told me that she had related to him that my father had never placed his hands on me & so I did the right thing.

For the next couple of weeks I heard nothing from Christopher. The inner man clown in me was texting & calling trying to find out what was going on with him but I got no reply. Eventually I got a message to say that he needed to see his son. Now this was funny! Like who was withholding his son? I was not trying to argue with anyone again & so I packed my son's stuff & he picked him up to spend the day.

To say I didn't find his request weird would be a lie but like I said before I was just trying to keep the peace. I remember him taking back my son later that evening. My son was about 3 years old at the time. I remember him running in the house excited to tell me about his day out. Apparently his father took him to the park.

Even as I was listening to my son go on & on about the park, it just felt as though something was missing from the story. The gentleman was always so busy, park date was not in his DNA. So to say that I was surprised when my son said he played with

Destiny at the park & that they went on the swings, would be a lie.

So the park date was a family day out with Michelle & her daughter & the gentleman & my son. The confusing thing was the fact that he constantly denied that that little girl was his child but he was secretly playing family. But we should all know by now that living secret lives was his speciality.

When he heard my son mention Michelle's name to say that she was also at the park & that she played with him, I'm sure he saw the look on my face & it must have prompted him to run because the next thing I knew I was throwing everything from my chest of drawers at him. I still can't believe I threw my nice black & white ying yang vase at him & broke it. He wasn't even worth that but his lies & constant deception drove me crazy.

Then to think that after throwing so many missiles & smashing everything, not one of the objects hit the target. Dem did always seh lefthanded people hand lean & clearly there was some truth to this. All I did was to give myself a mess to clean up after. Life unfair bad!

PASSPORT PLEASE

Once again I was called into another meeting at work. The topic of said meeting was my passport & whether I was now in possession of same. Unfortunately, I still wasn't & this was explained.

I could see the discomfort when I told them that my application was still pending. I was asked whether I had received any correspondence since the last document that I had provided & I confirmed that I had received a letter confirming receipt of my application & advising that same was pending consideration. I was asked to take in said letter.

I remember having lunch later that day with Victoria. She lived close by & so would pop in to visit every now & again. I remember the topic of discussion over lunch being my immigration woes. Victoria was British born & so was clueless to a lot of what I was explaining that was going on with me. I however remember how teary eyed she got when I told her that I might possibly have to resign my position before they opt to fire me. Once I said this the first thing she asked was how was I going to take care of myself & twanny.

You see she also knew that I received little to no support from Christopher so going back to a situation where I was without an income would be to my own detriment. I told her that I would take in the letter I had received from immigration & hopefully same would be sufficient.

So the following day as requested, I provided the letter I had received from immigration. It seemed to have done a little damage control but there was still the question of whether I should be working full time hours seeing that my initial visa was a student visa & the renewal application was also for a student visa. I knew I wasn't suppose to have been working more than 20 hours weekly but I acted clueless while they deliberated.

I was dismissed from the meeting & told to return to my duties. But for the next couple of weeks I felt nothing but discomfort. Everyday I showed up for work I was wondering whether this was going to be the day that I would be fired. There was also the fear of whether the company would see it fit to make a call to immigration in regards to my case. Now that wouldn't be good!

So it would come as no surprise that when I was called into a meeting for the third time about the same passport issue & was once again asked for an update on same, all kinds of red flags went up in my head & I thought to myself that it was time. I proceeded to submit my letter of resignation shortly thereafter.

I remember how upset Christopher was. His issue was the fact that he would now have to take on my bills because of the actions of his wife. I remember him complaining how much stress would be placed on him now because "people" decided to be vindictive & act stupid.

I didn't care for much of what he was saying because my position was had he not searched my house & taken out my darn payslip, this situation wouldn't have presented itself. So ultimately it was HIS fault. He handed his wife the ammunition she needed to once again try & make my life hell.

So for the next couple of weeks I was home unemployed & trying to figure out my next move.

J. O. B NEEDED

Weeks turned to months, two months to be exact, that's how long I was out of work. I remember when the first month end came & it was time for Christopher to cover the bills, I got nothing but lip from him. There was no urgency to pay the bills & I guess once again he had control over me.

I remember constantly calling him about my landlord's rent money his reply to which was that he needed to wait. The reality of my situation had finally started hitting home. I quickly realised that I had lost my financial freedom & was once again the gentleman's prisoner because of my inability to provide for myself.

He eventually covered the bills but not before telling me that England wasn't working out for him & so he was seriously thinking about returning to Jamaica. He explained that he would be in a much better position financially in Jamaica when compared to England. He went on further to say he had owned so many assets while he was in Jamaica & can hardly achieve anything in England especially because he was black.

Once he had finished explaining himself, I told him I had no issue going back home because I too was of the view that I was not living up to my full potential & that there was so much more that I could possibly achieve back home. So I think we were pretty much on the same page.

I was told that he would start seeking somewhere for us to live in Jamaica & that once that was done, we would start making preparations to return home. This all sounded like a very good plan to me because to be honest, I had had enough of England.

The gentleman would leave for Jamaica shortly thereafter. I was excited because in my mind he had gone to put the plan in motion. I would eventually receive pictures showing me a place that he had gotten. At first I was given the impression that the property was being bought but I later learned that this was never the case, he only had a rental agreement.

Now that he had found a place, I kept asking him how soon would we be leaving. Remember I didn't have my passport in my possession & so I would have needed to request same to be able to leave. Despite me asking, no information was forthcoming. I went as far as to start checking out the cost of the tickets & sending him the information but even then there was no further discussion around the topic.

With the departure option looking dim, I decided to try my luck at getting a job in the interim. Based on my ongoing passport issue, I would now need to find a cash in hand job. I remember Tiffany was working at this cab station & the weekly pay was not bad. So she encouraged me to find one such job.

I called a few companies from the directory listing but most had no vacancy. I would eventually call one who had a vacancy & needed someone to start right away. I was invited to visit the location for an interview which I attended & was immediately employed. I started getting the job training on the same day.

So what was this job about? I would be working as a dispatcher for a cab company. I would take bookings for airport trips etc & ensure that the jobs were given to the right drivers, basically the drivers with the posh cars. I would also have to attend to walk in & regular call in customers meanwhile trying to ensure that I kept good record of which cabbie was next on the list for a job because one slip up would result in a war. They didn't joke when it came on to their money. I also needed to ensure that I took down the correct information from the call in customers. The fact that I wasn't familiar with the area meant I oftentimes had to ask them to spell the name of the roads. This however improved over time.

This job gave me the opportunity to meet persons from different cultures & to also learn more about them. The cab office was owned by Pakistanis. The drivers were a mix of Africans,

Pakistanis, Algerians, Indians & Afghans. Surprisingly there were no Jamaicans.

There was never a dull moment in that cab office. It was like I was the class teacher who was responsible for a lot of "bad breed pickney". The arguments & disagreements were a lot & I constantly had to be playing the role of referee. It got so bad that I had to complain to the boss & he would "suspend" the culprits. Their punishment would be me not giving them any work for a day or two.

I remember getting my first week's pay. I was getting £200 per week, the salary was not bad at all. Once I got that cash in my hand, all the complaints I had about the job suddenly went away. To be honest just like the retail job, I would never have imagined myself working in a cab office but once again it was all about survival. I would eventually fall very ill one night & the cab office was to be blamed.

STACEY A PREGNANT YUH PREGNANT

I got in from work one evening & had a headache. I didn't see it as a big deal. I took some paracetamol & proceeded to lay down & I eventually fell asleep.

I remember waking up later that night feeling nauseous & before I knew it I had to run to the bathroom as I had now started vomiting. This feeling felt a little familiar, it felt like when I was pregnant but I knew this could not have been the case because I had been on contraceptives since my son was 6 weeks old.

Everyone in the household also came to the conclusion that I was pregnant. I remember telling them that if this was indeed true, then it was definitely a miracle.

I was up bright & early the following morning & made my way to my GP's office. After explaining my symptoms I was asked whether I believed I was pregnant. I replied with a very strong NO. I was however told that my symptoms were in line with early pregnancy & so I would need to take a test to rule it out. I gladly took the test because I knew pregnancy was not an option for me.

After the pregnancy test came back negative, I was then told that I had experienced a full blown migraine attack. I was like migraine?! I had never had this problem before. I was given a list of triggers so that I could try & identify the root cause & the only thing I could identify with from the list presented was cigarette smoke.

The cab drivers at the office were avid smokers. They were the type that used one cigarette to light another. Among themselves they smoked over a pack of cigarettes daily. The office constantly reeked of cigarette smoke.

The next day I went to work & had shared my diagnosis with my boss. He was very accommodating & had told the drivers that going forward there should be no smoking in the office. They were compliant for the most part but for the ones who somehow didn't get the memo, I would curse them in Jamaican patois & once they heard that, they knew to tek weh demself. I don't think they understood anything I was saying but the fact that I wasn't speaking to them in my usual tone painted a great picture for them.

Many days I would sit in the cab office & question what was I really doing with my life. I in no way felt satisfied with where my life was. On many occasions I would tell myself that this definitely was not what I worked so hard in high school for. There were many opportunities available in England but in the absence of a passport & proper documentation, those opportunities quickly changed to nil.

I remember my very good friend from high school Deon who had left for England a few months before me, was having some of the same challenges I was facing. Like myself, her passport was also at the Home Office pending consideration. One thing I can tell you about her though was the fact that she was a Jill of all trades. Wherever the hustle was, she was there!

Some days I would call her & hear that she was on a tutoring gig. Another time I would call & it would be an interior decorating one. Then there was jerking of chicken at Nottinghill carnival, then there was teacher at her church summer camp, then there was hairdresser combing natural hair, then there was dressmaker & the list went on & on. One thing I admired about her was the fact that she didn't see herself too good for any job, it was all about survival & making that money.

I wish I could have taken a leaf out of her book but my pride wouldn't have allowed me to do some of what she did. I remember the first time Simone took me to her cleaning job with her one evening. She had hurt her back at her other job & so I went to assist her that way the work would have been a little lighter & she would have finished quicker.

Honestly speaking in that moment I felt like I was a million percent better than going by people's desks & emptying their bins. Jamaican people would have said mi a gwan like mi stoosh but it wasn't even about being stoosh, it was more about me leaving my home country for a better life & all this really just didn't seem like it. It made me feel like I was moving backward, no real progress.

We would eventually get a new housemate, my cousin's friend. Remember now that we had rented a house for ourselves so any housemate we had, was chosen by us. We really couldn't afford to end up in a house with random mad people again. Although at one point my cousin brought in two tenants that were highly recommended by her that we had to part ways with.

The first was a very nice lady but it was obvious that her evening job was to sell sex. The house was heavily trafficked by a lot of different men. It all became a little too much & so we had to ask her to leave. The second lady was like one of them ghetto gangsters from back home. Remember we were renting her a room but you would think it was her house because she tried to "bad us up" on a regular basis. Everything we did in our own space was a problem to her. If she placed the broom on the left & we moved it to the right, this would have resulted in a big argument. Now the argument would take the form of some of those that we see on videos in ghetto communities. We would be classed in the worst way & the bad words would be as long as the river Nile. We eventually had to ask her to leave also. It took a lot of work because she was adamant she wasn't coming out but eventually we got her out.

Once we had gotten her out, it was peace & harmony. The new girl that came blended in well. She was also Jamaican but was in a better position than us status wise & so she had a good job. She worked for a prominent rental car company. Every now & again she would take a vehicle home & we took pleasure in getting dressed & going for drive outs. Car rides was a luxury for me because despite the fact that Christopher changed so many cars in the 5 years I was in England, I rarely drove in any of them. Public transportation was my best friend.

Even on days when it was snowing, my baby & I would be out in the cold in our layers of clothing trying to keep warm as we made our way home. So yea car rides felt like a privilege.

Everything was going well in the house until one Saturday while I was cleaning, the new housemate came to me & said "You know the person I heard you were, you are not", I replied by saying "heard?" She went on to say yes & now that I have met you I have realised that you are a completely different person.

So who could have told this person who I only recently met anything about me?

TELL ME MORE

What is it that you could have heard about me & from who? After all I have only just met you. These were my questions. Try & recall though that she was my cousin's friend but I didn't want to believe that my cousin was the person who had had a discussion with her about me.

She went on to say that she was told how living with me was horrible because I was nasty. She said my cousin told her that she was the one who did all the housework in the house. She told her that not even the bathroom that I used I would clean. Clearly by living with us, she now saw the truth & so felt compelled to say something to me.

By this time I had stopped tidying up & had taken a seat because I could not believe what I was hearing. She went on to say that my cousin had told her how badly my son's father treated both myself & my son, so I quickly said to her that that was no secret & I would be the first to tell anyone that because I don't pretend.

The next attack was on me. She told the girl that I behaved as though I looked better than her & I didn't. She said I was hunch & didn't have any shape & I couldn't dress. I sat there listening & to say I was hurt would be an understatement. I would have never expected this from my cousin considering the journey we had been on together in England trying to keep our heads up & stay afloat despite everything we were constantly faced with.

Now when I thought I had heard everything she went on to say that my cousin also told them (apparently another one of her friends was there) that she was the one who was feeding my son because his father wasn't doing anything. Now her attack on my appearance & character was one thing but MY SON! This cut deep! And you know what cut even deeper? The fact that it was a lie!

My cousin had never had the responsibility of feeding my child. If we are to be real I aided in feeding her. The most she had contributed to my son in regards to food would be a £1 bottle of milk. She is usually on the road & so if I ran out I would call her & ask her to buy a bottle on her way home, that was about it.

They say to give to Caesar what is due. As bad as Christopher was, he would take us grocery shopping monthly. So when I just moved in with her, the food she ate was what he had provided because she was really in a bad position financially. Also, on two occasions when we had to move house, it was Christopher who had to pay her portion of the deposit because she didn't have it & she repaid him later on. So as bad as he was, I would have appreciated if she stuck to the narrative that he treated me badly but don't say he wasn't feeding his child & you had to, when you knew you were struggling to even feed yourself.

While hearing everything I was laughing because I saw the personal attack on my appearance & character as a reflection of her insecurities. Like who had time to be thinking about looks? Everyday my focus was survival! I constantly looked a hot mess because of how stressed I was & so if you asked me I would never say I thought myself to look better than anyone, I looked horrible. So her utterances about looks was a big joke to me but when I heard that she spoke about my son & told a lie at that, now that was unforgivable.

After processing everything I remember how hurt & betrayed I felt. Over the 2 year period that we were in contact & had started living together, we had gone through a lot together & seemingly had each other's back. I remember that despite her being older than me, I took charge of the household because I was more mature by far. So I did most of the cooking etc. & ensured that the house ran smoothly.

When she got home the evening I confronted her about the whole thing. One thing I must say that I respected her for was the fact that she admitted her guilt. She then tried to explain the reasoning behind her actions but to be honest I can't relay any of what was said because I blocked it all out. At the end of the day nothing she said could have explained the level of betrayal or why it was even necessary. So at the end of our conversation I told her I wanted nothing to do with her & despite the fact that we lived in the same house, I didn't want to have any contact with her. I also told her that she was not to use anything in the house that belonged to me, no grocery from my cupboard, do not use anything for me that was in the fridge, not even a spoon that belonged to me in the kitchen I wanted her to use.

People who fail to recognise that children are off limits when it comes to certain things, I have no respect for. The fact that all we had in England was each other & probably a few friends, I thought that meant something & had value but I guess not.

So now it was every woman for themself.

FREE FLIGHT- GOOD OR BAD?

It was a hard pill to swallow but the cut off was necessary. Not even an apology made me rethink my decision. I could not get over the fact that she stooped so low to speak about my child.

Once I got in from work in the evenings, I locked myself in my room. I tried as best as possible to avoid her. It was harder keeping my son away from her. As you can imagine as a three year old he was all over in the house & he certainly didn't understand what was going on.

I went back to Christopher to ask about the proposal to return to Jamaica. Once again I wasn't getting any positive argument. So it was clear to me that if I really planned on returning home that I would have to do so on my own as there was no help forthcoming from the gentleman.

I would later learn that two of my maternal cousins were in England but they lived outside of London. We got in touch & they later arranged to visit London to spend time with my son & I. I remember discussing with them my new found desire to return home. Everybody that I shared the thought with had the same reaction & it went something like this " Weh yah go Jamaica go do? Nuttn nuh deh a Jamaica." I strongly believed otherwise though.

One thing I can vividly remember my dad telling his friends when I was about eight years old was the fact that he wasn't worried about me growing up in the ghetto because I was strong willed & was always a leader, never a follower. He also made mention of the fact that I knew when to remove myself from situations. So if I was friends with another child, the moment I saw them taking up "big womanship" I would drop them. And as you can imagine this taking up of "big womanship" was very prevalent in the ghetto & so soon I ended up with pretty much no friends.

I say all this to say that if I had made up my mind about returning home, there was absolutely nothing that anyone could have said to me that would have changed my mind. The only thing that could have resulted in a change, would be me getting back my passport with an extension stamped in it.

My cousins immediately fell in love with my son. I remember one of them offering to take him to spend time with her & her toddler in Birmingham. She explained that if I was really serious about returning home then she could take him for a week or two that way I could work extra hours & also save the money I would have spent for a babysitter. It sounded like a plan & I was in agreement.

I decided to call immigration to find out how I would go about canceling my application & getting my passport returned. I wanted to get all the necessary information so I could put a proper plan in place. I remember calling the Home Office & being transferred to this very nice guy named Tony, how coincidental. He explained to me that they wouldn't have sent the passport to me. I guess just in case I decided not to leave after it was returned but to instead remain illegal in their country. He said I would have to book my ticket and then call them back with the itinerary details & they would arrange for me to collect the passport at the airport on my departure date.

He went on to ask whether I had a date in mind when I wanted to leave. I could tell they really wanted me out of their country. I explained to him that I hadn't secured my airfare as yet & I also needed to figure out how my son would travel seeing that he can't get a British passport & neither can he get a Jamaican passport because the Jamaican Embassy says he is not a Jamaican.

Now this is where the conversation got interesting. Tony informed me that if I wanted they could pay the return airfare for both myself & my son & they could also arrange a travel document for my son to travel on. I told him that I would need sometime to process everything & would get back to him soon.

I didn't discuss any of this new information with Christopher. I remember going back to him asking about our departure date, again there was still no response. I brought up the topic of my son not having a passport & us having to deal with that seeing that we had planned on returning home. He was quick to provide a solution to this problem. What was his solution? He recommended that I allow his wife to adopt my son that way he could have easily been issued a British passport.

After I had gotten over the shock of his suggestion, I told him a long line of bad words. Like every other word out of my mouth was a swear word. I had never sworn so much in my life. Like why would I give up parental rights to my only child for a stinking passport?! At this point I was ready to end the conversation with him but I needed confirmation that he had indeed sorted out a place to live in Jamaica. So I asked him & he confirmed that there was indeed a place & that this was where he stayed the last couple of times that he had visited Jamaica & would be staying again when he visits in the summer. So just like that I was told that there were plans for him to travel again soon but I still could not hear anything about my airfare or any plans for me to leave.

It was crystal clear that if I was to return home, I would have to take matters into my own hands. I remember contacting my cousin in Birmingham & sharing with her all the information that I had gotten from the Home Office. She was of the view that they would come & detain me once they found out where I was. Her reasoning made no sense to me. After all I was canceling my application & opting to leave voluntarily, so why would they need to detain me? I am not on the run!

I told her that I would possibly be taking up her offer for my son to spend time with her. I told her that as soon as I had finished fine tuning the plan, I would let her know when I would need her to take him.

It was now time to work out the logistics & decide once & for all if I was really going to go ahead with this departure plan.

SIGN ON THE DOTTED LINE

It was agreed that my son would stay with my cousin in Birmingham for two weeks. We had arranged to meet at London Victoria. I arrived at the train station with my son. My cousin would arrive shortly after & I gave her my son & his bag. She once again brought up the fact that she feared I would be detained by immigration if I chose to go ahead with taking the ticket from them. She went on to say "Well at least if they come you won't have your son so they can't take you anywhere without him." The concern she had I genuinely didn't, but the more she spoke about it, the more I started wondering whether I was being naive.

Nevertheless, I decided to return a call to Tony to make the arrangements official. He asked whether I had decided on a departure date & I said yes September 15th. There was nothing special about the date other than the fact that I had arrived in England in September of 2001 & so I thought why not leave September as well.

Tony advised that he would visit me in a couple of days with some documents that I would need to sign & would also make the necessary arrangement for my son's travel document. It was all becoming very real. I was really making the move back to mi yard!

First thing I did was to purchase a barrel & I started packing as I went along. I also started picking up extra shifts at the cab office & would visit Victoria Mutual to deposit those monies worked. It would usually reflect in my account in Jamaica in approximately two days.

I remember calling my parents & advising them of my plans to return home. To say they were excited would be an understatement. I knew they always wanted me to return home but didn't want to tell me to, based on the fact that they didn't have anything to offer me & neither were they in a position to house me & a child. But the time had come for their dream to become a reality.

The first friend I made contact with was one from primary school called Melissa. I had told her of my plans to return home & had asked her the procedure to get my TRN & my NIS sorted out before I got there. She always knew someone & this time was no different. She told me she knew someone at both places & could have them sorted out. I also wanted to sort out my learner's permit so I could start my driving lessons as soon as I arrived. She told me that she could also have that sorted but she would need passport sized pictures. I agreed to mail the pictures to her so we could get all the balls rolling.

Tony made contact with me & advised that he would be visiting the following day with the documents for me to sign & to also take me to the Jamaican Embassy to request the travel document for my son. He asked me whether I had a picture of my son because the embassy requires one. I told him I only had school pictures & he confirmed that same was fine.

I checked in with my cousin & she confirmed that my son was good. She said he was having fun & was enjoying her son's company. I told her that I was contacted earlier by the immigration officer & that they would be visiting me tomorrow. She once again expressed her concern. She said she didn't like how nice they were being to me & that something seemed very suspicious. Once again I started second guessing my decision based on the concerns she expressed. But was it too late for me to change my mind?

The next morning I woke up & I remember just praying constantly & trying to convince myself that I made the right decision. I started getting ready as Tony was scheduled to visit soon. This was the only time throughout this process that I started feeling nervous & anxious. I kept replaying all the things my cousin had said & started thinking what if she was right? In all of this I totally forgot that I hadn't made contact with my lawyer to bring him up to date & inform him of my decision.

I decided to call his office while I awaited Tony's arrival. I was advised that he was out of office. I spoke with another lawyer at the firm & she told me that I should brace myself to be detained & If I didn't want to be detained then I should leave my house immediately before they arrived. She was like get off the phone now & get out that house! My heart was beating so fast I'm sure it broke Usain's record!

While contemplating whether to follow the lawyer & run or not, I heard a knock on the door. It was clear Tony had arrived. By this time I felt like I was going to pee my pants.

Tiffany's room was at the front of the house & so she could see through her window who was at the door. She apparently heard the knocking & had looked out. Despite the fact that we didn't speak, she came to my room door & said that there were two men at the door with immigration IDs on. She went on to ask if I knew why they were at the house. Although I really didn't want to speak to her, I told her I had a meeting with them. By the time I said this, she too was of the view that they were possibly planning on detaining me.

The knocks at the door became louder & the frequency increased. What do I do now?

BANG! BANG! BANG!

The knocks got louder & louder & soon my mobile phone started to ring. When I looked it was Tony & so I didn't answer. Maybe if I didn't answer my phone or the door they would just go away or maybe not.

I took some deep breaths & proceeded to open the door. Tony started laughing & said there you are! His colleague went on to say "Stacey I thought you had done a runner on us" & they both began to laugh. So I said not at all I am here. Tony chimed in & said I was just saying to my colleague that if you knew you were going to disappear on me you should have told me, that way I wouldn't come & miss lunch! We all began to laugh, me more nervously than anything else.

Anyway, they both came inside & we proceeded to the kitchen for them to explain the documents & for me to review & sign. The documents pretty much stated that I had agreed to withdraw my application & to leave their country voluntarily. It also had the details of my agreed departure date & my carrier which at the time was Air Jamaica. Everything seemed to have been in order & so I proceeded to sign. I was provided with my copies which I would have needed to take with me on my departure date.

Next on the agenda was for them to escort me to the Jamaican Embassy to get my son's travel document. The ride there was very comfortable & wasn't as awkward as I would have expected it to be. They asked me a lot of questions about Jamaica & expressed their intent to visit one day. Tony also asked why I decided to leave & I told him it was too difficult to survive without having the proper paperwork. He went on to say that he understood & added that my letter that I wrote was very admirable.

For a minute I thought letter? What letter is he talking about? I think he saw the perplexed look on my face & so he reached into his file folder & handed it to me. When I saw it I burst into laughter! This was a letter that I had written to them out of frustration asking them to provide some update or feedback on my long outstanding application. I noted in the letter that my interest wasn't to live off their benefits & public funds, I just wanted to be able to work freely so that I could adequately provide for myself & my son.

Tony then went on to ask what was next for me once I got to Jamaica, so I quickly replied get a job! He asked whether preparations had been made for my arrival & whether I had a place to live. I told him that my son's father was supposed to have sorted a place for us to live so we should be good. If I didn't know better I would think that Tony was genuinely concerned about my wellbeing.

We arrived at the Jamaican Embassy & I was ushered in like I was a diplomat & was taken to a secluded section. I was later escorted to the commissioner's office. Tony & his colleague were asked to leave us alone. The commissioner questioned whether I was being asked to leave by force & I confirmed that I wasn't. I was asked why I was agreeing to a Jamaican travel document for my son when he was born in England?! I explained that the law as is wouldn't have afforded him a British passport & I was not prepared to rely on the option of keeping him in the country for 7 years just so he could get one.

You see it was said that children born in England whose mothers didn't have status in the country could qualify for British citizenship if they remained in the country until they were 7 years old. My son was 3 years old going on 4. There was no way I could continue to live the way I was for another 3 years. So once again I confirmed to the commissioner that I was ready to go. With that being said I was asked to sit back outside in the waiting area.

We would eventually receive the travel document & were on our way. Tony gave me the document to have a look at. As was expected it would have remained in their possession & would only have been given to me on the day of my travel.

I remember Tony asking me whether I had eaten before leaving out & I told him no. I told him food wasn't my concern it was more the fact that everyone thought they were coming to the house to detain me. Both him & his colleague burst into laughter. He went on to ask why would they do that when I was the one who contacted them & asked to leave? I told him I really didn't know what to think.

Tony decided to buy me lunch. He & his colleague decided to try Jamaican food. We stopped at this restaurant in Thornton Heath. He asked me what was good to try on the menu & I recommended the oxtail. So we all had oxtail with rice & peas & fried plantain. My house was less than ten minutes away from the restaurant so once we had finished eating it was time to drop me back home.

Finally I was back home. Tony bid me farewell & wished me all the best with my endeavors & a safe travel when the time came. The last document I was given was one with instructions on how to retrieve my passport once I got to the airport.

It was now time to tell Christopher that I was going to mi yard!

DIAL TONE

So my travel arrangements were now finalised. It was now time to tell Christopher that I would be departing England on September 15th. He was presently on vacation in Jamaica, this just might be the news that will ruin his trip.

I remember going to the corner store to purchase a phone card. Once I got back in I made the call. He answered the phone & we had the usual chit chat. The moment I said to him that I would be returning to Jamaica on September 15th & he exclaimed "What!", & then the call just somehow ended.

I kept trying to call back & he kept rejecting the call. I was determined to continue calling until he answered even if it meant I was going to call all day. So I called & called until he eventually answered & he answered by saying "What!" He sounded mad as hell! By the time I could have said "Suh weh yuh hang up di phone fah?!" I heard a female voice saying "Das why yuh hitch up out yah ina di car because u a talk to that b&%ch!" The more I listened to the person rambling on I came to realise that it was his wife! So how me neva know seh a di whole fambily did deh a Jamaica?!

The next thing I heard was like they were wrestling for the phone after which I heard a voice which sounded like their son telling them to stop. I eventually disconnected the call. So I didn't get anywhere in relaying to him my travel plans but I ended up learning about his family vacation. So for months I had been asking about a ticket to return home & got nowhere but he found the money to have a family vacation.

He eventually returned a call to me asking me to go over what I was saying previously & so I did. He went off on a rant asking how I could have made such an important decision without his input. I had to quickly remind him of how long I had been asking him to purchase a ticket for me to leave & he refused to.

Once the rant was over he went on to say that he would change his ticket as he was slated to return to England long before my arrival in Jamaica. I asked once again about the house that he was supposed to have sorted out & he once again confirmed that everything was in place. I don't know why I found it so hard to believe him about this or maybe I do know why, HE WAS A NOTORIOUS LIAR!

I followed up later with my cousin to check in on my son & to also confirm that I wasn't detained. I updated her on the departure date & despite not being enthusiastic about my decision, she agreed that I had to do what I thought was best for my son & I.

I started advertising some of my furniture & other items for sale. I also had contacted my friends & told them to come by to take anything that they wanted for themselves. The emptier the house got, the more realistic the reality became.

Next on the list of persons to inform of my departure was Victoria. I remember hearing a loud Nooooooo when I told her I would be leaving England. Before I knew it I could hear her voice breaking, the water works had started.

FINAL GOODBYES

Time was drawing nigh. I was still working & trying to ensure I had enough money to pack & ship my barrels & to also ensure I had some money in my account to spend once I arrived in Jamaica.

It was time for me to meet my cousin to pick up my son. She told me that she had gotten him some stuff & had also bought him a suitcase that we could use on our trip back. Once I got to the train station I saw her coming down the platform, one hand pushing the push chair & the other carrying a grip. I remember my first reaction was "A weh she a go wid dah old time suitcase deh!" Immediately I started feeling so embarrassed when I thought of how far I was going to have to travel home with the grip.

As she got closer to me the first thing I greeted her with was "A weh yuh get dah suitcase deh?" I almost fainted when she said she bought it. Like seriously? You went & bought that? In these civilized times? My face usually says a lot more than I do so I wasn't surprised when she said "It look like yuh nuh like it." She went on to say that I didn't have to carry it by the handle like she was. She said it had a string & two wheels so I could pull it by the string. I couldn't hold the laugh when she proceeded to do a demonstration along the platform in the train station. Despite how ashamed I felt about having to carry the dulcimena suitcase, I told her thanks for everything & her assistance & bid her farewell.

It was now time for me to "luggo luggo" back home. The journey home required me to take one train & a bus & so it wasn't so bad. While on my way home I would receive a call from Victoria asking if they could get to spend time with my son & I prior to our departure. I agreed to meet them at Canary Wharf where we would have lunch & they would take my son with them thereafter to spend a few days. Another part of the agreement was for me to cook Jamaican food for them to have when they took my son back home to me. I had no problem honouring their request.

As my departure date grew closer, every weekend I was in Croydon shopping & stocking up. Most of my shopping trips took me to Primark or as my friends & I called it Primarni. It was our go to store because the items were very reasonably priced. They also had most of the latest style trends that other prominent retailers had but for far less. You will come across people who will tell you that they could never shop in Primark, I am not one of those people.

I remember speaking to my mother & she told me that Christopher had contacted her. Wonder what this could be about now?! She said he apologised for everything that happened to me in England & had explained that it was hard for him to help me how he would have wanted to because his wife watched his every move. She said he indicated that me coming to Jamaica would be a fresh start & that he would be better able to take care of my son & I from hereon. She told me that he had also agreed to take her to the airport with him when it was time to pick us up. A fresh start he said, I guess that was left to be seen.

For the next couple of weeks it was all about putting in the work to make the money. One of the cabbies that stood out in the office was this cab driver that we called 05. The talk in the office was that I was responsible for the change in his appearance & how he started carrying himself. They reckoned that the moment I arrived he started dressing sharply everyday. Not only did he started dressing sharply but he also upgraded his little betsy car to a Mercedes. Most evenings once I had finished my shift he would be ready & waiting to give me a ride home. Whether he had intentions or not, I would never know because he at no time stated any. It could be because I would constantly state that I had no interest in married men, a category that he fell into. One thing I can say though was that he looked out for me during my time at the cab office & so it came as no surprise when he offered to take me to the airport at a reduced cost once I was ready to leave.

Eventhough all this packing & planning was going on, I said absolutely nothing to Tiffany despite us being in the same house. She showed me her true colours & I had made up my mind about not wanting to have anything to do with her going forward. Next thing on the agenda was to contact my landlord & advise him of the fact that I was leaving & request my portion of the deposit. My landlord was also a Caribbean national & LOVED MONEY!

I made contact & the call was going very good until I started asking about my deposit at which time he started giving me some cock & bull argument which made no sense. As he continued talking & saying all the things I really didn't want to hear, I remember thinking to myself "Look how dah ole man yah a go mek mi trace him!"

He was refusing to return my deposit because Tiffany & her friend would still be living at the house after my departure. He reckoned that they might damage his property after I leave & he would need to ensure he has money to cover any damages.

So I asked him how did two adults become my responsibility? Am I their parent? I reminded him that the lease was signed by Tiffany & myself & so if a walk through was to be done prior to my departure & everything was in order, then he would refund my portion of the deposit. When it was time for Tiffany & her friend to leave, you do another walk through & if you feel as though things aren't in order then you hold on to her deposit. It was very simple. He eventually agreed & this was settled.

LAST SUPPER

I was expecting Victoria to take my son home later that day & so as was previously agreed I was to cook for her. If my memory serves me right I think I made curry chicken & rice. She & her husband ate & we chatted as though it was the last supper. When it was time for her to leave that's when the thunderstorm started. This would have been the last time she would be seeing us before our departure. I tried to fight back the tears but despite my best efforts, the water works also started for me. Her poor husband stood there looking at both of us like we were crazy.

It was winding down time & so everyone was scheduling their visit to say their goodbyes. Deon was next in line. She came to spend some time with us prior to our departure. She also agreed to make the airport journey with us on the day to say her final farewell.

I remember visiting my former housemate & hairdresser Nikki. She was a character! She was like "Stacey yuh cah go back a Jamaica wid nuh boring hairstyle enuh, yuh afi hot!" So it was decided that I would be given a two tone hairstyle. The top of my hair would be blonde & the back black or as old time people would say party a front & business a back.

We were there for hours trying to "ketch" colour but eventually we did. When I looked in the mirror the only thing I could have said was lawd jeezas. Prior to this my hair had always been dark. This was my first encounter with bleached hair.

I eventually got a call from Christopher asking how everything was coming along. He went on to say that he couldn't wait for us to get there as there was so much for us to do together. He added that Jamaica was fun! I started to wonder if he was ensuring the deal was sealed & I didn't change my mind about leaving. For a second, one would think he was employed to the Jamaica Tourist Board based on how he was promoting the island & listing all the things that awaited us to enjoy. I could see clearly the benefit of my departure to him. He could finally live two lives in peace! His wife wouldn't know what's happening in Jamaica & neither would I know what would be going on in England.

The day we long awaited was finally here. It was time to close the England chapter of my life after being there for five years. It was time to return to my home soil to see what Jamaica had in store for me.

AU REVOIR

And just like that five years of my life was spent in England. It was five very hard & interesting years but I wouldn't have changed a thing. Everything had to have happened how it did, it was all apart of my journey. Sometimes I would have asked myself why me? But one thing I've come to realise is that the big man upstairs makes no mistake & if he brings you to it he will bring you through it.

So it was time to close the door on this leg of my journey & return to the land of my birth. As to what was in store for me there, I had no clue but I always told myself that it can't be worse than England.

My high school friend Deon came by my house to make the journey with us to the airport. Shortly after her arrival I would get a call from 05 to say that he was outside. He came in to help us with the luggage & it was off to London Heathrow.

During the drive to the airport despite trying to appear upbeat & in good spirits, I couldn't help but to reflect on my time in England & I came to the conclusion that I really didn't accomplish much, only a baby. I also started thinking about what people would say about me returning home with just a few additional educational qualifications & a child, & the fact that I was pretty much coming back to start from scratch.

But had I cared a lot about people's thoughts & opinions, I wouldn't be leaving England. Remember they warned me that there was nothing in Jamaica so returning home was a bad idea. I guess I would have to wait & see whether they were right.

Here we were, London Heathrow. Deon followed us in to as far as she could before bidding us farewell. I am very bad at goodbyes & so it took everything in me to not buss some bawling ina di people dem airport. I'm sure I looked up at the ceiling about a million times to try & prevent the tears from running down. The last thing she did was to take a picture of my son & I as we made our way to our check in area.

Before we could go to the Air Jamaica counter though I had to collect our travel documents. The instruction I got from Tony was to go to a specific section in the airport where I would see a phone. I was to pick up the phone & dial 0 after which I would hear it ringing on the other end. He said once the person comes on I would proceed to give them our names & they would take the documents down to us. It all went just as he said & in less than a minute I was holding my passport that I hadn't seen in four years, the big old blue book. The picture in it was so ugly but I was happy to be holding it again.

We proceeded to the check in counter with our travel documents & the letters that Tony had given me along with our four suitcases. Those were the days when we were allowed two pieces of free checked luggage each. The next drama to unfold was the flight being delayed but if you had ever travelled Air Jamaica you would know that this was the norm. My flight was delayed by one hour, then two hours & then finally three hours.

The delay now meant that my flight wouldn't be getting to Jamaica until sometime after 9pm, so I had to make contact with Christopher to advise him accordingly. It was a difficult task keeping a four year old entertained during the very lengthy wait, but I tried. If "When are we going on the plane" was a song, I would know the lyrics by heart because that's the only tune my son was singing.

Finally it was time to take my seat on the big bird. Thank God I wasn't seated in the aisle on the return journey. I really needed as much things as possible to keep my son occupied during the nine hour flight. I hope seeing clouds would provide him with some amount of entertainment if all the other things I packed didn't work. We are off! See Y'all in Jamaica

JAMAICA LAND WE LOVE

WELCOME TO JAMROCK

If there was one thing we all knew about Air Jamaica flights it was the fact that they were very festive. From the celebration whenever the plane landed to the possibility of some verbal dispute among passengers, but the festivity I experienced on my journey back was very different. The cooling system wasn't working & so the aircraft was hot. It was like the blower was on but no air conditioning.

Imagine flying for 9 hours in a humid aircraft. It was very uncomfortable. The food on the other hand was great! But yes back to me being hot & sweaty. I was also wearing full black! MURDER!

When the pilot announced that we were approaching Kingston, I had to go to the lavatory to try & spray & freshen up myself. I can proudly tell you all that mi body did well stale! Remember I was now three hours behind on my travel time because of the delay. By the time I arrived in Jamaica it was a new day in England. So yes my body reminded me that an urgent shower was required ASAP!

When the flight landed, the gentleman in the far back gave out "Jah Rastafari, Ever Living, Ever Present." It was clear that he was being deported. He was being heavily guarded by British officials and once it was time for him to get off, his handcuffs were visible although they did try to cover them after with a jacket.

We made our way from the aircraft & into the airport. Try & recall that in 2006 there were no fancy gates so you were let out on the tarmac & you had to walk in. As I made my way into the immigration section I was quickly whisked away by a family friend who worked at the airport as an immigration officer at the time. It is good to know people in high places! I was able to avoid the long lines.

He then escorted me over to the baggage claim section & helped me with my bag & pan & also helped me to clear customs. As the porter walked out with my luggage & me behind, I heard someone say "Stacey" when I looked to my right it was my dad, I didn't even know he was going to be at the airport. He looked so different. So much had changed in the five years that I had been away.

As I walked further to the exit there stood my mom, Christopher & my primary school friend Melissa. If there was one thing that remained the same while I was gone, it was my mother's resentment for my father. The lady stayed very far from him & because of this I had to greet them with my sweaty self separately.

I was happy to see my parents! I was over the moon to be back home. Now remember I told y'all I was hot & sweaty & probably would start smelling very soon but that wasn't going to stop my mother from taking me on a meet & greet. So on my way home I was told that I would have to stop by my grandmother's house because everyone was expecting me. I tried to protest as it was late but I didn't have a choice in the matter.

I got to my grandmother's house & as expected everybody lock up in dem quarters. These people were early sleepers. Nevertheless, once I entered the house & said hello hello, people started appearing. It was great seeing everyone but I don't think my son was enjoying the meet & greet as much as I was. Whenever his grandmother or anyone else tried to touch him he would give out "Don't touch me, you are too black." Like what the hell! Where did that come from? When I told him that he was also black he said no he was white! Poor kid! The struggle of being born in white people country!

Finally, I was heading home! While in the car I could hear my mom trying to talk to my son & all I could hear was "I don't want to talk to you, you are too black!" Funny thing was my dad had embraced him earlier & had spoken to him & he didn't have this reaction at all. I knew it was only a matter of time before my

mother gave him the warning so when I heard her give out "
You have some lick fi get yuh see" I couldn't help but laugh.

And here we were, home. I no longer had to worry about
whether Christopher was lying about having a place for us, I
was now seeing it in the flesh, it was real. I don't think I had
mentioned how nice he was behaving, you would never think it
was the same person. Guess he knew he had a point to prove so
he could pretend like I was telling stories about my England
experience & none of it happened.

Guess we will see how long he will be able to keep up the nice
guy act.

DAY 2 ON THE ROCK

Once we arrived at the house & offloaded the luggage, it was time to have a much needed shower. Christopher made sure to point out that the house had hot water in the shower. He went on to say that he wanted the transition to be as seamless as possible for my son & I. O wow! Who are you again?! And where is the old version of you that I know?

My mother decided that she was going to stay the night & spend time with my son despite him wanting nothing to do with her because according to him she was too black. Christopher advised that he wanted to take me to the club with him. I was tired but I was also excited to be home & so I agreed to go.

When he said club he didn't specify Strip Club! I had been gone for a while but I surely remembered certain places & areas so when I saw him turning on Ripon Road, I knew there was only one club on that road. When we arrived & I said "Then a really gogo club you bring me come?" He replied to say that he doesn't go there for the dancing but rather for the music because they have a very good DJ & the vibe is usually good.

As I walked in the first thing that greeted me was the big stage & the girls dancing. It was very hard not to watch when the stage was a prominent feature in the club & took up the entire middle section. So where do you stand so that you focus more on the music & not the dancing I asked? He couldn't answer. From what I could see no matter where in that building you stood, the stage was right there in your face. The only way for you not to see the stage would be if you went to the private rooms for a lap dance. Truth is though he didn't lie about the quality of the music, it was a good vibe. I totally enjoyed.

The next day my primary school friend Melissa came by my house. She said she knew I might have wanted to go on the road & so she came to take me. We ended up going to Azans to pick up a few household items & then she took me to my dad to drop off some stuff I had for him. One thing wid my father enuh if you go to visit & plan to stay 5 minutes, prepare to stay all 2 hours because he has stories for days or better yet years.

He had questions about all these places in England & whether I had been to any of them. Pity him neva know a nuh tourist life mi did a live a England, a sufferer. I knew of some of the places he had made mention of though. He had visited England during his time working on ships & somehow remembered every bit of detail from his travels.

Once I had left my dad I visited 34 & also dropped off some stuff I had for them. It was now my grandmother's time to bring me up to speed with the happenings. I was now learning that she was previously diagnosed with cancer & had done her chemotherapy & was now good. I heard about my mother suffering a heart attack, my uncles who maliced her because they wanted to sell her house & put her in a home & she said no, my next uncle who cut off everybody because he believed they told his babymother about an outside child he had, the stories were ALOT! But out of all she said what stood out to me was the fact that she & my mom were sick & I didn't know. They reckon they didn't want to tell me anything because they didn't want to worry me especially because I couldn't travel.

Melissa took me back home & I decided to start unpacking & getting things in order. As I opened the drawer to the built in closet in my son's room, I found some items of clothing. When I took them out & threw them on the floor, they were all female clothing. Panty, battyrider shorts, tshirts, regular tops etc. I called Christopher to the room & said "A who fah clothes dem yah?" He acted clueless then went on to say he felt as though they belonged to the person that was renting the property before him. So I went on to probe further. "So for the how much months now you have rented the place you didn't check any of the drawers?" His reply to which was no because he hardly used that particular room. Let us pray I don't find anything else as I continue to unpack & set up this house.

STAY AT HOME MOM

It was time to have a discussion with Christopher on what was next for me. He would be leaving Jamaica shortly so we needed to get as much sorted as possible.

Try & recall that I had returned home mid September so school had already started. I needed to get my son enrolled quickly. The two primary schools that I would have been willing to send him, Jessie Ripoll & Alpha said they had no space. Once this was confirmed I knew we had to go the prep school route because I knew how rough primary schools could be & I could just see my son getting a hard time especially because of his accent & all, & the fact that he somehow wasn't a fan of black people. Dem woulda beat him up!

We checked quite a few schools & eventually decided on St. Theresa. It was the cheapest in the prep school category. My nephew was a past student & so I knew it was a good school. After completing the forms & paying the requisite fees, I was told to take my son in the following day for them to conduct an assessment.

Once that was taken care of, it was time for me to meet another one of my high school friends in Cross Roads. She promised to take me to her driving school to pay for my lessons. I remember stopping by 34 & asking them how the taxi business work to go Cross Roads. I was told to just stand on the opposite side of the road & just listen to what the drivers are yelling when they slow down.

Just like my grandmother said, a car stopped at my feet & the driver asked "Cross Roads?" So I hopped in. While in the cab I remembered my school days when these places were my stomping ground. While I was getting comfortable on the back seat sight seeing & well spread out, the driver stopped to pick up more passengers & I was told to "small up yuhself!"

I arrived in Cross Roads & walked to the post office where we had agreed to meet. My friend was already there waiting. She then told me that we were going to walk up the road to Retirement Road. I think she saw the look on my face & so she gave out "A nuh far man!" Mi seh the sun did well hot! A long time mi never experience hot sun & all sweat. When we arrived at the driving school, all fan mi did afi a fan miself. Di sun deal wid mi wicked! I made my payment for my 10 lessons & agreed to start in another two days. It was agreed that they would pick me up from 34 daily.

I made my way back to 34 & then made contact with Christopher for him to pick me up. My son was home with his grandmother. Christopher had already approached my mother about taking care of our son & him paying her on a weekly basis seeing that she would have been giving up her current babysitting gig which was her income. She agreed.

While on the way home with Christopher, I began discussing my plan to start applying for jobs. The gentleman asked why was I moving so fast. Fast? I asked. He said yes, I had only been back for a couple of days so I should just enjoy the break before running into work. He went on further to say why do I even need to work. I should look into being a stay at home mom & just take care of our son. He added that he would take care of all the financial obligations so I would have nothing to worry about.

Dah man here figet how him put mi through trials, tribulations & sufferation when I didn't have a job previously? It look like him figet! I told him it was not in me to stay home & not work. He suggested that I try it for a month & see how I felt after. Then he added "Besides if you go ina nuh office go work a bare man a go look yuh!" DING DING DING DING DING. Now we talking! I knew there had to be something behind the recommendation. I knew it was never about me but more about him & his insecurities.

Well while he was busy telling me not to work, my friends were busy fixing up my resume so that I could start applying for jobs. Full speed ahead mi seh!

THE CASE OF THE MISSING RUBBERS

I got up the following morning & took my son to St. Theresa for them to conduct their assessment. They needed to confirm whether he was on the same level as the kids in kinder 2 or whether they needed to keep him back in kinder 1. The kinder 2 teacher came to the principal's office & told my son that he would be coming with her. The teacher was a dark lady with dreadlocks. As she held his hand to take him over to the classroom, all I could hear was "She is touching me, why is she touching me? I don't want her to touch me, she is too black! Let me go!" Jeezas peace! What a piece a drama ina the people dem school! Mi did shame bad!

When she came back to the principal's office she told us he wasn't ready for kinder 2. I was by no means surprised. I hated the education system in England. I was accustomed to seeing babies in Jamaica getting textbooks to attend basic school & the books were used, they did school work. While in England everyday my son would come home from school with his hair covered in sand & whenever I asked him what he did at school he would say play. I went to his teacher one day to ask what they did on a daily basis & why his hair was always covered in sand. I was told they played & that at his age that was the way they learned, through playing. My initial thought was "A wah kinda foolishness this." Ramp whole day? Not in Jamaica!

So with the assessment completed he was expected to start school the following day & as was expected I was provided with a list of books that I needed to purchase. I was also slated to start my driving lessons on the same day my son would be starting school. The school was in close proximity to 34 so the plan was for Christopher to drop me off at 34 once we took our son to school. The driving instructor would then pick me up from 34 for my lessons & Christopher would pick us up once school was out & take us home. This was the plan for the next couple of days as he would be leaving for England shortly.

While packing out my clothes in the dresser drawers I noticed there was a drawer that had a lot of receipts, junk & over 2 dozen condoms. I had counted the condoms when I came across them initially without his knowledge. Each time I recounted, the number was going down. So I finally decided to confront him about it.

"A who a use di condom dem weh ina dah draw deh?" He replied "Huh? What?" So I went on further "Mi count dem enuh & the numbers keep going down & mi nuh use none!" He went on to say that a lot of times his friends pass by the house & beg one or two. Man come here come beg you condom? Yes Stacey all the time. Well if man afi a come & beg you condom then dem shouldn't a have sex!

As per usual dah man here think mi did born big enuh. I was just counting down to his departure so that I could start focusing fully on myself. The resumes were going out, & I was reaching out to people I knew because we all know a "links" run Jamaica & getting a job was high on my list of priorities.

VROOM VROOM, BEEP BEEP

It was finally time to start my driving lessons. I was so excited. I remember the days in England when I wished I could drive or even had a car for that matter. Getting your provisional licence was not an easy task in England & the entire learning to drive process was very costly. So between the tests & cost for the lessons, it was all outside of my budget. Besides, even if I got the licence I knew I would still be driving my two feet because remember now I could barely cover my living expenses so I definitely wouldn't have been able to afford a car.

I however placed learning to drive on my list of top priorities once I returned home. I ensured I had set that money aside because I didn't want to have to ask Christopher to pay for the lessons. You see after his unwillingness to assist in getting me documented in England, I came to the conclusion that he really didn't want to see me making any progress in life. He just wanted me on one level & that was me being dependent on him. So if I was going to become independent, it was a path that I would now have to chart on my own.

Anyway, after taking my son to school, my driving instructor came to pick me up from 34. I'm sure the man was grateful to see that he was still alive at the end of the lesson. I remember going down Deanery Road in the vicinity of the Clan Carthy High School field. The corner was very deep. As I was approaching the corner the instructor said slow down, as far as I was concerned I slowed down. Then I started hearing his tone getting a little more exciting "Slow down, slow down, slow down!" Long story short when I went around that deep corner, the vehicle was off the road & ended up on the sidewalk, oops.

I could see the poor man's anger like he wanted to say "Come out a mi vehicle!" So after we took the vehicle off the government's sidewalk, we pulled over to the side of the road. He went on to ask me why I thought the vehicle ended up on the sidewalk so I replied "Because I didn't slow down enough." So the gentleman said "Then yuh neva hear mi a seh slow down?" Boy Jamaican people impatient bad enuh & nuh have no tolerance fi foolishness. Hear how the man a deal wid mi & a mi first lesson!

Anyway the instructor concluded that I had a heavy foot problem & so he suggested that I remove my shoe & drive barefooted that way I can feel the pedals & gauge the amount of force I apply. I don't know if this was the best approach because to this day I can't drive in shoes. But the man was more focused on his life so barefoot driving it was.

The rest of the lesson went well. The one hour flew by very quickly. I am sure the instructor was happy to let me back off at 34 but unfortunately for him he would be seeing me again tomorrow because I had paid for ten lessons.

I remember entering 34 & my grandmother asking me how the lesson went & I replied "Mama mi nearly kill off di man!" Laughing spoil! So I would now spend the rest of the day with her while I waited on my son to finish school. Let us hope him nuh up deh a tell the people dem nuh touch him cause dem too black.

Christopher was scheduled to depart the following day, hooray. Oh sorry I really should be putting on my sad face. Now I can finally look forward to focusing on myself.

BYE BOO

Another day, another driving lesson. Before entering the vehicle mi seh "God, please control mi foot." I really couldn't afford to get another rough up. Clearly the instructor couldn't afford for me to put his life in jeopardy again either & so he decided to put a lot of cardboard under the gas pedal. No matter how much gas I was pressing, the van wasn't going more than about 50mph. People behind me were honking their horns & as soon as they got the chance to overtake they would do so but not before cursing & calling me a lunatic & telling me to get out of the way.

It was time for Christopher to catch his flight & head back to England. I found it so funny that there was no more talk about him returning to Jamaica to live & so I asked about it. The response I got didn't surprise me at all. He said there wasn't much happening in Jamaica & it was very difficult to do business here because of extortion so it makes better sense for him to be able to earn GBP & then send whatever is needed to take care of us here.

I couldn't help but laugh. I knew he had no plans to return to Jamaica. He only said it hoping that I would buy into the idea. He really didn't need to do all that though because I was more than ready to come back home & just in case he didn't realise that, well look I was now back home & it was all my doing. He had no input in making it happen.

As soon as he left for the airport I started lining up my business. I had phones & clothing that I had received orders for. You know how it go already, cah mek dem man yah know everything bout yuh pocket. So I reached out to the respective persons & arranged for them to visit & collect their goods.

His friend returned to the house to park his vehicle. Once he drove the vehicle in I noticed he was removing the license plates so I approached him & asked him what was that about. He said that Christopher gave him instructions to remove the plates & keep them in his possession until he returns to Jamaica. I decided to probe further. So did he say why it was necessary to do this? His friend replied to say that he said I was learning to drive & he didn't want me getting tempted to take out his vehicle. In my mind I said to myself "That ole fart."

But seriously though what would possess me to take out his vehicle? You know seh dah man deh neva gi mi nuh ratings! The biggest joke was when his friend handed me the car key & said that I was expected to start the vehicle at least once a week to ensure the battery doesn't run down. What a piece a libaty!

Christopher had two kingfish cars on the road at the time. They were used for rentals, charters & route taxi. He had arranged for one of the drivers to take my son to school & pick him back up daily & to take us anywhere else that we needed to go.

I had gotten a call to attend an interview over by UWI campus. I don't recall now what the position was but what I do remember was the fact that I got a follow up call to say I wasn't successful. The next job interview I went on was at a place called Niche Financing. The interviewer said he couldn't offer me a job at the moment because my accent was too deep & his clients wouldn't understand me. Cockafart! As far as I knew I was speaking standard english. What is there to not understand?! The next interview I went on was at a clothing store in Mall Plaza I think it was called Go West. They were the distributors of Guess clothing in Jamaica. The interview went well but when I saw the salary package for a managerial position, it wasn't worth my time at all. The owner tried convincing me not to focus too much on the basic pay because there would be opportunities for me to earn commission & bonus. Based on my observations from the little time I was there, the store was very slow which meant sales would be too. She cah trick me! So it was back to job hunting again.

Christopher wasn't concerned that I couldn't find work. He kept saying that I should stay at home & take care of our son. Well eventhough this was not what I wanted to do, I had no choice at this point. Until something came up & I could secure employment, stay at home mom it was.

I was bored out of my mind during the days while my son was at school. The little driving lessons gave me an escape but those were coming to a close soon. I remember asking my brother Junior to give me additional lessons on Sundays once I had completed those with the driving school & he agreed. He told me there was an area up by Mona where people learned to drive & said he would take me there. I was excited about that.

My feeling of excitement would be short lived as I would receive an email from Sophia. I guess the fact that she didn't have a number to contact me on didn't say to her that I was now out of her way & so she should just leave me alone. No No she HAD to find an alternate means of contact.

WEEEEE NUH LIVE NUH WEH

I'm sure you have all heard the saying that you have to take bad things & make joke. I got an email from Sophia which pretty much stated that I was "kotching" in Christopher's house & I needed to leave. She went on to say that she had already given him instructions to put me & my bastard child out.

Y'all know that once my child is mentioned I am going to cuss her out but I kept saying to myself that there was only one way that she could have known we were in Jamaica & that was through her husband. I guess when he was trying to "beg friend" he saw it fit to tell her my business.

Anyway, I told her to come & put us out. She said she knew the address because she was staying at the house while she was in Jamaica during the summer. So I told her that was even better as I wouldn't need to give her directions. So I went on to ask her " O suh a you did leave clothes here because you did plan fi come back? Hush mi dash dem weh." At this point I was finished arguing with her because I knew she couldn't be that stupid to want to come on my home turf & push badness. I have one sister who I knew for a fact would have fixed her business.

Now it was time to get to the root cause of the problem. I called Christopher & asked him whether he had told Sophia that I had returned to Jamaica. He tried to beat around the bush to say it wasn't like I thought it was. So how was it sir? He reckoned that she had asked for my son & which school he would be going to & that was when he told her that we had returned home.

She asked for the child who she constantly referred to as a bastard? I found that very hard to believe & I made my disbelief very clear to him. He went on to say that he wasn't hiding anything from anyone & so when she asked where we were staying in Jamaica he also told her the truth about that. He said he was given an ultimatum to put us out but he had already set her straight & told her that that was not going to happen.

So he tried to paint a picture as though he stood up for my son & I but I wasn't convinced. I still couldn't understand why he needed to divulge any information about my son & I when he knew for a fact that that lady didn't care much for us.

Anyway, it was time to start my free driving lessons with my brother. He came to pick me up on the Sunday evening as agreed with the learner driver big red L attached to his car. So I entered the car & adjusted mirrors & everything like I was a professional.

It was now time to pull off from the drive way. I don't think my poor brother was ready. You see I had gotten accustomed to the driving school van with the steering wheel that made you feel like you were in the gym working out based on the amount of effort you had to put in to get it to move & turn. So you know I put in that same amount of effort while in my brother's car & the car ended up over the opposite side of the road.

I could hear my brother shouting "brake, brake,brake!" Once he had gotten over the fright he began explaining to me about power steering & the fact that minimal effort was required for vehicles with same. He began showing me how just one finger could move his steering wheel.

Clearly I traumatised my poor brother & so I was told to exit the car. My brother said I wasn't ready for the road & so he would have to drive us to the practice location up Mona. He said I should only drive in open lots as far as he was concerned. This nuh sound good at all!

The first Sunday lesson didn't go so badly at all although I am sure he was tired of me running over the stones along the reverse trail. I had a very long way to go.

ANOTHER DAY, ANOTHER INTERVIEW

Once again it was time to attend another interview. This time I would be going to Sagicor. Once I arrived at the location I was directed by the receptionist to the area that I was supposed to report to.

I got to the area & the first question I was greeted with was whether I had a hair band to put my hair in one, my reply to which was no. I was advised that the company had a no colour policy & so the colour in my hair was a problem. I was very confused by their position, after all I had not been given the job as of yet. I explained to the lady that SHOULD I get the job it would not be an issue for the colour to be removed.

I don't think saying that was sufficient. The lady went for some rubber bands & brought same back to me & asked me to put my hair in one. The blonde colour that was in my hair was at the top, so even if I had put my hair in one, the colour would still be visible so I couldn't understand the request but nevertheless, I complied.

Next I was given a math test to complete. The test was fairly easy & was pretty much basic math. Once I had completed the test, I was then called in for the interview. When I entered the room I realised it was a panel interview, I absolutely hated those. But anyway let us see how this goes.

The first comment from one of the panelists was in relation to my hair & the colour. In my mind I kept saying to myself "It can't be that serious!" Once again I reiterated my willingness to lose the colour SHOULD I get the job. By this time I knew I wasn't going to get the job. It was very clear that my hair colour made a first impression that by no means impressed them.

So It came as no surprise when I was contacted to say that I wasn't selected for the job. To be honest after how I was treated,

I really wasn't interested in the job or working for them. Their behaviour came off a little discriminatory.

I remember a couple of my high school friends coming by my house to visit. They told me to get dressed they were taking me to Integration Thursdays over by UWI campus. I can vividly remember my outfit. White long asymmetrical off the shoulder top, grey jeans, red broad belt, long beads, red peep toe flat shoe & a red clutch purse. Proper white woman outfit!

Once we got onto the UWI campus, I didn't know we would ever reach the party venue. I walked through grass, dirt, back road & front road until I eventually heard music & realised we were close. We eventually got into the party & it was a good vibe & we were enjoying ourselves until the weed smoking became overbearing & some old tough back men wouldn't leave our poor asses alone. As soon as we started dancing, there they were. It was very obvious that these men were in no way, shape or form UWI students. I was told that they were men from the nearby August Town community who knew how to bypass security to get in.

Overall though it was good hanging out with my high school friends. It felt as though nothing had changed. Melissa had also reached out & told me that she would be taking me to a club called Quad the following day. I was really excited about seeing more of the party scene.

Y'all know that I pretty much did nothing fun in England & so I was open to enjoying every bit of my country. Let us see whether Quad was what I remembered Mirage, Asylum & Cactus to be.

SIGNAL DI PLANE, PARACHUTE, LOG ON

And just like that, in the blink of an eye it was Friday & I was very excited to be going to the club later. I remember speaking to Christopher at some point during the course of the day & telling him that I would be going to Quad.

I remember when I said it it was almost as if I had cursed a bad word. His reaction came off like "Who gave you permission to go to the club?" Anyway, I knew I wasn't asking him to go but instead telling him that I was going & so I didn't concern myself much about his reaction.

I started putting my outfit together, black short tailored shorts, black waist coat vest & gold peep toe shoe. You all know by now that my alias in high school was dancie because of how I loved to dance. Well that didn't change & still hasn't changed to this day.

I wasn't worried about being out of the loop with the dance moves because we kept ourselves abreast while in England. You see we would get these dance DVDs of various big parties & by watching we would be able to keep up with the fashion trends & also the dance moves.

We use to practice the moves at home that way when we would visit a club called Graneries in England we could show out. The club was mainly supported by "Yardies" but there was a fair share of white & black British present as well.

Melissa visited my house to pick me up. She said she would have been coming a little earlier because there was another party/fish fry that she wanted us to stop by first. She said she had promised to support a friend.

Anyway, I noticed she was driving in the direction of Duppy Gate so I asked her where was this get together & she said over by Mobile Reserve (police base for those who don't know). So I asked her if her friend was a police officer & she confirmed he was.

We got to the location & I was greeted by a sea of men. When we walked in, there were only two other females & we made it four. Immediately I became very uncomfortable.

I remember seeing a gentleman walking over to us & based on her reaction to him clearly he was the person who had invited her. He was then introduced to me & I did the pleasantries & started wondering when wi a lef!

Everything I was offered I declined. Mi nuh want nuttn fi eat & drink! One bagga man & four women? No sah I needed to stay very alert. Next thing I knew I saw Melissa with liquor in hand. So I tapped her shoulder & said "Hi memba seh a you a drive." She laughed at me & told me that one likkle juice wasn't going to do her anything.

Anyway, I was back in my corner once again counting down to leave. I don't know what the man was telling her but all I could hear was kicckky kicckky kicckky. Clearly the words were very sweet. I started thinking to myself "You know seh dah man yah is not no fren." By the time the thought crossed my mind, I saw when the man proceeded to push his hand up under her skirt which was a mini by the way, & again all I heard was kicckky kicckky kicckky (laughter for those of you who might not be familiar with the terminology).

When I saw this play, I was now ready ready because I didn't want anyone to think that there was any open invitation to feel me up. The one thing that kept going through my mind was the birds of a feather saying. So I quickly told her that I was ready. The police man quickly announced that I was boring & told her that she shouldn't bring me back. That's fine sir!

During the car ride to Quad I wanted to say something about the feeling up I witnessed because I knew she had a man & the man feeling her up was not him. Afterwards, I thought to myself that we were all adults & people were free to live their lives as they choose. Me just know seh me & har nah go back no weh together.

Got to Quad & the vibe was right. I liked the three floors concept. The club in England, Graneries had the same concept but the crowd was always on the dancehall floor & the same was true for Quad. Good thing I was keeping up with dance DVDs in England, I didn't feel left out at all.

If I was uncertain about where I was, I knew I was definitely in Jamaica because mi bottom couldn't eat grass in peace. Every minute there was somebody behind me trying to wine it off. I had to stop dancing, turn around & ease dem off but while I was doing this, mi see my friend over di corner lock off wid one man. I guess her motto for the night was go hard or go home.

DID I GET THE JOB?

I had made a pledge to myself never to go anywhere with Melissa again so when I saw her calling me after the Quad night out, I thought twice about answering. Anyway, I answered & gave her one of the half asleep tones.

She went on to say that the project she was on at the bank to which she was employed was being expanded & they were looking for other people to join the team. Once I heard that the call was about a job, mi wake up quick quick. She gave me the details of two individuals & instructed me to email my resume to them. I didn't delay, I jumped on it right away & sent the email off.

On November 16, 2006 I received a call from a Mrs. Smellie who told me she was calling from NCB & would like for me to come in for an interview the following day. She queried whether the proposed time was convenient for me & I confirmed that it was.

Lawd mi did nervous! I absolutely hate interviews. I started researching the company just in case I was asked anything about it. I asked Melissa whether there was anything that I needed to know or if there was anything she could remember from her interview, her reply to which was that I should just relax & answer what I'm asked as best as possible.

I don't think I slept a wink the night before. I got up & got my son ready for school & he was picked up by his driver. I then arranged for the driver to pick me up to take me to the interview. Remember now I didn't really know anywhere so when I told him I was going to Trafalgar Road he replied "A dah road deh right down deh suh name suh enuh, walking distance." Walk in heels to an interview? I don't think so! Please be on time was my next request.

I remember calling my friends & asking them what people wore on interviews here. I somehow felt that my choice of clothing might have been a problem in the past. I loved my cropped trousers & asymmetric skirts & these were acceptable office wear in England. My friends told me to try & stick to skirt suits or dresses with sleeves. I was encouraged to avoid wearing pants.

Okay skirt suit it was. Only this skirt suit was an asymmetrical cut one with a waist coat vest. My late friend Mario (RIP) use to card mi hard later on in the years about that outfit. He would always say "Hey unuh memba when Stacey bus the corner dah morning deh wid di fire blonde hair & the lambada skirt & every man a seh bombaat a who that". I would constantly correct him to say that my skirt was an asymmetrical cut not lambada.

I arrived at the Atrium & informed the security that I was there to a Mrs. Smellie. He called through to Mrs. Smellie, confirmed my arrival & she cleared me to enter the building. I was given a pass & was directed to take the elevator to the 4th floor. Once I got off the elevator, I followed the signs to the department I was headed to.

I came upon a brown door that was closed. I don't think I was mentally prepared for what awaited me on the other side. I proceeded to open the door & as I walked around the corner I was greeted by what could have been approximately twenty pairs of eyes. The department had an open floor concept and so there were no cubicles or offices. There was just an array of desks & bodies seated behind them.

Everyone was just staring. I approached the person at the very first desk, said good morning & asked to be directed to Mrs. Smellie. He quickly pointed me to her. I was now with Mrs. Smellie, proceeded to introduce myself & she asked me to take a seat. She then took up her phone & made a call to someone who she referred to as Mr. Mac. I could hear her briefing him on the project for which they were employing persons & proceeded to inform him that he was being asked to conduct an interview. I don't know whether the phone receiver was loud or whether this

Mr. Mac was being loud but one thing I knew for sure based on what I was overhearing, was that he was not amused by her request. He complained bitterly about being put on the spot & being asked to conduct an impromptu interview that he was not prepared for. Eventually I was escorted to his office by Mrs. Smellie for my interview.

This was the most unconventional interview I had ever experienced & I think this was mainly because he wasn't given the opportunity to prepare. He pretty much went through my resume, asked me a few questions about living & working in England & also queried the reason behind me returning home. The interview pretty much felt like a conversation & I was very appreciative of this.

Later that day I would receive another call from Mrs. Smellie confirming that I had gotten the job & informing me that I was slated to begin working on the morning of November 20, 2006 at 8:15am.

WORKING GIRL

I was up bright & early Saturday morning getting myself ready to go & meet my cousin at my grandmother's house. The plan was to have Christopher's friend Trevor take me there & I would leave my son with my sisters while my cousin & I would make our way to go work clothes shopping. One part of the plan didn't work, my son was adamant he wasn't staying with them & so I had to walk with my human handbag.

We got to the clothing store & I was impressed with the variety & also the quality. My cousin while trying to guide me explained "Stacey, buy a black skirt & a black pants because that can mix & match with different tops. You have to ensure that you have at least one week's worth of clothes to start." I followed her guidance & did as was suggested.

The fact that I was going to start working meant that the offer that the gentleman had made my mom to pay her to take care of our son would now kick in. She had previously given the lady for whom she worked notice to say that whenever I gained employment, she would have to leave to take care of her grandson. Well the time had come, I had now gained employment.

First morning of work & I was very excited. Today I would be given details of the project that I would be working on along with the salary. I got to work bright & early & made my way to Mrs. Smellie's desk. She queried whether I had a bank account with this particular bank as same was needed for me to be paid through. Fortunately for me I had one. You see my brother was also employed to the bank & so once I had returned home, I had visited with him & had opened accounts for myself.

So the fact that I already had an account saved me from having to visit a branch that morning to open one. I was told that I would be given temporary access passes in the mornings to enter the building. Remember now I was being employed to work on a project which basically meant the employment would be temporary, so I guess they didn't see the need to provide us with ID cards.

It was time for me to ask the million dollar question because I noticed the longer I waited the more I heard about everything else except this. "Mrs.Smellie, what is the salary for the job?". When she replied & said $7000 weekly I almost fell off the chair. I replied & said okay with a smile but if she could hear the conversation going on inside my head, she probably wouldn't have bothered giving me the job. The job I would have been doing was to provide courtesy calls to customers whose credit facilities were late for payment.

Next task was to assign me a desk & I ended up right behind Mario, the guy from my previous post who called my skirt the lambada skirt. He was acting all shy & reserve. Once I was assigned the desk then I had to wait to get set up in the system. While I was waiting on that process to be completed, Mrs. Smellie walked me through the office introducing me to everyone. Immediately I could tell the members of the boys' club that targeted "fresh meat", I was ready for them.

But just in case I wasn't I remember my brother calling me later that evening to give me their files. He told me who to beware of. You see these were all people with whom he had worked at some point during his career in the bank. For the most part he referred to many of them as his "bredrens" indicating they were more than just coworkers. Outside of giving me a heads up, I remember my brother also asking me how I got the job because he had sent in a resume for me previously & was told that I didn't meet the entry level requirement because I didn't have a first degree. I remember saying to him "links" & laughing.

Later that evening I spoke with Christopher & when I told him the salary for the job, he laughed hysterically. $7000??? $7000 Jamaican dollars? He asked. He went on to say that he could pay me much more than that to stay home & take care of our son. He then went on to ask "So you really a go put on your clothes & go work fi $7000?" & I replied with a very strong YES! He started laughing again & made the comment that the clothes I would be wearing to the job costs more than the salary I will be paid & he burst into laughter again. If this wasn't enough he added that my mother would be getting paid more than I was for looking after our son & the laughing continued.

I didn't care much for what he was saying or his reaction. One thing I knew for sure was that I would be getting dressed tomorrow & heading out again to go work for my $7000.

TRAINING DAY

For the next couple of days I was placed beside a girl called Maxine to observe how she worked & also to take notes on how to use the system. It wasn't the best training method but it was the one being employed & so I had to make the most of it.

I had my little notebook & I wrote down the different menu options used to check different things in the system. It was almost like I was in school taking notes. The training continued for the rest of the week after which Maxine told them I was ready to go on my own.

I was now in receipt of my first payslip. The figure on same was a little over $4000. How could this be? Where is the $7000? When I went through the payslip I realised there were deductions for tax among other things.

I remember calling my brother Junior later that evening, he was an accountant & I was telling him about my salary issue. He quickly said "Stacey go back to them on Monday, you are NOT suppose to be paying income tax as what you are earning is way below the tax threshold."

Armed with this information I was ready to go & defend my additional $3000 bright & early Monday morning & that's exactly what I did. I remember approaching Mrs.Smellie, showing her the payslip & telling her that based on my investigation I was not suppose to be paying income tax. She looked at the slip & agreed with me. She made a call to the human resources department & they corrected the issue.

I couldn't understand why I was the only person defending the $7000. All the other project workers took their $4000 & didn't say a thing. But now, by me opening my big mouth, they would all benefit & be paid the agreed $7000.

I remember one of the smooth talkers in the department coming over to set me up in one of the applications but like I had mentioned previously, I was warned about them. So while setting me up he decided to ask a lot of personal questions, age, kids etc. In my mind I kept thinking "Sir jus hurry up & do weh you a do & gwan over yuh desk."

Try & recall the open space concept that I described previously. So someone sat in front of me, two people sat to my right, one person behind me & another to my far left. Other than the person to my left, in these covid times everyone else would have been in breach of the social distancing protocol as there wasn't enough space between us. I say this to say that you could hear people's business even if you weren't trying to.

So it came as no surprise when the gentleman putting me in the system said "O I like your hair & your hair colour" & I replied with "Then a the first you a see it?

I have been here for a while now" & all I could hear at the desk in front of me was kicckkyyy kicckkyyyy kicckkyyy. Mario couldn't stop laughing.

They quickly recognised that I was never going to become one of their workplace statistic & so they did the next best thing & became my bredrens. They guided me along the way, told me to go & open my equity account & start purchasing stocks, told me to join the staff credit union & start saving just in case I needed to borrow later on & to also take out the life insurance product that they offered to cover not only myself but my family & any other guidance or heads up that could have been offered, they gave it to me. All in all I can say that they provided solid advice & guidance & I was very appreciative of it.

I remember receiving a call from one of my paternal brothers (I have six). He queried my plans to go back to school & pursue my degree. God know mi neva have no school plans & I told him just as much. He went on to say that he wanted my niece to also start university but her complaint was that she had no company. He then proposed to pay $50,000 towards my tuition every year if I decided to apply for university, pretty much to be my niece's company. This amount at the time was approximately 50% of the fees. I told him that I would think about it & get back to him.

PEACE & TRANQUILITY

We have all heard the saying "Weh yuh nuh know cah hurt yuh." The fact that Christopher & I were in separate countries, I was clueless as to what was taking place in England & that cluelessness made peace reign between us most of the time.

He was now able to live his double or is it triple life peacefully. The fact that there was a time difference also worked in his favour because most times whenever he called me it would be like 1am or 2am in the morning in England, everyone was asleep. So as far as he was concerned, he had things under control. He was also trying to prove to my family that he wasn't the person I had made him out to be, so he was Mr.Nice Guy almost all the time.

I revisited the offer made by my brother for school & whilst I had no immediate plans, my friends encouraged me to take up the offer. I remember in my discussion with him he had indicated that my niece was looking at doing school online with the University of Phoenix. He told me to look at their course offerings to see if there was anything that I would have been interested in.

I looked at the courses but I immediately told him that online learning was not for me. I told him that I didn't think I had the discipline required to stay on top of things on my own & preferred the classroom setting. So it was agreed that I would apply for a degree program at the University of the West Indies.

Work was going well. Every Saturday I would be at Tick & Save buying a new top or bottom to add to my work clothes collection. At least the $7000 was doing something for me. Christopher had offered to bring me some clothing for work but this possibly wouldn't have been received until sometime in 2007.

He had promised to return to Jamaica for Christmas 2006 but later informed me that his son was accustomed to having him around on Christmas & it would be too sudden for him to change that tradition. So wasn't my son also accustomed to seeing you at Christmas as well sir? Even if it was for a couple hours but I guess the first born has been getting it for a longer time so only his feelings were taken into consideration.

Anyway, I was not going to let that get me down. We all know Christmas in Jamaica was all about fun, family, food & excitement. So I looked forward to exposing my son to that tradition. Just like I had looked forward to introducing him to our food. Out of everything he tried oxtail & stew peas were his favourites. Ackee was & still is a no no for him.

So for the next couple of months everything went smoothly. We celebrated Christmas, did the whole watch night service tradition for New Years & celebrated my 22nd birthday shortly thereafter. I finally started feeling relaxed but I'm sure you all know by now that my relaxation moods are usually short lived & this time was no different.

I received a call from the gentleman's relatives here in Jamaica asking whether I had heard that his wife had put him out the house. In my mind I said to myself "but a regular thing that." Anyway, I continued to listen to see where the story was going. She went on to say that his wife's sister best friend Mary was pregnant & that his name was called. Now I was by no means surprised because remember this same young lady had called me in England to tell me that I was to check myself for germs because he had given her & another one some kind of infection. So clearly they were sleeping together & unprotected at that. A couple weeks before I departed England, I had also seen her shopping one Saturday in Croydon & she really looked pregnant. I remember mentioning it to Christopher & asking him whether the child was his & he told me to stop asking him rubbish.

The family member went on to say that Christopher was now living at Mary's house although he has denied that the child she was carrying was his & reckons that he didn't have anywhere to go & so he was just renting one of her spare rooms. Once she said that, it all made sense because if I should call him at certain times of the day, his phone would go unanswered. So he definitely was calling me when everyone was asleep just like he did while he was at his wife's house.

But if you are renting a room as you claim, shouldn't you be free to answer your phone & speak to whoever you want without it being a problem? Unless there was more to the situation than he was saying & we all know that with him, there usually is A LOT more.

I decided to ask him about the pregnancy & he took God off the cross & nailed him back on & said the child was not his. He even called the name of some guy & said that the person was the child's father. He went on further to say that the guy also lives in the house & they are all cool because he knows he is just there as a tenant renting a room.

WHAT'S IN THE DARK

My mother always told us to be honest about our doings because whatever was in the dark would come to light & when it does, the light would be very bright, almost blinding. She spoke no lie.

Christopher maintained that he had a business relationship with Mary. He also maintained that he was at her house solely as a tenant & nothing else.

One night while he was speaking to me & I guess he expected Mary to be asleep but I guess she wasn't, she snuck up outside the door listening to our conversation. The next thing I knew I heard a long line of swear words & what sounded like something being thrown & then of course the call was disconnected shortly after.

I kept calling back his phone but as expected he didn't answer. Like why would his "landlady" be cursing him out for speaking to me?! It just didn't make any sense at all. I continued calling his phone non-stop but still no answer & so I decided to just wait until he called back.

I remember hearing my phone ringing at about 2am local time & the caller id said unknown & so I figured it was Christopher that was calling back. When I answered, the female on the other end went "Bitch, Slut" so I replied with "Take a look in the mirror, you will see the real bitch & slut!" The person then hung up.

I immediately called Christopher's phone & it rang unanswered on numerous occasions until it was eventually answered by guess who, Mary! So once she answered I proceeded to ask for the gentleman her reply to which was that he was sleeping. I went on further to say "Wake him up, it's urgent!" She replied with "Why would I wake him up to speak to you?" By this time it was even more obvious that she was the person who had called me earlier.

I went on to say to her "You called me earlier, so it's clear you have something that you want to say to me, here is your chance, go ahead." A who tell mi fi go seh suh? Is like my girl feel like she did have mi file & couldn't wait fi read it out to mi! The first thing she said was "Your man wants me!" She then went on to say I wasn't to think that he wants me just because I am "kotching" in his house. She made it clear that Christopher was only allowing me to stay at his house because of our son.

Now this was a white girl with no black or Caribbean background, suh weh she know bout kotch?! That reference made it very clear to me that Christopher had a discussion with her about me. Try & recall that his wife also came to me with the kotching reference. So the gentleman had clearly placed it on a billboard that I was kotching in his house in Jamaica.

Anyway, I asked her if that was everything that she wanted to get off her chest, before she could answer I fired back & told her that he only wanted her because he could play her for the fool she really is. I then disconnected the call.

I remember my mother walking into my room & asking what was going on & who was that cursing. I was so happy I had the call on speaker & she was able to hear some of what was going on. I couldn't sleep for the entire night. I couldn't wait to hear from Christopher so I could unleash my rage.

He eventually called & when I confronted him about everything Mary had to say he started laughing. He went on to ask if I was sure she was the person that called because he can't understand why she would be saying those things. I had to remind him that not only did she call but I also called back his phone & she answered. He seemed to have been missing out that little bit of information. He went on to say that he couldn't understand what was going on & that he would go & speak with her & call me back.

For a minute I thought he wasn't going to call back seeing that he had been busted, but surprisingly he did & totally flipped the script in the process. The gentleman called back to say he spoke to Mary & none of what I am accusing her of is true so I needed to go figure out which man woman was calling me about their man.

EXCUSEZ MOI?!

So are you going to sit there & defend Mary? Are you going to tell me that I'm delusional & she didn't call me & neither did she say the things I am saying she said after she answered your phone? These were a few of the many questions I had after realising that Christopher was actively defending Mary.

I remember my mother stepping in & telling him that she heard the conversation & the person on the phone was definitely British based on the accent. It was only at this point he adjusted his stance & started saying that maybe Mary was indeed lying because the call log on his phone had been erased.

I also pointed out to him that no Jamaican woman was going to call another female about her man & use words such as bitch & slut. That lingua is definitely white. The language on that call would have been very colourful had it been a Jamaican on the other end.

After all the excitement & him trying to take the focus off himself, I quickly took him to task about the "kotching" argument. He went on to say that he had no such conversation with Mary & that I was to keep in mind that his wife's sister was her friend. He alluded to the fact that the reference came from the wife & they were the ones discussing me. So when I said to him "Suh a yuh wife tell Mary fi seh my man want har to?" He quickly dismissed this saying that Mary was just trying to get under my skin.

I remember him trying to demonstrate that he had nothing to hide & that everyone was aware of our relationship & where things stood between us. Apparently the best way he could think of to make such a statement was to use my picture as his display picture on MSN Messenger.

Mi nah go lie di yamhead inside of me did feel big when mi see it. Mi a seh yea big statement this. Now they will know better than to call mi phone cause a me di man want, a me di man a post up! Did the thought ever crossed my mind that he just might have blocked or deleted Mary & his wife temporarily in order to put on this fake show? NEVER! Unuh nuh see seh a circus mi did belong!

Finally, I had received a response from the University of the West Indies confirming that I had been accepted. I was so excited! I quickly called my brother to inform him of my acceptance & to also give him a heads up on the payment deadline mentioned. I placed the call & after sharing all the information, my brother proceeded to say "My girl yuh salt!" By this time I was very confused. "Salt? What do you mean?" He replied by saying that he had already helped some of his other nieces & nephews with their school expenses & so he was not in a position to help me.

I felt hurt, confused, angry & a host of other adjectives all rolled up in one. Remember he was the one who had reached out to me & made me an offer, so how is it I am now "Salt"? I could understand if I had called him begging but he was the one who approached me with the proposal. Try & recall that prior to him contacting me, I didn't even have any university plans on my radar.

Anyway, I put on my big girl panties & decided to call Christopher & tell him what had happened. The fact that I had now been accepted, I was now very interested in attending & so I now had to work on a plan B. Remember my salary was only $7000 weekly so I was in no position to even avail of a loan to finance my course of study.

After explaining to the gentleman what had happened with my brother, he burst out into laughter. I couldn't understand what was so funny. He then went on to say "You always a try go round me & do things wid your family & dem always a flap yuh" he then proceeded to start laughing again. As you can imagine I didn't find any of this funny. Once he had satisfied himself laughing, he agreed to pay the tuition for me to start my degree. UWI here I come!

AND SHE'S OFF

After returning the form to confirm my acceptance, the university sent me a package which included a form to be completed with details of my sponsor & the source from which they would be paying my tuition.

By the time this came about Christopher had lost his 9-5 job due to carelessness. He worked as a CCTV officer for a security firm. He saw it fit to take a small television with him to work one night. They used the same CCTV cameras to monitor his movement & decided that he watched more TV than he did his actual job that he was being paid for. So just like that he was fired. He didn't have a case because the use of electronics was prohibited & this was clearly stated in his contract.

I explained the situation to my maternal brother Junior (same one mi nearly kill when he was teaching me to drive), & he agreed to sign the forms to be my sponsor & provide me with the requisite payslips & bank statements. Once all this was submitted, I had now confirmed my place at UWI to read for my degree in Management Studies.

Next on the agenda was to try & get a time change at work. They had us working shifts of 10am-7pm & 11am-8pm. Most of my classes would commence at 5pm & so my current work hours wouldn't have been suitable.

I remember going to work & approaching my supervisor about the matter. I took proof in the form of the acceptance letter to back up my request. She didn't hesitate to honour the request. One thing I can say about the organisation was that I didn't experience any challenges during my course of study. Time off was afforded to me to sit exams & even when it came time for me to do this one particular course that was only offered at 9am on a Tuesday morning, I was given the time to attend the classes.

All in all the university journey was rough because it meant my days started at 8:15 each morning & went up to 9pm each night. Once I got home my second shift would start as my son was adamant that nobody could help him with his homework other than me. So he would wait up for me to come in from school to assist him. Most nights I was BEAT but I had to take care of my motherly duties.

I remember my work neighbour Mario introducing me to redbull after hearing me constantly complain about wanting to sleep sometimes in class. Like clock work at about 3:30pm most days we would walk over to then supermarket Superplus & stock up. I would drink my redbull by 4:30pm & then make my way to school. The redbull worked! The drawback though was the fact that I took forever to fall asleep in the nights eventhough I knew my body was tired.

Mario was really a friend in need & deed. He knew I didn't drive & so whenever he could, he would arrange with other persons he knew that were attending UWI & ask them whether they could have given me a ride. It was through this practice I was able to meet Yolande who has now become a very dear friend. I remember she shared her timetable with me so I would know the days she had school & we could arrange our journey to class.

As luck would have it she was pursuing the same degree program but she was a year ahead of me. She took me under her wings & provided much needed guidance. We also started choosing courses together so we could support each other especially when it came to those group work assignments. I HATED them! There was always that one person who did nothing & someone else would have to take on their part of the project.

Now while school seemed to have been going well, another problem was on the horizon. I no longer had a lot of free time to constantly keep up & keep in touch with Christopher. Most evenings when I got in it would be like 2am or 3am his time & remember now that my priority once I got in was to help my son with his school work. I sometimes had assignments that I needed to complete for class the following day & so my focus really & truly wasn't the gentleman & understandably so.

Apparently he too had noticed the change & had taken me to task about it. I outlined what my days were like & all the demands. I was told that people MAKE time for what was important & I was tempted to say that's exactly what I'm doing but remember now he had the handle because he was paying the tuition so I had to play nice.

After trying to work out in my head how I was going to squeeze him in the already tight schedule, I only heard when the man gave out "A Mario a tek up yuh time, think mi neva know you woulda go work go find man!" The only thing I could do after hearing this madness was laugh. I asked him how he came to this conclusion & he reckoned I was always talking about Mario & him getting rides for me etc. So I asked him why he didn't use that bit of information to look into himself & recognise how selfish he was to have a car parked at the house & I'm not allowed to drive it, strangers have to be coming to my rescue along with Ontime Taxi Service.

And just like that I was given the keys to the Lexus jeep. VROOM VROOM. BEEP BEEP.

SHE GOT HER OWN

Based on the guidance offered by my work neighbour, I started window shopping for cars. The Honda Fits were very popular at the time but after my previous Honda Fit Saga, I was positive I no longer wanted that car. What Honda Fit saga am I referring to you might ask? Well it went something like this.

So 2007 was coming to a close & you know that meant that my birthday was on the horizon. I got wind of news that Christopher was planning on buying me a car for my birthday. He however could not decide on which car to purchase so he asked his friend Trevor to shop around on his behalf.

His friend however took the easy route out & decided to just tell me what the plan was & asked me what car I wanted. The car that was popular at the time was the Honda Fit. So I told him that I would take one of those. He then went on to say that we should visit the car dealership to view it & then confirm whether that was my final decision.

So we went to visit Newline Motors on Constant Spring Road. When we got there Christopher's friend walked right up to the young lady with whom he was in dialogue re the purchase. He introduced me to her & coincidentally we had the same name. He made it clear to her that Christopher was not to know that I had visited the location & neither was he to know that I knew about the car being purchased as the plan was for it to be a surprise. She laughed & said the secret was safe with her.

Now the fact that there was this man willing to buy me a young 22 year old girl a car as a birthday gift, somehow piqued her interest. So the calls & emails to Christopher about the sale of the car developed into something else & before I knew it her name was another to be added to the list of females he cheated with.

Not only was her name added to the list but one night while I was at home wondering where he was as his soon come back turned into hours upon hours & all calls to his phone went unanswered, I would then get a call from a third party to say that my babyfather was involved in some argument outside a club in New Kingston. Suh a when him reach a club? Weh him a argue bout & wid who? were my questions only for me to be told oh no he isn't arguing but there are two females arguing over him.

So I am at home trying to locate the gentleman & he is out & about with another woman. So when the details were revealed one of the females involved in the argument was my namesake from the car dealership. I was even more confused now like how did car dealership girl get so invested that she was now arguing over Christopher?

Unuh know seh mi neva get the car though?! But the man ended up getting a woman. So it was a win win for him. I guess the sales rep saw a bigger opportunity where she could market herself rather than the car. The young lady was ambitious! She was looking long term & thinking about how she could set herself for the future. What is the sale of a little Honda Fit? Herein lies the reason the Honda Fit was no longer my choice vehicle.

Anyway, I remember driving pass a car dealership in Cross Roads & seeing a nice small hatchback car on display. The dealership was Executive Motors & the car was the Mazda 2. I remember consulting my brother Junior to get feedback on the brand. Being a typical Jamaican, he believed only in Honda & Toyota & told me not to venture into the Mazda market because the vehicle would be a hard sell should I decide to sell & the parts would be expensive & hard to source.

If you have known me long enough then you would know that I will seek advice but ultimately the final decision will always be solely mine. So whilst my brother was saying no to the Mazda, I was scheduling a test drive. Once the test drive was completed, I was even more convinced that I wanted the car.

I got my proforma invoice & headed back to work. I showed it to my work neighbour & he did the calculations. He told me that I would need to pay $180,000 to the car dealership & the credit union would finance the balance. He also advised me to start making preparations for my insurance payment along with my fitness & registration. Poor me neva buy car yet & as such I was clueless to the process so I was appreciative of the guidance he offered.

The next thing I needed to do was to brave up & ask Christopher for the car deposit. When I tallied my two shillings I could cover all the other expenses but I needed that $180,000 to deposit to the car dealership. I remember starting the conversation with "Like how you did promise to buy mi a car & you didn't, you can give me a deposit towards one?" There was a pause & then came the question "How much money are we talking?" So I told him the amount & he confirmed that he would be willing to give it to me.

My work neighbour helped me to do my loan application & in no time same was approved. I remember Christopher asking for his name to be added to the car title as co-owner. So because you gave me $180,000 you have shares in the car? Please note that the total cost of the vehicle was $1.8M. I knew for a fact that I wasn't going to add his name & so I quickly told him that it wasn't possible because I was getting a staff loan from the bank & clearly he isn't staff.

I had witnessed too many cases of jointholder nightmares to fall victim to it as well. It's all good when the asset is being acquired but when the relationship isn't working out & people have to part ways, that's when the nightmare begins.

I remember when it was time for me to collect the car from the dealership it was my work neighbour who took me there. Once again I was accused by Christopher of being involved with him all because of how he looked out for me. I knew there was no truth to the allegations & so I didn't see the need to try & defend myself.

I was so excited when we got there & I saw the car well polished & awaiting my arrival. I didn't own a house as yet but nevertheless I felt a sense of pride collecting my first car.

And just like that December 2008 I collected my brand new 2009 Mazda 2.

DADDY IS HOME

You know what was funny, I got so excited whenever it came time for Christopher to return to Jamaica. It was almost as if I expected us to have the time of our lives once he arrived. The truth is our lives were usually very miserable once he arrived.

You know what else was funny? I would cry everytime it came time for him to leave. Whether they were tears of joy or sadness is the other question. Looking back now I'm blown away by my reaction because there was never a time that the gentleman visited & we were at peace for the 4 or 5 weeks that he was here, our peace lasted for 1 week at most.

It was weird how he would always make preparations for us to be at war. I remember the first time I came across a rent receipt for a property on Hope Road. I couldn't understand why he would have needed to rent an additional place. I remember confronting him about the rental & his reply was that same was rented to ensure he had somewhere to go when he & I had arguments.

So how do you automatically assume that we would be arguing? Is it because of the things you know you planned on doing? Is it because of the lies you know I will uncover? Why would one make preparations for misery & problem?

The first hurricane I experienced since my return to Jamaica was Dean. I remember us being without power for a little while after due to the JPS light wires that had fallen. I remember us being in the house hot & miserable, mosquito attacking us every chance they got & pieces of cardboard being our fan. I remember the gentleman saying that he was going to drive by his rental apartment to see whether the power was back in that area & if it was, he would return to pick up my son & I so we could stay at that location for the night. It sounded like a very good plan.

I remember listening to my son being miserable & whining & complaining constantly. I kept wondering what was taking Christopher so long to return. Remember now I had no phone to follow up, my phone battery was dead. My son & I waited, & we waited & we waited until we somehow fell asleep.

I got up in the middle of the night & I realised that he was still a no show. I was so angry & couldn't wait to hear what lies he was going to return with. He eventually surfaced the following morning & advised that he went to the apartment, the electricity was back, he started watching a little TV & fell asleep on the sofa.

What the hell? Watch TV? Sleep? You were only suppose to see if there was electricity, turn right around & pick us up. You didn't even need to go inside the apartment. You can see the building lights from outside. I couldn't believe how selfish the gentleman was. Even if he didn't consider my discomfort in the heat, what about your child?

This was the start of a very interesting visit. Next on the list of drama were some emails I came across from a female who he claimed was just a friend & former co-worker. Now from what I read miss thing was clearly upset with Christopher about a lot of things & as expected his relationship with me was one of the things that she was also upset about .

Boy when mi a read har email dem enuh, she class mi up enuh. One would think that she & I had issues prior based on how she spoke about me & this was not the case at all. I had to respond to the email & thank her for her feedback on me. I explained to her that despite what she thought about me, Christopher was never going to leave me for her.

A who tell mi fi go seh suh? My girl came out guns blazing telling me that prior to me coming to Jamaica she was the one sleeping in my bed. I had to tell her that she was one of the many that was sleeping in it prior to me so she wasn't to consider herself special.

I must have struck a nerve because her next move was to call Christopher & make a complaint. He knew better than to come to me about her because he knew that he had previously told me that she was just a friend & former co-worker. Not to mention the part where he said she had a man that she lived with.

Later that night he left his phone careless & I went through it only to see a string of messages from her. The girl was big mad! She did a dun him! As I scrolled I remember seeing her saying how she regretted getting rid of her child because he convinced her that the child could not have been his & that it was for her man. I think my heart stopped for a little.

So you mean to tell me that the gentleman knew she lived with her man & even if he decided to get a little sex from her, he honestly didn't see it fit to use protection?!

EVERY DAY IS WAR

You know the devil use to tempt me whole heap? After mi search email & phone & nearly ketch heart failure & also got a proper tracing, can you believe mi go repeat the same action & nearly dead again?! God would not have pushed me to do this again, it must have been the devil.

So I once again got access to Christopher's emails & there was a new female on the block. There were quite a few emails between them which basically spoke to her having problems with her current man. At the start of the email trail it seemed as though he was just being a friend but that didn't last very long because soon after they were arranging to meet up.

The first thing I did once I got her name was to search for her on Facebook. Once I placed a face to the name & I saw that she was a browning with long hair, I said yup mi a get bun again. He had a type for the most part & browning with long hair was it. He even confirmed this because at times when I would accuse him of being involved with someone he would proudly say "She is dark skinned, you should know that's not my type."

Now it's one thing to be giving me bun but to be bold with it is another thing. I remember getting a call from my sister one day while I was at work. "Stacey can you believe seh Christopher deh ina mi workplace wid woman & a nuh like him nuh know seh mi work here, yuh nuh see seh him bright!" I could hear him in the background laughing & telling my sister to calm down claiming that the female was just a friend. I heard when my sister said to him " So if she is your friend why when mi ask har who she, she never seh she was just a friend?" I heard the gentleman say "Because you rush the girl & frighten har." I quickly described the girl I had recently found out about & my sister confirmed that it was indeed her.

I remember calling the gentleman's phone after my sister said he had left her workplace & it took a while for him to answer. When he eventually answered & I asked him what the hell he was playing at & why would he even think of going to my sister's workplace with his woman? It was clear he was not alone as his response to my question was that he would call me back & he hung up the phone.

I proceeded to call back & he refused to answer & so I called non-stop. When he eventually answered again I said to him "Suh you a hang up phone in a mi ears caus yuh woman in a yuh van?" and before he could respond his passenger replied "Yes I'm in here." The call was again disconnected & despite calling back almost a million times, he didn't answer.

In my mind I was saying to myself but dah gal yah bright eeh before she keep quiet she a talk up like a fi har man. In reality though whose man was he really? I think the only person who really could say he was theirs was his wife & even her saying it would sound like a big joke.

He did not come home until 3am the following morning. I guess once again his "argument hideaway" rental property came in handy. But a coulda next year him come in a di house, me & him did a go war. So he tried to take his time when entering the room hoping not to wake me up but him clearly nuh know seh woman nah sleep until dem release dem anger.

So as soon as he opened the door & stepped in the room, I sprung up like a Jack in the box that had been wound up & said "Which part you a come from them time a morning yah? So you a disrespect mi fi yuh gal? All a carry har go mi sister workplace? A big fuxk$@g disrespect that enuh!" He replied by asking if he wasn't allowed to have friends. So I asked him why he couldn't speak to me in her presence if she was just a friend? His excuse was that he felt embarrassed especially after how my sister disrespected the girl in front of people.

You see the gentleman knew I was very dependent on him & as such no matter how much shit was tossed in my face, the only thing I could have done at the time was to just wipe it off & wait to be slapped again. I kept trying to understand why someone would constantly go out of their way to hurt someone they claimed they loved. It felt more like he hated me based on the things he would put me through on a daily basis.

But then he would show up with a suitcase filled with clothes & shoes, a new phone, a new laptop, a new camera, pay my tuition, buy me some jewellery, book an expensive vacation & just like that I was once again of the opinion that he loved me all because he bought me some things or did something nice for me. Did I even know what true or real love was? I doubt I did. If I didn't even know what it was to truly love myself how could I really tell if or when someone else genuinely loved me?

Looking back at it I think by Christopher doing something nice for me, I equated that to love when all it was was manipulation.

We don't intentionally hurt the people we love.

READY AGAIN

So I cleaned the shit that was thrown in my face & I was ready again. Ready again for what you might ask? More shit? Or just a regular peaceful life? The probability of either happening were the same so I had to stay ready.

I remember my tuition not being paid that semester because the gentleman reckoned that my sister & I "diss" him in the presence of other people. So because he was confronted by my sister about his blatant disrespect, he flipped the script & immediately we were somehow in the wrong.

It was a good thing I had the little job because I remember having to take a loan that semester to pay my tuition. I remember thinking to myself "yuh cah spite me" but that moment of celebration came to an abrupt end when I received a message from the landlord that the rent was outstanding.

I called his friend Trevor as he was the one who usually paid the rent on his behalf. The rent had to be paid at a lawyer's office in Downtown Kingston & neither myself nor Christopher had any interest in going there so we would usually rely on his friend to make the payments on our behalf. I remember asking his friend whether he had given him any money to pay, his reply to which was no. I told him that I had gotten a call from the landlord in regards to an outstanding payment. He promised to speak with Christopher to get him to do what he was supposed to.

I appreciated his friend's help in getting him to take care of his responsibilities but his friend encouraging him to do the right thing opened another door. This was the door where we would both now be accused of being involved. You see the gentleman had a lot of "yes" men around him that he called friends. They didn't care too much for me because they didn't appreciate the fact that I would go against a lot of the suggestions they made to him.

I remember the time they were "boosting" him up to purchase some rims for his vehicle at a cost of three hundred thousand dollars. I asked him if he was stupid & pointed out to him that he could have used that money to buy a little car to put on the road to operate as a taxi to which he agreed. His friends were not pleased.

Most times they would arrange for him to get these services done with people they knew, & would plan with, to overcharge the gentleman & then they collect their cut after. These were the people he idolized, these were the people who were always placed as priority before my son & I. A lot of times we were home trying to have family time & this was impossible. The house was heavily trafficked.

For a very long time I blamed his friends but eventually I came to the realisation that had the gentleman not entertained them & had he put a stop to it, they wouldn't have felt comfortable to just show up whenever they felt like it & in most cases overstayed their welcome, at least for me.

I later learned that a lot of the times it was the gentleman who would ask them to come by our house. Why? Because he had somewhere to go, usually some rendezvous with a female & he would use his friends as an excuse to get out the house but once out, he had a different agenda.

One night I was home alone with my son. It was getting late & Christopher had not come home. All calls to his cell went unanswered. I remember calling his friend Trevor to find out if something had happened seeing that they had left the house together. When Trevor answered his words to me were "Stacey, gwan a yuh bed, nuttn nuh happen to him." This statement was followed by a chuckle. He was correct. The gentleman surfaced 6:00am the following morning.

As he walked through the door he was greeted by my anger.
"Weh yuh did deh? You a tek this thing mek a f@$king habit?"
And just like that World War 3 started.

I AM TIRED

The lies rolled off his tongue & came from his mouth like flood waters during heavy rains. First I was told he was at the strip club with his friends. Remember now I called one of his friends when I couldn't reach him & he was nowhere near him. Once I had brought this piece of information to the fore, I was told that that particular friend was not there but the others were. I went on to ask if the club doesn't closes? Why would he just be coming in? At this point I was told that he went to check on his rented apartment & fell asleep once he had turned on the air condition.

I was just tired of it all. I kept going around in circles. I had no days off from hurt & pain, & despite me constantly vocalising how his actions were affecting me, nothing was done. He just continued to do whatever he felt like doing. He had no regard for anyone else.

I remember constantly being on edge & feeling like my brain was going to explode. So I decided to start keeping a diary of all the things that were happening. Writing it on paper & reading it back to myself brought on a lot of emotions but I realised that in a weird way it helped. I also left the diary in plain view because I also wanted him to read it. Probably this was the only way to get him to understand what he was putting me through seeing that talking to him was not working.

One day I walked in on him reading the diary. He went on to say that he could not believe that he was really putting me through all these things. Then he said "Wow!" I thought that this revelation would have resulted in changed behaviour, it didn't. His remorse lasted for just that moment & then it was back to regular programming.

I recently came across that diary & I read one entry & began asking myself why did I subject myself to all this? I could hear the hurt screaming at me & feel the pain knocking me down as I read the words on the page. Eventhough I have worked on healing from everything that I went through with Christopher, seeing pages upon pages of entries of me screaming & begging just to be loved, respected & appreciated really weighed heavily on me.

I remember taking a picture of one of the pages & sending it to my friends & saying "that time when I was getting mad & kept a record of the things he did to me" & I laughed after sending the picture but deep inside it was like I had opened the wound once again. I had to quickly put the diary away, back where it belonged.

The weird thing was reading it didn't make me mad at Christopher. I was mad with myself. Like how could you sit & allow someone to treat you this way for so long! But you see when I love someone, I LOVE them. Similarly when I've stopped loving them, I've stopped loving them & nothing that they do can rekindle the feeling. So I always gave people a lot of chances because I know when I'm done, I'm DONE.

Despite my reaction to Christopher's sleeping out, he continued. Some mornings he came in at 6am, other mornings it was just in time to take our son to school & if he slept out on the weekend, he would usually surface about midday the following day.

I recognised I couldn't beat him so I decided to join him & embrace what he was clearly going to continue doing. So I said to him "Can you at least try to come in before sun up so the neighbours don't see you waltzing in & know you slept out?" Our neighbours were very nosey but failed to be nosey when they heard me screaming for help & my son screaming for his father to let me go, but that's another story. He agreed to start coming in before the sun comes up, I guess we will see how that goes.

I knew he was going to do whatever he wanted to, nothing I said or did would stop him & he didn't care about me enough to stop himself, so might as well endorse his behaviour but just ask that whatever is done isn't done in a disrespectful way.

He came in in good time for a couple of nights as agreed but that didn't last long. It was back to his old behaviour. I remember confronting him about it one Saturday morning when he came in & his attitude was pretty much that he doesn't care. At that point I swear I lost it. The closest thing to my hand was a saucer & I threw it at him & it hit the wall. From there I just started smashing all the framed pictures of us & ripping the pictures to pieces. Was this going to solve anything? No! But in the moment it helped to release all the anger I had built up inside.

When my son walked out his room & said "Mommy what's wrong?" At this point I recognised that I had to do something even for his sake. I couldn't continue on this path.

NEXT BIG MOVE

I started working out my next move but it was rather impossible when you don't have the finances part worked out. Everything takes money.

I remember moving out & going back to 34. Now this was a nightmare. I had gotten so accustomed to being on my own, that being in a 7 bedroom house filled to capacity with people felt like torture. I had no peace. When it wasn't people asking to borrow clothes, handbags, money then it was the ones eating out everything that was bought for my son & myself.

Whilst I was there Christopher displayed no interest whatsoever. He really didn't care what was happening with his son & myself. After being at 34 for about a week, I remember telling my mother that I really couldn't stay there any longer.

My mother decided to place a call to Christopher to ask him what kind of father he was allowing his child to leave the comfort of his own space to go "kotch" with people, a situation he wasn't familiar with at all. His response was that I could have moved out & left our son, I didn't have to take him. So she asked him who would have looked after him when he decided to go & sleep out with his women, that one numbed his tongue, he couldn't respond.

I didn't hide anything that was happening in that house between the gentleman & I. My family & selected friends were all aware of the ups & downs. Christopher called it telling the whole world our business & not having any privacy but I called it releasing the tension so it doesn't stay inside me & drive me crazy. He had something to be ashamed of, I didn't.

Anyway, I moved back in & was greeted at the door with the words "Mi did a wonder how long it did a go tek you fi come back! You a move out like you can survive pon yuh own." The statement was followed by a laugh. He constantly reminded me of my dependence on him but I knew one day to come I would be able to stand on my own.

I never felt defeated by him constantly putting me down & making me feel like I was less than, instead it motivated me more to prove him wrong & show him that I could & would succeed with or without him.

It was hard trying to focus on school when there were so many things happening but I knew that getting my degree would provide a stepping stone to possibly getting on staff at work as I was still on a contract.

I worked flexitime shifts at work for the most part but on days when I had school, I would go in to work for 8:15, other days would have been 10am but I was switched to 11am at one point. I remember seeing this number calling Christopher's phone almost every morning by 10am.

It was almost as though he told the person the time I went to work but he clearly forgot to tell them that the time had changed. So I took a mental note of the number. The third morning I saw the number calling again I asked him if he wasn't going to answer his phone his reply to which was no because it was just people calling him to beg money. He went as far as to say "Answer it nuh & see" after he saw the look on my face.

Clearly I didn't answer that morning but one night as he got ready for what looked to me to be a very hot date, I saw the number calling again & so I decided to answer. After all, he did say I could have answered previously.

When I answered the phone I could hear like the person paused but she went ahead & asked for him. So I told her he was unavailable & asked her what business she had with him. She chuckled before saying that she was waiting on him to come & pick her up to attend a party. I think at the time the party was French Connection, yes high end party.

She went on to make it clear that she knew that I was his son's mother & that we were no longer together. So I asked her if that's what he told her & she said yes. She also went on to say that based on the amount of time that they spent together, she had no reason to think otherwise. So I said to her "Well all he has told me about you was that you are a beggar, so don't you think if we weren't together that he should have just said you are his woman?"

I think calling her a beggar struck a nerve. She went off telling me that her father was rich & she wasn't in need of anything not even from Christopher. She went on to speak about the size of her house, where it was located & the circles within which she operated.

When the gentleman came out the shower & saw me with the phone, I think he had a mini heart attack. It was almost like he got possessed by a spirit. He grabbed the phone from me & started saying hello, hello & right there in my presence he told her that he was getting ready & would be there shortly.

Then suppose mi did a cuss the girl & hype up miself? Mi woulda get flop big time. Anyway, I clearly went on to argue with him about what had just happened & the fact that all along he lied about who was calling him. He went on to say that this girl's father had money, they lived in a mansion up Belvedere & he wanted to know what it was like to be with someone like that who didn't need him for anything. He explained that in a situation like that he would know that the person would love him for him & not for what he could do for them.

Did he really just look me in the face & say all this? O yes he did! And what was I going to do about it? Absolutely nothing! After all what could I have done? I was dependent on this man to do almost everything for my child & I.

As expected he didn't return home that night. Bawl until mi drop asleep was my go to remedy. When he surfaced the next morning to eat & leave, yes eat. My house was the restaurant! So he would eat, get dressed & he was gone again. So yes when he showed up to eat, he tried starting another argument. I realised this was his new strategy that he would employ whenever he wanted to go & sleep out. I stopped him in the middle of his sentence & said "Look I am not going to do this today. If there is somewhere you need to be, just go. You don't need to start an argument to go & do what you want to, just go & do it."

The last thing I said to him before he left the house was "Just remember those tables, they do turn & what a day it will be when they do."

RICH KID ON THE BLOCK

It was very clear that the gentleman was smitten by his new "rich" girlfriend Paula. He was smitten to the point that he couldn't stop talking about her.

I was told where she lived, the size of the house & the fact that the house even had a gaming room & a pool. I was told the vehicles that her father had & the fact that he had just gifted all his daughters Honda Fit cars.

Now imagine this man was technically "cheating" on me & pretty much felt comfortable to brag about the person he was cheating on me with to me. He would usually have denied his involvement with any females I asked about but not this time, he was like a proud dad.

One day I overheard him speaking to his friends about a party that he was planning which would have been held in New York. Once he had finished his conversation with them I started asking questions as I didn't know him to be a party promoter. He said Paula had a lot of connections in the entertainment industry & they were planning on going into business to keep parties. He went on to say that money was in it to be made & he was all about making the money.

Clearly I started questioning why Paula had to be involved in the process & I was told that it was her idea. I started thinking to myself if she had all these brilliant ideas, the connections needed to pull them off & her daddy's money to do so, why wasn't she doing these events & making money from them all along? I don't think he had stopped to ask himself these questions, he was just all about doing whatever was necessary to impress her.

The event was slated to be held at the Amazura Night Club in New York. I didn't have a U.S. visa at the time so you know I was excluded out of everything. I am sure I would have been excluded even if I had a U.S. visa though.

Just like that the gentleman packed his bags & was off to New York for his show. From what I heard it was a success & everything went well until there was the talk about some money that couldn't be accounted for. I remember laughing to myself & thinking "Brute! Yes man dem rob yuh!"

Despite the ongoing money dispute, things were still going strong with Paula. Apparently someone else took the money that couldn't be accounted for, it was clear that the thought that she might have taken it didn't even cross the gentleman's mind. After all, her daddy had money & as such she wouldn't need to trouble his or so he thought.

I remember one night after he came in from being out with his friends or so he claimed, his phone just kept going off. The phone was on silent & was hidden under the mattress. The constant sound from the vibrations woke me up but Christopher was fast asleep. He was out cold. I started following the sound to see where exactly it was coming from & voila I found the phone.

I took some very deep breaths before venturing into it to search it. The first thing I wanted to establish was who the hell was calling at 3am in the morning. When I looked at the call log I realised the calls were from Mary. The next thing I went to check was the phone gallery. I don't know if I was ready for what I was about to see.

I would have learned by now that once I ventured in the gentleman's phone, something or things were definitely going to be there that would "lick mi for six" & this time was no different. First thing I saw were pictures of Paula all posed up in her underwear. The more pictures I looked at two things became very clear 1. He definitely took the pictures & 2. They were taken at his rendezvous apartment.

The pictures didn't give me that much of an heart attack mainly because he was very upfront about his involvement with her. It was the baby pictures & videos from Mary that almost gave me a stroke because since his family broke the news about the pregnancy he has constantly maintained that the child was not his. Well everything in this phone was painting a completely different picture.

Deep down I knew he was lying about the child not being his but seeing all these pictures & videos where he was being kept up to date about the child, made me feel some type of way.

The worst part was the fact that I had to just put back the phone where I found it & get up the following morning & pretend nothing had happened. I couldn't open my mouth because had I done so then I would have given him a reason to retreat to his rendezvous apartment. I hated the fact that when he was not around my son would constantly ask for him & ask when he was coming back & would sometimes get upset when he didn't return. So for my son's sake, I kept my mouth shut.

TAKE IT OR LEAVE IT

Paula had become a permanent fixture. She was fulfilling all the fantasies that the gentleman had which I had no interest in being a part of.

I tried as best as possible to keep my focus on school. After all my degree was probably the only thing that was going to rescue me out of this very dependent position that I was in.

I remember applying for a job at another financial institution when I saw that there was no significant change in my $7000 per week salary despite me being employed for a few years. I remember telling my then supervisor that I was seeking a job opportunity with the competition. She queried how far long the process had reached & I informed her of the fact that I was made an offer. She immediately got up from her desk & told me that she was going to speak to the general manager because I was a good worker & she wouldn't want to lose me.

After that meeting, I got my first promotion. I was now on the official salary scale for the organisation. This was only the beginning for me as I was promoted on two other occasions afterwards.

Christopher didn't like the fact that I was progressing. I remember the sense of pride I felt when I could now say to him "Just pay the rent, I will cover food & the other bills." I remember him saying that me making this move as soon as I was able to said a lot to him about who I was as a person & my character. He went on further to say that this was an indication that I wasn't with him for what he could do for me. I was happy he finally got this revelation as I was tired of being accused of being a gold digger.

The gentleman somehow felt that females were only interested in him because of what he had. I remember pointing out to him that he was the one who used his material things to impress & attract people & so people would rarely be around him for his good looks.

I must have struck a nerve because he clapped back quickly with the fact that Paula was in the picture & she didn't need him for money. So I guess he was saying she was there for his good looks?! That was the biggest joke because I knew for a fact that he had to be spending heavily to maintain rich kid & her lifestyle. He was also working overtime trying to impress her family.

I grew up hearing people say Jamaica very small & is not who you know but who knows you. It was customary for me to share details of the gentleman's new women with my friends. I remember sending Paula's picture to a friend of mine & she burst into laughter when she saw it. She told me that her father was their family friend & so she knew her & her brother & sisters. Just like that my friend could have given me her file & in that moment I realised that she wasn't better than me & had absolutely nothing over me. It only appeared like she did because of the pedestal the gentleman chose to put her on.

I remember searching for comfort & I somehow found it in a long time family friend. I had never seen this person as nothing more than a friend but on those days when you are made to constantly feel like you are not enough & less than, speaking to someone who makes you feel like you are important & valued will switch on a whole host of emotions.

With everything else that was going on, I welcomed the distraction. The usually short conversations started becoming longer & they were something that I began to look forward to.

It was crystal clear that regardless of how I felt about the situation, Paula was not going anywhere. She had become a permanent fixture in Christopher's life. She had also become his priority & as such his visits to Jamaica were no longer centred around my son & I but instead his new found love.

He spent more time away from us than he did with us eventhough we were all in the same country. It was probably best for us to bring the curtains down on this toxic relationship.

CASE OF THE MISSING PASSPORT

Christopher had been away & was due another trip back. His flight was slated to arrive in Jamaica the Friday some time after 5pm. I would receive a call at approximately 9pm that night to say that the flight was canceled & he was being housed in a hotel. He went on to say that due to the cancellation he wouldn't arrive in Jamaica until the Monday.

I remember being at work & getting a call from my mother. She had called to inform me that Christopher was home. I remember looking at my watch & seeing that it was a little after 1pm. I quickly said to my mother "He is not coming from England. He was already in Jamaica & just decided to surface."

Once I got home & saw the gentleman I was very blunt & I told him that he was in Jamaica from Friday but needed to spend time with Paula & so he lied about his flight being canceled. He looked at me like I was crazy but deep down inside I knew I was correct.

For the next couple of days I kept trying to locate his passport but it was nowhere in sight. It was no longer being housed in the dresser drawer where it would have normally been. It was now being locked away in his safe, one that I didn't have a combination for.

One day as I laid in my bed, I looked up at the top of the built in closet where Christopher's suitcases were. The first thing that caught my eye was the luggage tags & then came the thought that the tags would have the date on them. This was the fastest I sprung up out my bed. I could feel that I was on to something. Just as I expected, the luggage tags had on the original date that he was supposed to have arrived in Jamaica. The lies were never ending.

As soon as Christopher walked in I confronted him with the newly found evidence. He laughed in my face & pretended as though I was crazy once again. He went on to say that I was to recall that the luggage went on the aircraft on Friday hence the reason why the tags would have Friday's date. My next question was "So they didn't bother taking the luggage off the aircraft when the flight got canceled?" There was a pause. I don't think he had a rebuttal prepared. I think he just expected me to believe the lies he was spitting out.

If the luggage tags weren't enough I later found receipts where he had gone to the phone shop to purchase chargers & other accessories on the same date he was apparently NOT in Jamaica. When I asked him about it he reckoned his friend Trevor made the purchases on his behalf with the expectation that he was supposed to have been coming in later that day. So I asked him how did Trevor pay using his card that was in England? The fact that I sat & took a lot of disrespect & mistreatment, I think Christopher thought I was also stupid but that was where he went wrong.

The next items to be found were room keys which according to the labeling belonged to the Altamont Court Hotel. I didn't need to see anything else. The case was closed & Christopher was guilty as charged.

I was so miserable & unhappy. My dermatologist was my new best friend. My seborrheic eczema which I was told was triggered by stress & anxiety, didn't get any time off. It was constantly at work & while it worked overtime, I had to pay a pretty penny trying to get it under control.

Some days I felt so disappointed in myself. The question of how much more was I going to take resided permanently in my thoughts. What resided next door to it was the fact that I was still nowhere near where I needed to be financially to make a clean break & walk away. I never stopped believing though that one day things would change & the change would be for the better.

WHAT IF IT WAS THE BIG A?

Have you ever sat & thought about some of your life experiences & could almost immediately recognise all the bullets, missiles, grenades & bombs that you dodged? God is Good!

I remember getting ready for work one morning when I heard my phone ring. When I looked at the screen I saw unknown caller so I knew the call had to be Christopher. I answered & yes it was him. He went on to ask whether I was feeling anyway "funny". Funny? I asked. What do you mean? Funny down there he replied. Down where? I asked. He then went on to say do you have any vaginal itching, odour or discharge. By this time I was rather confused but nevertheless I replied & said no I don't. So I asked what was the issue his reply to which was that he had gone to the GUM clinic & his results came back positive for TV. Now until that day the only TV I knew about was the one I watched. So my lack of knowledge had me thinking that this TV was something linked to & possibly caused by yeast. So my uneducated response was that I would call my doctor & schedule an appointment & check to see if something was wrong with me. Clearly I am thinking I was somehow the problem.

So I called up my gynecologist & told him I needed an emergency appointment & he said no problem I should make my way to him. I called in to work & told my then supervisor that I would have been coming in late as I had an emergency. I got to my doctor's office worried, panicking & an overall hot mess. My doctor calmed me down & asked me to explain what was going on. I went on to tell him that my partner called to say he had tested positive for something called TV & I needed to find out If I had it or could have given it to him. Doc then went on to ask how many sexual partners did I have. So I replied one. Doc then went on to say "Stacey remember anything you tell me is confidential so you can answer honestly". He repeated the question & I once again replied one. He then asked whether the person who called me was the one partner that I was referring to, my reply to which was yes. I remember doc bursting out in laughter. I was not amused! Did this man not realise I was on the brink of a nervous breakdown?! Doc went on to say Stacey do you know what TV is? Do you know anything at all about it? I replied with a very strong NO!

Doc then went on to explain that TV was a STI & was transmitted through sex. He then went on to say that I would have had to have sex with an infected person in order to pass it on to my partner. He further explained that me having just the one partner meant that I couldn't have been the carrier. By this time I am seeing every colour in the rainbow. Doc gave me the all clear & sent me on my way but not before opening my eyes to how differently this situation could have played out. I was way ahead of him! I had already played out a million different scenarios in my head by now.

I got in my car, shed a few tears then turned my air conditioning all the way up to cool down my now bright pink face. I returned a call to the gentleman, he answered on the first ring. "Did you go, did you go? What did he say? My reply to which was " Gwan go mek two more call & see if you can find out a which front shot yuh because your germs that you have has nothing to do with me!" He was at a loss for words. When he finally found words, the only thing he could manage was "Call you back."

That drive back to my office although less than 20 minutes felt like 24 hours. I felt so betrayed! To think I was being loyal to someone who didn't even respect me enough to protect himself & by extension me. How do you continue being involved with someone like this? How do you interact hereon with someone who could have literally brought death to your door in the form of aids? This was my wake up call that my exit from this situation was long overdue. Like how much more was I going to subject myself to?

When Christopher eventually found an explanation it was in the form of maybe the TV was as a result of his previous prostate issue because I was the only person that he was sexually involved with. Do you see what happens when they think they have you fooled? They also speak to you like you are a damn fool!

We owe nobody anything but we owe everything to ourselves. Be grateful for the bullets God blocked for you & show him your appreciation with changed behaviour & removing yourself from the situation. It was time for me to show God my changed behaviour.

I THINK WE NEED A BREAK!

After my close encounter with what could have been a life changing situation, my sexual appetite for Christopher dwindled. Despite his best efforts trying to convince me that his diagnosis was somehow linked to a previous health problem, I was not going to buy into that foolishness. We had already determined that you were diagnosed with an STI & there is only one way of contracting it & that's through sex.

I remember trying to have sex with him after the incident but this time with protection of course but the whole encounter just felt very off because whilst I might have been present physically, mentally I had checked out.

I proceeded to have a discussion with Christopher & told him that I needed a break. I told him that I needed to see what else life had to offer & to decide whether where I was with him was where I really wanted to be. I just needed some space as I had a lot going on in my mind that I needed to sort through & figure out.

Initially there was some resistance but whichever one of his females he went & discussed it with, I would like to thank them. He came back to me to say that he had spoken with someone & they told him that it was best for him to give me the break I had requested & allow me to explore & figure out what exactly I wanted. The person had also told him that had he not allowed me this time to myself then it was possible that I would rebel & subsequently cheat. This sounded like someone who was trying to create a vacancy for themselves but nevertheless whoever you are, thank you.

I had kept in touch with my long time family friend Mark. I had told him a lot of what had been happening. Similarly, I also told him when I requested the break. The break would see me speaking to him more regularly & eventually we started hanging out. It was a breath of fresh air.

Mark & I would eventually discuss an overseas trip to Canada. After being previously denied a U.S visa, I had no interest in applying for any other. I just always felt like my lack of assets would have resulted in me being constantly declined. Mark had however assured me that the Canadian process would have been different. He also agreed to assist me with the application. This gesture left a lasting impression especially when I thought about how little Christopher did for me to aid my growth process. Left to him I would have remained on the same level he met me, that way he could maintain control.

2009 was coming to a close & as we usually do when a new year is approaching, we start thinking about all the changes we would like to make. Whether they were actually going to be made was left to be seen. I know mentally I was in the mood for change or changes.

I kept Christopher in the loop about everything that was happening with Mark. Something I would later come to realise was a mistake.

2010 THE YEAR OF CHANGES

I remember celebrating my 25th birthday with a dinner at home with my family & a few friends. Mark wasn't invited & understandably so because I was still living at a property for which Christopher had the lease. So despite what was happening between he & I, respect was still due & so I brought no one to his property.

The discussion continued with Mark about the Canadian visa application & before long I had gotten all the documents needed to facilitate the submission. He had taken the initiative to submit the application on my behalf. Once this was done it was time for us to await the decision.

Every now & again Christopher & I would speak & on the odd occasion there would have been some mention of Mark. I remember sharing with Christopher how Mark's mode of dress differed from his, BIG MISTAKE as he would later use the conversations I had with him to try & paint a picture to Mark that I was mocking & ridiculing him.

One evening after work I decided to swing by Mark's house. I had gone on campus earlier only to be advised that my class scheduled for the day had been canceled. While I was at his house sitting in the living room might I add, I would receive a call from Christopher asking why I wasn't at school. I was a bit taken aback by the question, like how did he know I wasn't at school? He went on further to say if I was now putting man before my education. The entire conversation I was at a loss for words because I kept trying to figure out how he knew where I was.

He went on to explain that his friend Trevor saw my car parked in a scheme & called him to ask what I was doing in that area. I was told by the same friend later on that this was a lie & that

Christopher had actually placed some kind of tracking device on my car.

I briefed Mark on what was happening & told him that I was going to leave. While I was driving out of the scheme, I would see Christopher's vehicle driving in & heading in the direction of Mark's house like WHAT THE HELL! I quickly called Mark to update him on the fact that the gentleman was heading his way. He told me not to turn back & that I should continue on my journey home.

I would receive a call later on from Mark to say that Christopher told him to leave me alone because he wanted back his family. It was during this conversation that he painted the picture to Mark that I had an issue with his mode of dress & that I had told him about his sneakers & socks dressing & we both laughed. He also conveniently made his licensed firearm visible for Mark to see while telling him to leave me alone.

I was livid! What is all this about? I did say to him give me a break, so what is all this madness & why was it necessary? I figured it was intended to be used as a turn off as not everyone likes the babymother & babyfather drama & I knew for a fact that Mark was one of those persons. He said the fact that Christopher came crying to him as if he was the cause of the issues between he & I, rested heavily on him & he felt the need to leave me be & we revert to just being friends.

As expected, Christopher & I had a massive argument. I was adamant that I was not going to allow him to dictate how the situation played out between Mark & I. By this time I now felt the need to rebel. I felt like an angry teenager who had now planned on breaking every rule their parent had set. I was not going to allow Christopher to have his way & I made this known to him.

I would later receive news that my Canadian visa had been issued & the discussion now was a travel date. Mark & I had agreed to travel in May of 2010. He had arranged for us to stay at his friend's house in Brampton. Christopher was advised accordingly & he had provided me with some cash to purchase items for our son.

My trip to Canada allowed me to meet the Robinsons people who immediately became friends. They were the hosts of all hosts & the fact that I was meeting them for the first time didn't mean anything. I was treated as though they had known me for a long time.

While in Canada I saw another side to Mark, the controlling side. He tried to control how I spent my money & what I spent it on & this was a turn off for me. After all I was on vacation & I took the money as spending money, I didn't take it with the intention of returning home with it. This situation & his attitude became a deal breaker for me & as such we decided to put the little trial run to rest. I know one person who was happy about this & I'm sure without me saying y'all know who it was.

I AM DIVORCED, WILL YOU MARRY ME?

May 2010 was really shaping up to be an interesting month. After closing the chapter with Mark, Christopher would provide me with a document shortly thereafter which basically confirmed his divorce from Sophia. The one thing I had been waiting to hear for at least the past nine years was now being said.

So it should come as no surprise that I said yes when the gentleman suggested that we should get married. The planning started immediately. The date had already been set, February 5, 2011. I know there is the question of why would I even think of marrying Christopher, let us put it this way, I wasn't thinking.

For the next couple of weeks all the conversations were about wedding plans. I think I had somehow blocked out everything that had happened between this man & I. I had always seen myself as being his wife & that was all I was now focused on.

I went on to the David's Bridal website & selected my wedding dress along with the bridesmaid dresses. Christopher had arranged for his cousin in New York to visit the store & collect them for us. I had started designing the invitations & selecting the souvenirs. I remember my schoolmate Roxanne had recently gotten married & so I had asked her to recommend some of the vendors she had used for things such as decor, venue, food etc. She provided her recommendations along with her blessings.

So let me provide you with the run down of the groundwork that I had now managed to cover in record time. The dresses were bought, Mona Visitors Lodge was booked for the reception, UWI Chapel was booked for the ceremony, Dwayne Watkins was booked for photography, New Levels Decor for the decor & Taniesha Williams for the cake. The guest list was done & selections were made for bridesmaids & made of honour.

The selection for a master of ceremonies was still pending but I had Ity Ellis at the top of my list of potentials. If full speed ahead was a person, it would definitely have been me. I don't know if the speed was due to me fearing that Christopher might possibly change his mind at some point. After all, I didn't wait this long for him to come & have second thoughts & I wasn't going to give him that opportunity either.

I started making calls to my family & friends & brought them up to speed with all the happenings. Most persons appeared happy & receptive to the idea of me getting married to Christopher but I could hear the skepticism in the voice of others. It was almost as though they wanted to ask if I was getting crazy but instead of doing this they opted to appear supportive.

I remember reaching out to my high school friend Kadian & sharing the news with her only for her to inform me that she was also planning on getting married in February of 2011. My level of excitement immediately increased once I heard that my friend would also be getting married a couple days after me. My next call was to my sister Annette to discuss all the places she would need to accompany me, to meet with vendors.

The first meeting we attended was with the decorators. Just listening to the ideas & envisioning the execution brought on anxiety. Like where was February 5th? It needed to hurry up & come. Our next meeting was with the photographer. We went through costing, timing, coverage & location among other things.

One thing you should have gathered by now was how excited I was about becoming Mrs. Christopher. Excited to the point that I started planning a wedding without even being given a ring. Like who does that?

WITH THIS RING

Christopher was scheduled to arrive in Jamaica in August of 2010. His cousin was also scheduled to visit for vacation & would be taking along the dresses with him.

Whilst I awaited his arrival I was busy doing the groundwork. By June I had the wedding invitations in my possession. Despite me having my guest list ready, I somehow didn't feel the urge to distribute the invitations as yet. I remember my sister asking me what I was waiting on & reminding me that I needed to give my guests ample notice so they had time to prepare. I heard everything that she was saying but I still didn't feel ready to distribute the invitations especially because I was still without a ring. I wanted to wait until at least that little piece of jewellery made it's way on my finger.

The wait was finally over, the day had come. I anxiously awaited Christopher's arrival. Once I heard the gate opening I knew he had arrived. Once he walked in the door our son was the first to run to him & give him a hug. Once the greeting was over, my son went to ask about his toys & games that he had requested. My son was adamant that he had to get his stuff now & so he had to start sorting through his luggage to take out all he had for him.

Once he was done doing that it was time to deliver my ring. I remember him going down on one knee, opening the box & asking whether I would marry him. I remember laughing while he placed the ring on my finger. The ring never look too bad at all.

We were booked to check in to Sandals Ochi Rios on the weekend at which time we would also be doing our engagement photoshoot. Christopher had brought me a dress which he said he had wanted me to do the photoshoot in. I remember he also bought me a matching Bridget Sandals to complete the outfit. We were all packed & ready to go.

We arrived at the hotel & received a very warm welcome. We were offered our welcome beverage while we checked in. Once the checking in process was completed we were escorted to our room. Once we got to the room it was time for us to get properly reacquainted. Our first night went very well. We were scheduled to have the engagement photoshoot first thing in the morning.

It was the morning of the photoshoot but I don't think I was prepared for what was about to unfold. I was in the shower when I heard this loud uproar like arguing. I couldn't make out everything that was being said but the little I made out was "Stinking gal, yuh bright & out of order." So I cut the shower short & went outside to try & figure out what was really going on.

When I listened to the voice on the other end of the phone I recognised it to be Mary's. I heard when Christopher said "Hey gal yuh brite & out a order, me coulda tek your clothes & carry come gi my woman?" "Yuh feisty & stink." The arguing went on for a little while. The more I listened to them argue the more they sounded like man & woman.

Once the call had ended I proceeded to ask Christopher what the argument was about. He said Mary had called him to say that she was missing some items of clothing & she was of the view that he took them out her house & carried them to Jamaica to give to me. He went on to say "Yuh nuh see seh she brite? She wear nuttn weh me woulda wah gi you?" As he continued to rant & rave I went on to ask him how could he have been accused of taking anything from Mary's house when he had told me he had gotten a place for himself. Just by asking that one question, he started cursing me out as well & before I knew it we were having a full blown argument.

I was such an emotional mess, I decided to call the photographer to possibly reschedule the photoshoot but before I could have done so, I got a call from him to say that he was on the hotel property & was ready to shoot. The pictures from the engagement photoshoot taught me my first lesson in the lies that pictures sometimes told.

When I posted those pictures, no one could tell what had happened couple minutes before they were taken. They painted the picture of a happy couple but were we really? As the congratulations came in, things were still a little tense between Christopher & I. Oh what an engagement this was. I remember Christopher purchasing some Jewellery from the duty free shop at the hotel & gifting same to me. I guess this was intended to be a peace offering & to smooth things over. It somewhat did the trick although in the back of my mind I kept replaying the incident with Mary.

Who would I really be marrying? Would it be just Christopher? Or would it be Christopher & Mary & a host of others?

LIFE WITH A SEARCHER

Once I returned to work the very observant persons in the office noticed my new piece of jewellery & expressed their congratulations. While they were expressing their congratulations I had already started thinking about the decision I was about to make & whether it was the right one. Nothing about Christopher had changed. He was still sleeping out & coming in at whatever time he saw fit & he was still always on the road every night with his "friends" leaving my son & I home alone. My mother was usually at the house with us Monday to Thursdays. After she too had spoken to him about the staying out late every night, he started coming home early but once she left on Fridays, it was back to his old behaviour.

One night I jumped up out of my sleep, checked the time & it was a little after midnight. I don't know why, but the first place my eyes went after, was to where my work handbag would have usually been & guess what it was missing. I then noticed that the bathroom door was closed & the light was on. I got up & proceeded to knock the door at which time Christopher replied that he was using the bathroom & I should use the other.

I opened the bedroom door & closed it to give him the impression that I had exited the room but I was still standing there. The next thing I knew I heard him opening the bathroom door & as he stepped out with my handbag in his hand I asked him if he had found what he was looking for. He quickly dropped the bag to the floor & started shouting YOU HAVE MAN! YOU HAVE MAN! So I asked him what led him to this conclusion. He said he used my phone to text a number pretending to be me & he called the number as well & a male answered. So I asked him to show me the messages & the number he called. After all if you are going to accuse me of something you should at least afford me the opportunity to clear my name. But I guess if HE said I was guilty of something then I was because what he proceeded to do was to throw the phone in the wall smashing it to pieces.

Now this phone that he apparently searched was a phone I had a Lime chip in. It was during that time when Lime had these sim cards that gave you a lot of free minutes. My dad's phone was on the Lime network so it worked out good for me. Everybody used that phone to call Lime numbers because it was free. I wasn't the only one who used it hence the reason I asked to see the messages & number that the gentleman made reference to. The reality was that there were no messages or calls. He got caught searching my handbag & was now trying to take the focus off himself.

I remember him shouting at the top of his voice " Yuh nah tell mi who you a f$%&?" I laid in the bed & remained silent. He went on to say of all the times I could have cheated, why would I cheat now when we were engaged to be married?

Remember I had mentioned earlier that this argument started at 12am & it went on until 3am. Bear in mind I had work later that morning, so I decided to just tell him what he wanted to hear. I was honestly just tired & wanted to sleep. So I proceeded to tell him that whatever texts he saw must have been from some guy I met on campus who likes me. I was just over the madness.

Once I had said this he went on top of his voice shouting & acting crazy. This resulted in my mother waking up & coming to the room door to ask what was the problem. As soon as my mother got to the door he blurted out "Stacey have man, she have man a f@$%." My mother proceeded to ask him if he had seen me with a man. Instead of answering he decided to storm out the house.

While outside he once again started talking at the top of his voice that I had a man & I was cheating & look at when I decided to start cheating, when we were close to getting married. My car had blocked in his vehicle & I heard him shouting my name for me to come & move my vehicle so he could drive out.

I got out of bed & went outside to move my vehicle. Once I got outside I was once again greeted by shouts from Christopher

"Yuh nah tell mi who you a f@#$?" I refused to engage in any further conversation with him. I got in my car, drove out the driveway & allowed him to exit. I drove back in only to see him driving in back behind me.

He continued with his rant until 3am, I guess by this time he must have entertained himself enough because the next thing I knew he was telling me that it was all a joke. He didn't see anything in the phone but he wanted me to believe he did to see whether there was anything I wanted to confess to him. This was the biggest eye opener for me.

The following morning I shared with my mother that the entire thing was made up & she was shocked. She reminded me that at one point through the entire ordeal Christopher also appeared to have been crying. She had so many questions & after voicing them she said "Stacey tek sleep & mark death because if him can bawl & carry on when him know a lie him a tell, mi nuh put nuttn pass him." She went on further to say "This is not for you. You have a job & only one child, try & get yourself out of this."As bad as it sounded, she was indeed correct.

The possibility of this wedding taking place looked very dim.

IT'S OVER

Christopher had spent a month in Jamaica & had returned to England as at the end of September. Things really didn't get any better between us while he was here. It was one argument after another.

I remember a friend telling me that I was selling myself short & I deserved a lot more. This was after he had seen Christopher on more than one occasion in his apartment complex with various female companions. I was well aware of the fact that I deserved more but the mistake I made was to sit expecting Christopher to be the more. He had already shown me exactly what he was bringing to the table, why did I still expect salmon when chicken back was constantly being served is besides me.

I remember speaking to my friend Deon about everything that had been taking place & when she asked me the question "Stacey, how much more are you going to take?" the question struck me like a bolt of lightning. It took me a while to respond. It really made me think why everyone else could see how bad the situation was except me. It also made me question myself as to when was I going to open my eyes & accept just how toxic the situation between Christopher & I was.

One thing that I did constantly throughout my ten year relationship with Christopher was to pray. Sometimes I believe that prayer was the only thing that kept me sane. This time was no different & after praying about the situation, I felt it was time to pull the curtains down on the relationship.

It was time for Christopher & I to have a conversation about our future & whether we were going to have one. I remember telling him that based on everything that had happened during his last visit, I think it would be best for us to call off the wedding because nothing about him & his lifestyle had changed & I doubt there will ever be any change. As soon as I had said this he quickly replied that he wasn't ready to get married again. He said he had been married for basically all his life & was only just knowing what it was like to be single & he wanted to explore his single status some more before getting married again.

He went on to say that he purposely did things that he knew would have pushed me to call the wedding off. He said he didn't want to seem like the bad person to my family so eventhough he didn't want to proceed with the wedding, he also didn't want to be the one to call it off. I went on to ask him whether he had stopped to think that we could have just had a discussion like two adults. He said he didn't see that happening because he knew I would have been upset had he said he didn't want to get married. So I shared with him the fact that I too was having second thoughts & also didn't want to get married so had he been man enough to have a mature conversation with me, I would have agreed with his position to call the wedding off.

I went on to tell him that there was no hard feelings & I felt this was the best thing for us to call it quits & go our separate ways. The silence was deafening once I had said this. As I was about to end the call, I heard him say that he wasn't ending the relationship, he just wanted the wedding to be called off & we could revert to just being in a relationship. I remember laughing out because this request was very funny. Once I had finishing laughing, I declined his offer & told him that I wanted to put an end to everything; relationship & engagement. He quickly said okay & proceeded to end the call.

I felt a little hurt & might have shed a few tears but I felt more relieved that I had found the courage to do what I had just done. September 2010 marked the end of this tumultuous relationship & the start of what was going to be a co-parenting nightmare.

THE WEDDING IS OFF

It was now time for me to spread the word that the wedding was off. The fact that most persons weren't surprised by the news said a lot. Now I was thankful that I hadn't distributed the invitations. Once again I was reminded to always trust my gut feeling.

To say that it wasn't embarrassing calling my vendors & informing them of the fact that the wedding was off would be a lie. I felt awful & saying the words, hurt like hell but I quickly reassured myself that it was all for the best. We had pretty much lost all the deposits with the exception of the cake & the decor. For a minute I felt bad about Christopher losing his money but I felt better once I replayed his voice telling me that he didn't want to get married. These were all just consequences of a decision that was jointly made. This thought process cleared my conscience.

It was time for Christopher & I to have our first conversation since the break up. He pretty much laid out the ground rules as to how we would operate going forward. He agreed to continue paying the $35,000 rent but I was responsible for all other household expenses. I was given strict instructions that I was not allowed to have any male visitors at his property. I told him I had no objection to his proposal.

I was happily adjusting to my new norm. No need to constantly be reporting to anyone, no need to be arguing with anyone & for once I could focus solely on school & my son. Things were also making a turn for the better at work. My contract had expired & I was informed that I would be placed on permanent staff as at October 2010. This bit of news was right on time as I would now have the responsibility of paying my university tuition going forward.
I saw it fit to celebrate making staff after four years of being on a contract & not knowing what my fate would have been at the

end of each. My new permanent status would also afford me a host of other benefits that would definitely be needed to aid in my transition as a newly single woman.

It was now November 2010 & I remember getting a call from Christopher advising me of the fact that he was planning on returning to Jamaica in December. I was trying to understand why I was being brought up to date on his travel plans. He went on to say that he would no longer be wasting money on another rental property & so he was giving me a heads up that he would be staying in the house with my son & I.

Can this man be anymore spiteful? When we were together he rented another property everytime he visited Jamaica & would spend most of his time there. Now that we are no longer together, this is the time you choose to stay in the same house as me?

As quickly as it got on my nerve was as quickly as I got over it. I knew where he stood for me, he was my son's father & nothing more. Him constantly being in my face & my space was not going to change my feelings.

A DECEMBER TO REMEMBER

Christopher made his appearance just like he had said. You could cut the tension in the house with a knife. Being around him & in the same space felt so awkward. I knew he was doing all this to try & get under my skin but I had made a pledge to myself that I wasn't going to allow him to.

My mother remained at the house with us during the week as per usual. My son was eight years old at the time & clearly didn't understand what was going on. I remember him asking why I was in his room & his bed & before I could answer he would tell me to go to my room & my bed. I told him that I would only go to my room & my bed if he would come with me & he agreed.

So there you have it I had successfully negotiated for my son to be the barrier between Christopher & I for sleeping purposes. This worked for the most part except on the odd occasion when Christopher thought I would be willing to entertain his touch. The touches were met with very strong resistance to send a clear message that I was not interested. I ensured I slept in very fitted clothing that not even the fan breeze could blow & expose me. I just didn't want the gentleman to feel like I was extending any form of invitation because I wasn't.

Despite the fact that my son was suppose to have been a barricade between us, ever so often he would be moved & I would feel a bigger body next to me. Once again I would have to make it clear that I was not interested in whatever was being offered. My sleep is very important to me & so I took the decision to retreat to my son's room with my mother to see whether I could finally get some uninterrupted sleep.

I had finally decided to reapply for a United States visa. I decided to just make my appointment & go without telling anyone. After the disappointment I experienced previously, I was approaching with caution. Anyway, I went to my interview & was granted the visa. What a joy! I remember getting home & sharing the news with my mother her reply to which was "Then you leave yah like you gawn a work & a really up a embassy yuh go? A same suh you woulda go a foreign & mi nuh know." We both burst into laughter.

I couldn't wait to get my passport back so I could show Christopher that he might have laughed at me before when I was denied, but voila I got the last laugh. Things were aligning & I was thankful that finally there was light at the end of the tunnel.

My sister Andrea was slated to get married on December 18th. Christopher was previously invited but wasn't sure whether he would have been in Jamaica to attend, well guess what? He had now confirmed his attendance. The wedding was to take place in St. Elizabeth. We would have been travelling in a convoy. Travelling in Christopher's vehicle with my son & I were my nieces & nephews, about four of them to be exact.

The drive down seemed like it was never going to come to an end & when it finally came to an end, our guest house was closed for the night. Apparently we were too late to get checked in & was told to return in the morning & so the next mission was for us to try & find somewhere to sleep for the night.

We eventually found a motel whose room rating I would give probably a 3 out of 10. It was horrible! but life is about experiences. This experience was definitely a first & last, one to never be repeated. Think about how distressed we must have been & also tired after travelling for hours but all this didn't stop Christopher from trying to see whether I would be receptive to his advances. Once again it was strongly rejected. I was standing my ground, I was not going to fall back into the trap I had just escaped.

The wedding day came & I had so many mixed emotions but nevertheless I carried out my maid of honour duties effectively.

My siblings somehow tried to talk me down & also encouraged me to give Christopher another chance but I sent them packing.

It was this search for sympathy that would result in lines being crossed between him & my sister Annette & would result in she & I not being on speaking terms for a couple years.

CHAPTER 26 ON THE HORIZON

I had received my DHL delivery at work, my passport with my U.S visa had arrived. I remember going home & having a very loud conversation with my mother about it because I wanted Christopher to hear. When he couldn't hold it anymore he came outside to ask whether I was the one that had gotten a visa & I confirmed. The look on his face said it all, he definitely wasn't happy for me. Despite the fact that his face told me all that was on his heart to say, his mouth gave out a that's nice comment.

The tables had made a 360 degree turn because instead of me being stuck at home with our son, I was the one now going on the road. I considered it important to paint a very clear picture to the gentleman that I was living my life. Sometimes I really didn't have anywhere to go but my friends & I would agree on finding somewhere to hang out & chat & kill time. It felt so good just going about my business & not having to answer to anyone.

January 2011 & it was time to celebrate my 26th birthday. My friend Deon was visiting from England & it was time to gather the girls & my son of course & head out for a meal & drinks. It was time well spent. Despite the brave face I was putting on, I was hurting like hell inside. Hurting not because I wanted to be back with Christopher but more because I felt as though I wasted my time. Imagine someone expressing how badly they had always wanted to get married to you but couldn't because of their situation but the moment when they actually could, they somehow changed their mind. I don't know why this was still bugging me even after I had seen for myself that the decision made was the best for all parties involved. Probably it was just the feeling of rejection that had me worked up. I guess I am human after all.

I remember being gifted a snake chain set for my birthday from Christopher. The thing I remember saying after being given the gift was "If you are giving me this with any expectations, please to take it back." He quickly replied to say that there was none & that despite what I was still the mother of his child.

Christopher had returned to England but he left a lot of waves in motion. The first wave came after people started asking me if there was something going on between him & my sister Annette. I was very curious as to why anyone would think this but I later learned that Christopher's vehicle was a constant feature at my sister's house while he was here.

I remember speaking to one of my other sisters Annmarie & telling her what I had heard. When she said "Girlllll" I knew for a fact that she had information to offer. She said Christopher had been going to my sister Annette & seeking her assistance in getting me to give him another chance. She said in exchange for this, Annette made quite a few requests of Christopher. Annmarie confirmed that Christopher had been giving Annette money & whatever else she would ask him to take for her when he was travelling. Annmarie went on to say that Annette & her daughter had gotten a suitcase of clothing on Christopher's last visit. All this information had my head spinning especially because it was crystal clear to me that Annette was acting in her best interest because she was yet to have a conversation with me in support of Christopher.

I went directly to Christopher to ask him what exactly was happening. He confirmed going to Annette & soliciting help from her to get me back. He explained that since making this request of her, she had made quite a few monetary & other requests of him. He proceeded to share a conversation between him & Annette. I think he thought this new information would somehow work in his favour in his bid to get another chance. It didn't! You see in the messages my sister was asking for money once again & he replied by saying you are always asking me for things, suppose I was to ask you back for something. She went on to ask something like what? He replied by saying some of that thing. She was quick to say it wouldn't be an issue. He would just need to book somewhere & she could meet him there after work.

Now if this wasn't bad enough when Christopher switched the conversation to say that he was just trying to focus on getting me back & just needed her help with that, she got mad! This was her response "Stacey don't want yuh! You deh here a gwan like ediat over har when other good woman like miself deh here. You know seh all when unuh deh she did have all credit union account a save ina weh you neva know bout? A use she did a use yuh fi yuh money."

As expected I confronted Annette about the situation. The first thing she did was to laugh before saying "Mi did tell Christopher seh I don't want to get involved in nothing enuh because mi nuh want him tell nuh lie pon mi."

I do know Christopher to be a notorious liar & manipulator so I wouldn't think it impossible for him to fabricate the story but when he made mention of me having a savings at my credit union, that was the statement that sentenced her. She was guilty as charged. She & I were very close so she knew things that my other sisters didn't & things that Christopher wasn't privy to.

Everybody was shedding their skin & revealing their true colour & I was very appreciative of this.

FAMILY VACATION?!

The Robinsons had been inviting me back to Canada for a visit with my son. My Canadian visa was still valid & so I decided to submit an application for my son. What I didn't know however was the fact that I wasn't able to make the application on my own as his mother, I needed a letter of consent from his father.

The embassy made contact to say that I needed to visit for an interview as they were not able to approve the application with what was presented, they needed more information. They also advised that they needed a letter from my son's father along with a copy of his ID. Here we go.

As luck would have it he was in Jamaica at the time. Once I briefed him on what was happening, he quickly said "So you were planning on taking my son on his first major vacation without me? I need to be a part of it." It was impossible for me to now say no he couldn't be a part of the vacation when the entire vacation happening depended on him. So with a heavy heart I agreed for us all to go.

With that being said we visited the embassy with the additional documents requested & waited to be interviewed. Once we got into the interview room, we were like one big happy family. Christopher was very chatty answering all the questions as if he was the one taking us on vacation. When he was asked for his ID & he presented his passport you could see how big he felt when the interviewer said "O you hold a British passport, so you know you don't need a visa to travel right? Only your family would require one." I heard when he chuckled before replying that he was aware of the strength of his red book.

The interviewer approved my son for the Canadian visa & we were asked to wait in the lobby. In no time we were called back in to collect the passport with the newly issued visa. Once we got outside & was making our way back to the car, I remember Christopher saying "Look how you did a try do things without me & it couldn't happen. If I didn't agree you wouldn't have gotten through." Saying he was pompous would be me trying to explain his reaction mildly because his behaviour was pompous times a million.

Now that Christopher had made it clear that he was not going to allow me to take our son to Canada without him being there, I had to call the Robinsons & advise them of the new development. Once I had spoken to them, they advised that they had more than enough room to accommodate Christopher. They knew he & I were no longer together & so had arranged for him to have a room separate from me.

He left for Canada a couple days before my son & I. Our flight was a disaster. The check in process was lengthy & when we finally got on the aircraft there was someone seated in my son's seat. The flight was filled with persons heading to Canada for farm work. The seating issue was eventually resolved as it was determined that the gentleman was indeed in the wrong seat.

Once we arrived in Canada & I began sharing with the Robinsons the whole seating issue, I remember hearing Christopher giving out "That's why I only fly first class enuh." As soon as he said my eyes just automatically rolled. He went on to say that he wasn't going to allow his son to experience anymore hassle & so on our return trip he was going to upgrade our tickets to first class. Wonder if a me him did a try impress?

One thing I will say again about the Robinsons, they are the definition of hostess doing the mostest. Our entire vacation was planned out. We would be going to Niagara Falls, Canada Wonderland, Movies & a host of other fun activities. They would also be hosting their annual summer barbecue. I was happy to be able to be apart of it that year.

Once we arrived at the house, my son & I was shown to our room. Our room was on the opposite side of Christopher's.

Everything seemed to have been going well until it was time for bed & Christopher came to my room to complain. He said it didn't feel good us being in separate rooms & he felt embarrassed about the situation. I quickly reminded of the fact that we were no longer together & it wasn't a secret. The Robinsons were well aware of the situation & as such there was absolutely no reason for him to feel embarrassed. I was not going to pretend the situation was what it wasn't just to stroke his ego.

The vacation was going well & my son was having a grand time. The time had come for the Robinsons' annual backyard barbecue. The food was good & the vibe was right. You should all know by now that once there was good music, I was definitely going to dance. Once I started dancing I caught the attention of a few of the men that were present. One person in particular had gone to the Robinsons to ask them who I was. Christopher heard the conversation & somehow decided that he needed to show ownership & so the next thing I knew he was standing right next to me. Every step I took to allow some space between us was followed by a step from him to try & come closer.

I felt so annoyed that I decided to go inside & sit down for a bit. I remember Mrs. Robinson approaching me & expressing how annoyed she felt by Christopher's behaviour & the fact that he wouldn't allow me any space to just enjoy myself. I don't know whether he was coming close to me with the expectation that I would dance with him but I was not prepared to do that as I didn't want to be sending any mixed messages or signals.

I remember having to ask him to leave my room on a few occasions during our stay. He made it seem as though he was playing games with our son & there was absolutely nothing wrong with that but once it was bedtime, it was time for you to retreat to your room. I remember him arguing with me for a second time about the sleeping arrangement. Why was this even still an issue? I really didn't know. What I knew for a fact though was that despite what he had to say, he was definitely going to sleep in his room, & so he did.

Our vacation was coming to a close & so we were winding down. One night we all sat in the kitchen discussing various topics. I remember Mrs. Robinson asking Christopher whether he would have been open to assisting me with purchasing a property should I decide to. He quickly replied to say that he wouldn't have a problem assisting seeing that his child would have been benefiting. He also went on to say that at least he would know that his son would have a roof over his head should anything happen to either of his parents.

I quickly asked the question whether the assistance would have been offered with the expectation that we would somehow be getting back together, his reply to which was no. He added that he had moved past that & had no expectations. He added that anything that was being done was being done in the best interest of his child & had nothing to do with me.

What a time to be alive. When we were together this man had me viewing properties all over Jamaica with the hope of us purchasing one. Each time a property was identified that I considered more than suitable for us, Christopher would stall when it came to paying the deposit despite him previously agreeing with the vendors that we were seriously interested. So for him to be agreeing to aid in the purchase of a house that he wouldn't be living in really sounded like an empty promise to me but I guess we would see.

It was almost time for us to fly back to Jamaica. Our vacation was coming to an end. Christopher decided to upgrade our tickets to first class to avoid any potential hassle on the return journey. It would have been my first time flying first class.

Once we had gotten to the airport & completed the check in process, we were taken to the first class lounge where we were feted. Food & champagne were provided while we awaited our flight. Seeing that this might have been the first & last time I would be travelling first class, I made the most of it.

As soon as I returned home I started the discussion about the house deposit. I was not going to allow the momentum to die down. He said he wanted to do something for his son, well let us see it.

HOUSE ON THE HILL

I already had a new development that I was scoping out. It was currently under construction with a completion date of August 2012. I had shared the brochures & the development plans with Christopher so he could see the property that I was planning on purchasing & that he had agreed to pay a deposit for even if it was said in jest. He gave the development the approval nod & advised that he would have started giving me some funds to save towards the deposit. The deposit required was $1.4 million dollars.

Over the next couple of weeks Christopher would instruct his friend when to provide me with cash that he had collected on his behalf & accumulated from his bus & taxis. On the odd occasion he would also remit funds to his friend Trevor to pass on to me. I could not believe what I was witnessing. Christopher was really staying true to his word.

Before I knew it I was purchasing a manager's cheque to take in to the developer's attorney to deposit on my unit. I felt very happy being able to actually see this dream of home ownership coming to fruition. Now it was all about patiently waiting for the development to get to a certain level of completion so I could commence the mortgage process.

I remember calling Mrs. Robinson & sharing the news with her that I not only had received the promised deposit from Christopher but I had also done a down payment on a property. She was very surprised that Christopher kept his word, we all were, but maybe, just maybe he saw the value in setting a foundation for his son, a foundation that he & I were never afforded. I refused to think that he was doing any of this because of me & his wanting us to get back together.

He had previously made it crystal clear that he had moved past the thought of us getting backing together & this was solely about his son, for once in my life I was going to believe him. I hope I won't be disappointed.

THE CASE OF THE CIGARETTE LIGHTER

I got in from work one evening & saw my laptop in the middle of the bed & a USB cord next to it. The cord didn't look familiar but I figured it must belong to some device for Christopher & he must have been the one using the laptop previously.

Anyway, I proceeded to the bathroom to change my clothes. As I sat to use the toilet I noticed a black object on the caddy, an object that wasn't there before.

As soon as I had finished using the toilet I went to take up the object. When I touched it, it was very hot & when I flipped the cover I realised it was a lighter. But what was a lighter doing inside the bathroom? Nobody in the house smokes. And why was it hot?

I concluded that it must belong to Christopher & so I placed it back where I had found it. Later that night my mother came to me & said there was a camera in the house. So I said camera? Where? She went on to say that she wasn't sure where Christopher had placed it but there was one. I started thinking to myself that my mother was being paranoid. I asked her what led her to that conclusion & she went on to explain that when she was tidying up earlier, she found a sheet of paper which had on instructions on how to set up a camera. When she said the camera looks like a cigarette lighter I almost passed out.

This was the same cigarette lighter that I had just seen in the bathroom. I ran to the bathroom to retrieve it & showed it to my mother. I immediately went on the internet to try & understand how it worked & that was when I realised there was a camera lens under the bottom.

Now when I first noticed it, it was indeed laying down flat but I honestly didn't notice the lens. I was more alarmed by the fact that it was so hot when I touched it. So the gentleman had made sure to position it so I would be recorded once I entered the bathroom. I was sick to my stomach when I realised what he had done.

Remember the USB cord that I saw on the bed beside the laptop when I walked in? It fitted the camera perfectly. So clearly he had just charged up the camera shortly before I got home. I was so mad! Like why are you spying on me? When you could have seen my body freely, whenever you wanted, you opted to devote your time to everyone else's . Was this a case of "Cow neva know the the use of him tail til it gawn?' Or was it just a case of obsession?

I took the camera out the bathroom, went outside & smashed it to pieces & then drove my car to a dumped up empty lot nearby & threw it over there.

Later that night when Christopher came in he kept patrolling the bathroom like he had lost something. I watched him go in & out almost a million times before asking him if he was looking for his camera. When I said it the look on his face was priceless, guilty was written all over it.

He went on to say that the camera had nothing to do with me & that he had bought it to put on his bus because the conductor was stealing from him. I proceeded to ask him at what point did the bathroom started looking like the bus?, there was no response. When he managed to find words I don't think he found the right ones because he actually thought the right thing to ask was "Where is my camera?" "Where is your camera?" "Where do you think it is?" I immediately started laughing. Laughing when I was angry was my new thing because God knows how many times I've thought about doing this man something drastic, but he just wasn't worth it.

I finally answered him about the location of his camera. I told him I threw it away. When I said this he got so mad! He started ranting about how much money he paid for the camera & the fact that he had bought it for his bus & I had no right to throw away his property.

My closing argument was "If It was intended for your bus, then it shouldn't have been in the bathroom. You used it to invade my privacy, so it had to go where it belonged, in the trash."

PRIVATE INVESTIGATOR

Who was spying on me? Who was feeding Christopher with information about what took place on a daily basis in the office? Who was providing Christopher with my co-workers names? These were all questions I had after I was constantly accused of exiting the relationship because of my involvement with the men in my office who he was able to refer to by name.

I had a pretty good idea who it might have been but I just needed the proof. The friendship between Melissa & I had gone sour & I figured she was the one who had been supplying Christopher with information. After all we both worked in the same department. We didn't have an argument or anything like that but I had come to realise that she & Christopher had been communicating behind my back & a bit of information that I had previously shared with only her, somehow made it's way to Christopher's ear. Once I had made the connection, I slowly distanced myself from her.

The department sports day was coming up & we had all gathered at our sport's club field to practise. While we watched the men training, I brought up the topic of Melissa & was bringing my friends Kim & Ven up to date on the fact that I was of the opinion that she was the one who had been carrying office business to Christopher. Once I had said it they both immediately agreed. Kim was the "hot head" & so it came as no surprise when she confronted Melissa & told her that we knew she was the one going to Christopher & calling people's name. Melissa's response to the accusation was that she didn't know what we were talking about. I joined in to say "You do! But just wait, it soon blow up in your face!" Kim was just ranting & raving & "throwing words" as we would call it at her.

By the time I got home I received a call from Christopher asking why my friends & I were troubling Melissa & instructing me to stop. The gall of this man! I told him that it was just a matter of time before they were both exposed. I started thinking how I could make the connection between Melissa & Christopher & then I remembered that I had a friend who was employed with the phone company. I knew she wouldn't have been able to provide me with any hard copy evidence but I just wanted confirmation that I was indeed correct about the connection.

I provided my friend with both Christopher & Melissa's telephone number. When I heard the girl say Staceeeyyyyy!!! I knew exactly what was going to follow. She confirmed that there was constant communication between them, phone calls, text messages you name it.

This was really the year of shedding dead weight & getting rid of unwanted baggage. Despite the fact that Melissa & I didn't speak like we used to before, I was still civil with her. At this stage there could be no more civility between us. She had burned every bridge that ever connected us.

This was the same friend that helped me move out of the gentleman's house when he & I had a disagreement. This was the same friend who had called me on numerous occasions telling me where she saw him with different women. This was the same friend whose defense I came to when Christopher & his friends were saying I should not associate with her because she had a bad reputation in the streets. So how did he suddenly become so attractive to her that she would want to assist him with his vendetta against me? How did someone who she had only known since 2006 gained her loyalty over someone she had known since 1994? One word; MONEY.

DO YOU KNOW HER? SHE KNOWS YOU!

As you would have gathered by now Christopher was once again in Jamaica. These days the house had become very interesting. Christopher would blast gospel music every Sunday morning & sometimes during the singing of the songs he would burst into tears, prayer & worship.

To the person looking in from the outside, he was changing his life & working on finding his way back into church. To me, it was all just for show. I didn't believe any of it.

I remember one Sunday after his praise & worship episode & him leaving for church, I noticed he had left one of his phones behind. He was watching something on the phone after his praise & worship session had ended & for a minute I thought he might have been watching a church service. Boy was I wrong. I had gained knowledge of the unlocking code for the phone after seeing him entering it one night. I took up the phone & unlocked it & was greeted by probably one of the largest penises I had ever seen. All this time when I thought he was watching something church related he was actually watching porn. So you do praise & worship, bawl living eyewater & cry out to God, then proceed to watch porn before leaving for church?! This was my confirmation that his behaviour now was just for show, he was the same person.

I remember sitting in the bedroom one night watching TV & minding my own business. He walked in with his phone, proceeded to show me a female's picture & went on to ask whether I knew the person. I looked at the picture which was on the person's facebook account & I told him I didn't know the individual. He asked me to look again & once again I told him I didn't know the person.

He went on to say that based on the things that the person was telling him about me it was obvious that they knew me. I knew for a fact that he was lying but I didn't want to just leave it to my assumption. I wanted to show him proof that I knew for a fact that he was lying.

I had remembered the name from the facebook account & so I decided to send the individual a message. On September 10, 2011 at 10:50pm I wrote the following message to Prudence:

"I was just told by Christopher that you apparently know me & based on some stuff you told him it would appear as though you really do. I'm curious as to what you might be telling him as I don't have a clue who you are."

She replied the following morning to say :

" I don't know you hence I couldn't have said anything to Christopher about you. And even if I knew you there's no way I would be telling him anything because I'm a woman too. I'm very disappointed at him right now for using my name under false pretence."

It was clear he just wanted me to know who he was dating now. I guess he was trying to make me jealous. Jealous of what is a question that I didn't find an answer to.

Once Prudence had confronted him about his antics & using her name under false pretence, he came to me & said he had wanted to ask me about any possible job opportunities that I might have known of for Prudence's sister who was seeking a job. He said he thought that by convincing me that I was supposed to know Prudence from somewhere, that would have made it easier for him to ask the question that he had really wanted to.

When I thought I had heard all the garbage that could exit the mouth of a human being, he spitted out more. He added that Prudence was working less hours at work & as such was having difficulties making payments to her car loan & he wanted to know what could be done to reduce her payments. Like seriously? Are you Prudence's messenger? Why are you coming to me with the lady's business? Just in case this wasn't enough he also proceeded to show me a BB messenger conversation between him & Prudence about her acquiring his last name. He went on to say to me that they would be getting married in December & I told him congratulations.

I remember sharing with Prudence all that he had just said & gave her a heads up & told her to thread carefully as he was a notorious liar. She replied to say that she was well aware that women don't usually run from good so the fact that I left is a signal that something must be wrong.

I constantly encouraged Christopher to go & stay with Prudence. I just wanted him out of my face & space but he needed to remind me daily that the space was his & I was just "Kotching in it." When we were together he was never home, now he hardly leaves the house, how ironic! I tried to make sure I left the house as much as possible though because the constant nagging was getting on my last nerve.

Clearly Christopher thought that constantly being in my face would have weakened me & resulted in me taking him back but instead it did the complete opposite, my resentment for him grew day by day.

ALL THIS TO FEEL MY VAGINA!

Like I had mentioned before, I was living my life. I was going out as often as possible even if it was only to Jo Jo's to eat roast conch & drink a heineken, I was there. I just wanted to be in the house only when it was time to sleep. The fact that Christopher was rarely leaving the house now was even more reason for me to leave. I felt stifled. Even if I was trying to have a life it felt impossible as I wasn't even afforded privacy to have a telephone conversation without him trying to be in earshot.

I left the house on Sunday September 11, 2011 like I had done many times before. Before getting home my mom had called me to ask whether she was to come by the house that night or wait until in the morning. I told her that it was up to her. After saying this she decided to make her way to the house now.

Later that night the worst thing that could have ever happened to any woman happened to me. I was attacked by Christopher in the presence of my child. I remember being in my phone minding my business when Christopher plunged on me & proceeded to put a pillow over my face. At the time I had a blackberry torch phone which had a little weight. It was in my hand at the time & the only thing I could do was to constantly swing the phone in hopes of it hitting Christopher. It eventually smacked him in his mouth & I managed to get the pillow off my face.

I started screaming & my son ran into the room & started crying & asking Christopher to let me go. No matter how much he cried & screamed not even this was enough to get Christopher to stop.

I remember screaming & crying for help & when I apparently screamed too loudly, Christopher pushed his hand inside my mouth & was just pulling as if he was trying to rip out my tongue & my teeth or whatever else. I guess this was also to try & silence me but even if I was silent, my son was screaming at the top of his lungs.

245

When I thought he was coming to his senses & had finally recognised what he was doing to me & in front of his child, he took it one step further. He proceeded to rip off my underwear & inserted his fingers inside me while commenting that I was wet like a man had just ejaculated inside me.

My mother arrived at the house & heard the commotion. She was so frightened that she completely forgot that she had a set of keys. She started shaking the grille & shouting out for my son to let her in. While all this was happening, the neighbours stood in their driveway like spectators. Nobody even attempted to call the police.

Once my mother had entered the house & started shouting & asking what was going on, Christopher ran into the bathroom & locked himself in. My mother started banging on the door before saying "You see if mi did ever come see you a fight my daughter, mi woulda beat you up." She started banging on the door again. I guess she was still hoping that he would come outside but he didn't.

Once it sounded like we were out of the room, he came out the bathroom, ran out the house & drove out. What had really just happened? I was in a daze & still trying to process everything. My son was inconsolable, after all he was only nine years old.

It was one year since we had exited our relationship, it was also my vagina & I was free to do with it whatever I saw fit. So even if you felt as though I was having sex with a dozen men, it was my choice & that should have been okay with you. Why? Because we were not together! I didn't once do any kind of back or forth that would have sent any mixed signals or fostered any false hope. I maintained my stance that we were over & I had no interest in getting back together. So what was all this?

Later that night Christopher placed a call to my mom asking to come & collect some of his things. He said he didn't want to be in any "tanglings" with the police & so just wanted to grab his things & go. Funny he would mention police because they were actually called but were a no show.

Where do I start with my son? How do I get him through this? That was my main concern.

RUMOURS OF WAR

I was unable to go to work the following day as I was still traumatized by the entire episode. There was also a hole underneath my tongue & I don't think I need to explain how that came about. I had to be having liquids only.

I called a few of my closest friends & brought them up to speed on what was happening. They were all mad as hell because if it was one thing they knew for sure it was the fact that I was never leading that man on. I say this because this would have been the easiest explanation for Christopher's behaviour but looking back on everything that was done even prior to the attack, I think obsession is the best explanation. I think it's that feeling of him owning me & so if he wasn't going to have me, then no one else should.

I received a few phone calls from my office & once again Melissa was at it. Apparently Christopher had made a call to her to say that he had beaten me up because he caught me with a man. Now as my FRIEND from primary school & I use the word friend very loosely because we all know by now that she was anything but that, she decided to spread the word around the office. Now her telling everyone that I was beaten up wouldn't have been gossip enough, so the narrative was that I was beaten up because I was sleeping with someone in the office & yes she called someone's name.

My phone was blowing up when the news broke & the majority of who were calling were not concerned about my wellbeing but was more interested in validating Melissa's story. I was told that she told every & anyone in the office that she thought would listen. She didn't even realise how she was being used.

Christopher was always of the view that had I not gotten a promotion at work, I would never have left him because I would still have been completely dependent on him. So he had said on more than one occasion that my job aided the break up. So what he was using Melissa to do now was to try & tarnish my reputation & possibly get me to lose my job. But they were both silly because the case they were building would never have been considered grounds for any kind of dismissal.

My phone was ringing again & I was getting annoyed but when I answered this particular call I was devastated. It was from my son's school. They asked me to visit to pick him up as he had been crying all morning & was telling his teacher that he had to go home.

When I picked him up & asked him what was happening, he said to me that he needed to stay at home with me to try & protect me from his father. This broke my heart & caused me to burst into tears. I tried to reassure him that I was okay & he didn't need to protect me, he just needed to focus on school.

The following day I would get a call from my son's teacher once again asking me to come & pick him up. When I went to pick him up this time his teacher told me that he had shared with her what had happened to me. She went on to ask whether I was doing okay & I told her that I was far from okay but I was trying to be. She told me that she had counseled my son for a little in a bid to try & help him cope with the stress & anxiety that he was experiencing. She recommended that I mention to Christopher what had been happening with my son because he was the one who needed to reassure him that there would be no repeat of his behaviour.

As you would imagine the gentleman & I was not on speaking terms but nevertheless I sent him a message relaying to him what our son's teacher had recommended. He spoke with my son & apologised to him for what he had witnessed & assured him that it would never happen again. I don't know whether this was ever going to be enough, well maybe I do know, It wasn't.

This was the start of the deterioration of their father son relationship.

NINE DAY WONDER

It was time to face the music. I had returned to work & was greeted by stares, whispers, more stares & more whispers. I would be lying if I said it didn't bother me because it did but I knew that this too would pass.

My son was back in school & thankfully I had not received any calls to pick him up. If I wasn't grateful for anything I was grateful for this.

Where Melissa sat in the office, I had to walk pass her desk when entering & exiting. Everytime I entered she would hang her head, she couldn't look me in the eye. One thing I knew for sure though was that she had no remorse for her actions. People were still approaching me to tell me that she was the source of the gossip.

I remember speaking to my sister Annmarie. She was the fighter in the family. Remember now that everyone in my family knew Melissa. In the conversation with my sister she expressed her disgust at Melissa's actions. Just when I thought that she was a changed person, I heard her say "She figet seh mi know which part a Allman Town she live? Mi will go round deh go beat har up enuh!" I quickly told her to remove that thought from her mind as she would be giving them what they wanted as that would be more detrimental to my job than what they were currently doing. Before hanging up she left me with the nugget that people talking would just be a nine day wonder. I asked her what she meant by that, she said by the tenth day someone or something else will become the topic of discussion, my situation would have become stale & played out.

Annmarie was right, the stares & whispers had gradually gotten a little less. Melissa however was on a high. In her mind she had tarnished my reputation & she had something over me because she was silly to believe that Christopher had a genuine interest in her. That man had been using & manipulating her but she was either too blind to see what was going on or her hatred for me was so strong that it motivated her to leave herself careless to be used.

I had been quiet for a while but it was time for me to take back my power & so I started telling people the motivation behind Melissa's actions, the fact that she was involved with my ex. Once I brought that to the fore, people started looking at her differently because most people knew that she & I were supposed to have been friends. So the question was how could she have done something like this to her friend?

I don't think I had mentioned the fact that she was also known to my son. She was a regular visitor to my home. My mother & I was having a conversation about Melissa & as expected my mother was burning her out wicked. Unbeknownst to us my son was in his room but was clearly listening to our conversation. I remember him coming out his room to say "I know her, I don't like her anymore."

If there was one thing I learned throughout this entire ordeal, it was who my genuine friends were.

WAS IT WORTH IT?

One thing about Christopher, he was going to use you to do whatever he wanted you to & then he was going to play the victim & throw you under the bus. This has always been his modus operandi. So it came as no surprise when he decided to share how everything got started with Melissa. This story went a little something like this.

Melissa didn't have a contact number for Christopher, he changed his sim cards very regularly. She decided to look him up on facebook & she was successful in finding him. She proceeded to send him a message to complain about me. Her complaint was about the fact that I had stop speaking to her & she didn't know why. She also complained about me hanging with new friends who according her didn't have good reputations & me getting engaged & soon to be married & she had not received an invitation.

Let us put things into context. Melissa sat three desks from me in the office, she saw me everyday. Now if you had this burning issue why wouldn't you have come to me directly? Why would you go in search of a man who lived millions of miles outside of Jamaica to try & resolve the problem?

Anyway, it was during that facebook conversation that she was informed by Christopher that I had called off the wedding. He told her that he was of the view that I had called it off because I was involved with someone in the office. As my friend who called me on more than one occasion to tell me where she had seen this same gentleman & with various females, why didn't she call him out & tell him exactly why I left? No instead she supported his position & told him that she thinks she have an idea as to who the person was & she would do some further investigations & let him know. This was the start of their plotting.

While she thought that he had placed her on a pedestal, in his confession he spoke so badly of her. Not only did he speak bad about her character but he also said that she wasn't his type, her breath stank, she was like a giant over him & she had size 12 feet. He admitted to using her for what he thought was accurate information. But why would she want to spend the time to get accurate information? She just wanted to tell him what she thought he wanted to hear that way I would be out of the picture permanently & she would be in.

The thing that confused me though was why did she feel that she needed to go that far? I had left the man for over a year with no plans of going back, he told you that I had left him, so if you really wanted him JUST TAKE HIM. I wasn't in your way & neither was I a threat.

To hear Christopher say that she told him that she always wanted a man like him & couldn't believe that I had him & left, was very disturbing mainly because she was privy to a lot of things that that man had done to me. She knew a lot of the lows that I suffered at his hands but I guess she was more focused on some of the perks that I might have previously enjoyed which she would possibly see as highs for her now.

Once I had gotten the email from Christopher in which he expressed how he really felt about Melissa, I forwarded it to her. It was time for her to see that she was played for a fool.

THOSE TABLES, THEY DO TURN

Growing up I would always hear my mother & grandmother say that it was wicked people whose eye water was always near.

Melissa clearly had gotten a slice of humble pie once she read the messages that I had forwarded to her. Her mood had suddenly become very sombre because she knew people had now started looking at her differently since learning about her plot with Christopher & then I had recently burst her bubble when I shared the messages showing what Christopher had to say about her.

So to say that I was surprised when she walked over to me on my lunch break with her cow bawling would be a lie. She now wanted to cry cree because the big spotlight was shining on her.

It was the regular practice for Kim, Ven, Tash & myself to sit at the back of our office building after we had eaten our lunch. We would consider it "Taking breeze." We were sitting outside as we would usually do when we saw Melissa exiting the building & walking towards us. Her face was already wet from the tears that were flowing. She came over to me & asked whether she could talk to me & I asked about? & she said the situation.

O so now you want to talk to me when it suits you? Despite everything that she had done to me, I didn't shun her. I got up & walked to another section of the building & decided to listen to what she had to say.

The first thing she said was that Christopher had told her that I had cheated on him with one man in England. I couldn't see how this was relevant but I replied with " Okay, him lucky a only one because there should have been a whole lot more." She continued by saying that she was sorry about everything & that she can see clearly now that he was using her. I replied to this with a strong yes he was. I can't remember saying anything more in the conversation, I mainly listened because quite frankly I didn't want to hear. When you were running my name through the mud You weren't sorry, so why do you even care now? Is it because your name was now being run through the mud?

I listened to what she had to say & I said okay & once again reiterated how she left herself open to be used before walking away. I wasn't even going to try & ask her why she did it or what kind of friend she was. When people show you who they are, BELIEVE THEM.

YOU CAN'T STAY HERE

Since the attack, my mother & I had been sleeping in my son's room with him. We all left Christopher to himself. Once more we woke up & heard a lot of movement over his room. When we came out in the living room, we were greeted by black garbage bags. The first bag I opened, I realised it was packed with items of clothing that belonged to me. What was this about now?

As he heard us outside in the living room, he brought out another bag & placed it on the floor. When I asked him what was this about, he replied you can't stay here anymore. Before I could say anything I heard my mother say "So weh you expect she & har pickney fi go? A better you behave yourself."

One thing I knew for sure was the fact that I was not going to engage in anymore arguments with Christopher. As he packed the bags, I walked by & went to shower to get ready for work.

When I got home the evening, I noticed that not all my stuff was packed. I don't know if he ran out of bags or if he got tired because surely enough I had a lot of belongings.

When he came back in the house that night, it was time for a different argument. This time he was asking me back for the $1.4M that I had deposited on the house. I knew it was only a matter of time before this request would have been made but I told myself that I was never going to return that money. That money was my pain & suffering settlement for all that I had endured over the 10 year period that I was with him.

I quickly told him that I had no money to return to him. As soon as I said this his voice got louder but as for me I was very calm. When he said I am going to get my lawyer involved, you need to return my money, I immediately started laughing. I proceeded to ask him if him Christopher had handed over any money to me? Because the reality was that he didn't. All the monies I got was

256

given to me by third parties. He had no paper trail of handing over any money to me. So he could talk & curse all he wanted but I was no fool, I knew for a fact that he had no case. Besides, Sophia had sold their house in England a couple years aback while he was in Jamaica & had held on to all the money & when she decided to give him his portion, she made sure she had enough left to secure a house for herself. So yes Christopher that's what we are accepting for our pain & suffering, house deposits.

Christopher & Prudence was now an item & I had absolutely no problem with this. What I had a problem with was him taking her to my son's school whenever he picked him up. I remember my son referring to her as the lady & her daughter. The poor child was confused by all that was going on around him but all I could do was to pray that the constant confusion would come to an end soon.

I had come to the realisation that there was no way I could wait until August of 2012 to leave Christopher's place & so I started shopping around for a place to rent. The rental market was ridiculous as most of the places that I had viewed, the rent was more than a mortgage payment. So I decided to start shopping around for another property to purchase rather than sitting & waiting on the one that I had deposited on to be completed.

I was moving in silence. While I was being cursed everyday about returning the $1.4M, I was busy looking for somewhere else to use it as a down payment on. While he tried to bring me down every opportunity he got, I was busy working on my plan B. The garbage bags remained packed & I didn't even attempt to unpack them. I just left him to do whatever he wanted to.

At the end of the day the only thing that lasts forever is salvation, so this too shall pass.

SHEER COINCIDENCE

It was time for the bank's annual sports day, the one we were busying training for previously. I say we as if I was a participant, I wasn't but I was the assistant coach/team manager/nurse. The day was a very busy one as I went from collecting the team members lunches to peeling their oranges, to providing them with their glucose & fluids, to nursing wounds, trust me I was on the go.

The uncomfortable part of it all was the fact that Melissa was apart of the team & so it was very difficult to avoid her when she was constantly with the other participants. Nevertheless, I made it work & held a straight face.

We had ran out of gatorade & I had volunteered to visit a wholesale on Old Hope Road to purchase a case or two. My friend Ven & I headed out to make the purchase. As I was travelling along Trafalgar Road I saw a black honda fit which after looking closely at the plates I determined belonged to Prudence. I noticed the car was headed in the direction of my house & so I decided to follow it. Every turn she made I was thinking to myself, please drive pass my road but that was not going to happen because the next turn she made was onto my road & she stopped right at my gate.

Next thing I knew I had jumped out of my car & Christopher & I was at it. I remember smacking him in the face & asking him what the f$%& Prudence was doing at my gate? While all this was taking place, Prudence sat in her car. I remember grabbing stones from on the road & throwing them at Christopher, at this point Prudence reversed her car & drove off. The disturbing thing was while all this was happening the only thing Christopher was doing was laughing. Writing this book & reliving these memories allowed me to come to the conclusion that in some twisted way Christopher thrived off drama. Like he created the situations, sat back & waited for them to play out. I had told him on many occasions that I didn't argue with his females because of him, I argued with them because they always chose to try & provoke me or I needed to defend myself. It was never about him but in some sick way he thought it was & he got a kick out of it.

Case in point; He knew that my reaction on this particular day was never about the fact that he was involved with Prudence. It was about the fact that you have asked me not to bring any men to the house but you thought it was okay for you to bring your woman. If he wasn't sure as to why I reacted the way I did, I ensured I told him myself. Despite telling him this he somehow went to Prudence & made it appear as though my issue was with her, & with him being involved with her. He also told her that I had been investigating her & that was how I knew her car. Clearly she bought into the lies he was spilling because the next thing I knew I received a message from her which went like this:

" I'm sure you are smart enough to know that if you use my information at your institution for your personal use, you can be fired. You don't know me & I don't know you. I know people & I'm sure you do too. Let's keep it that way. I just made a formal report. I've never been involved in any mix up in my life. If you are acting this way over Christopher maybe you should reconsider leaving him then, because obviously he's worth keeping."

My response to Prudence went like this:

"Listen Prudence don't mek Christopher full up your head of crap. Everything I know about you is what Christopher told me! He is worried that we might be corresponding hence the reason why he is trying to build strife. If you & Christopher are together as he claims then you have no business at the house that my child & I lives & that is what I am f$%^ing pissed about. I told Christopher I'm going to F him up & he knows why so don't let him pack your head with shit & try to manipulate your head. I have no beef with you. Christopher is the one stalking my life despite the fact that we are supposed to be over. So everything as it relates to you, Christopher told me. Nobody is worth me jeopardizing my job for. If I'm jeopardizing it, its on my own accord. If I had anything to say to you you were at my gate, I could have said it directly. Me nuh want Christopher so don't get it twisted."

You see what he had gone & done? I didn't once mention having an issue with Prudence or planning on doing anything to Prudence but he somehow went & planted that seed to cause a problem between us when one didn't exist. When I confronted him about going to her & lying & making it seem like I had an issue with her, he sent me a few messages & they went like this:

"Look she is doing what she is doing because of what you did to me today. She don't see why you did that & me & you nuh deh. So she claims that if I can't defend myself against you then she will. She is my woman now & it's her duty to protect my interest. I am sorry this is going down like this but she needs to satisfy herself that me & you nuh in a nuttn. Look I had to tell her whatever just to look out & she said she will say something to you & she will let you stop all this crap."

Look out for what sir? What are you telling her to look out for? You knew I had no issue with the lady, so why were you creating one? Take note of his speech, "If I can't defend myself against you she will." A woman yuh want fi fight over you? How is it that you have suddenly become so defenseless when only a few weeks ago you were holding me down, ripping off my underwear & forcing your fingers inside of me?

You don't get to play the victim sir, you are the aggressor!

LET ME JUST DROP THIS BOMB & GO

Time was winding down for Christopher to leave, I couldn't wait! I had to be limiting my house hunting efforts based on the fact that I didn't want him to gain knowledge of it. So I had to lay low until he left.

I know I haven't mentioned it much but despite all the drama that was going on in my life, school was still happening. I didn't quit & I had absolutely no plans of quitting. I was struggling to balance life stress, trials & crawses with university but I was never going to give up. I had one year left to complete my degree & there was no turning back.

It was the day before Christopher's departure & I recall there was some kind of disagreement but I can't remember clearly what it was about. What I do remember though was when he turned around, looked me in the face & said " O & by the way Dianne's child is mine." The devil on my right shoulder was saying tek the bokkle & claat him but the angel on the left said smile & say congratulations. So I smiled & said congratulations. I could see how puzzled he was by my reaction. Maybe this statement didn't evoke the response he wanted & so he added that he wasn't even worried about the house deposit that he had given me anymore because he knew I wouldn't be able to purchase a house on my own. So you are waiting on me to fail? Okay but I'm going to make sure I don't.

Just in case y'all don't remember who Dianne was because I know Christopher has gone through a lot of women, Dianne was the one he took to my sister's workplace & had constantly maintained that she was just his friend. He even denied that her child was his but suddenly now the time had come for him to confess.

I remember his friend Trevor telling me how badly he felt about how everything had gone down. He said he wished things could have been handled differently especially after seeing how my son was affected by it all. He went on to say that he remembered speaking to Christopher when he told him that we were going to get married & encouraging him to tell me about his son with Dianne. While I listened to Trevor I recognised that I was the only one who didn't know for sure that the child was his but everyone else was well aware. He said he told Christopher that it wouldn't have been right to enter a marriage with me when there were so many skeletons in his closet. He ended by saying "But you know him nah tek no talk from nobody."

At the end of the day though, I was never naive & so in the back of my mind I knew it was his child. Besides I remember finding some baby boy clothing in his suitcase one year & he told me that his niece had asked him to take them to Jamaica for someone. There was also the time he picked me up from work & the passenger side of the windscreen was filled with little baby hand prints. So I would have been stupid to have believed him when I saw so many signs that painted a different picture.

Christopher had finally left & I was breathing a sigh of relief. I felt like I would have thrown a party just to celebrate his departure. I knew it was bad when even my mother said thank God when he left. Remember now that Christopher had made it clear to me that he was awaiting my failure, so there was no time waste. The house hunting was now in full swing.

It always amazed me how after heading out in the early hours of the morning to purchase the Gleaner newspaper by the time you started calling at 8am, everything listed was gone. Seriously, at what point did people make contact & secured the properties? I kept wondering what I was doing wrong.

I also started checking out some of the real estate companies website to see what they had available. I remember viewing a few properties but they weren't to my liking. A co-worker of mine had told me about checking the Gleaner online on Wednesdays. While going through the ads, I saw a listing in the same area as the apartment that I had deposited on. It was a little after 8pm but I decided not to wait until in the morning as that didn't work in my favour previously.

I called the number which was answered by a male. His background was very noisy. I proceeded to tell him that I was calling about the ad for the apartment. He told me that it was his drinking night & he was at Medusa's. He gave me the address for the property & asked me to meet him there the following day to view the apartment.

I was so anxious I didn't even sleep properly. I just wanted Thursday midday to come & it did. I got to the apartment complex & as soon as I walked inside the unit, I said to the gentleman I WANT IT! This property was located at number 5 & the one I deposited on was at 12A, I definitely saw this as a sign.

He made sure to temper my expectations & he did so by telling me that he wasn't going to give a sale agreement to just one individual, he was going to give sale agreements to as many individuals as possible & the property would go to whoever monies he received first.

My next call as I left the complex was to my attorney. I told him that I had found another property & he needed to request a refund of my deposit urgently.

LEGAL TRICKSTER

I was following up with my attorney everyday to confirm whether he had gotten back my money. Everyday it was another story & I soon realised that he was trying to stall me.

I was introduced to this attorney by a realtor that I had been using previously. She was the one who had introduced me to the property that I had previously deposited on. I remember advising her that my circumstances had changed & I needed a place immediately & so I would have to cancel the sale I did with her. She promised to try & see whether she could have found me another property that I could move into now. She had shown me a few but none to my liking. I had told her about the one I had found & she asked me for the address & I provided her with same. I remember getting a call back from her later that day to say that it wasn't to her liking because it had too much concrete & not enough green spaces. I told her this wasn't a deal breaker for me as my son was accustomed to the concrete life. I knew it was more about her commission for her but I was going to do what I deemed to be best for me.

So because they both worked together, the fact that the realtor was now going to lose her opportunity to earn a commission, I could sense that the attorney was using delay tactics to try & sabotage my pending deal, but I was never going to allow that. I was on him everyday like white on rice until he eventually told me that he was in receipt of my refund but same was paid to him via cheque & the cheque would take 3 days to clear because it was from another bank. I knew this was factual & so I started counting down the 3 days.

Once he had received my refund, he sent me a bill where he was charging me for a sale that wasn't completed. He also billed me for visits he reckoned he made to the vendor's attorney. When I perused the document the man had created some charges which were not previously discussed with me. They amounted to approximately $250,000. A my closing cost money him a try shorten? There was no way I was going to allow that.

I made contact with him & told him that the only thing I was willing to pay for was the vetting of the sale agreement but everything else listed were not negotiated at the time I retained him & so they weren't applicable as far as I was concerned. Also, how could you want to charge me your fee on a sale that didn't close? Are you crazy?

I called my brother Junior & told him what was happening with my refund & he agreed that the attorney was being disingenuous. He told me to send him a message stating that I was not in agreement with the fees & I wouldn't be paying them. My brother also told me to inform him that I would be reporting him to the legal council.

The following day I would receive a letter from the attorney advising that he would be withdrawing his services with immediate effect. I had no problem with this but I was still without my refund & the 3 days clearing period had long passed.

When I called to ask what was happening with the refund he tried to tell me that the cheque wasn't cleared on his account. I quickly said to him "Mr.T before you lie to me think back about where I work & the fact that I can easily prove that you are lying." After I said this he went on to give me a story about his mother being sick & hospitalized & him having to go to the hospital. I gave him a stern warning that if I didn't get my refund in hand today, I was going to make another call to the legal council. I emphasized on the ANOTHER. Truth be told I hadn't even placed one call but the tactics worked, I got my money.

I quickly called Mr. M & asked to be provided with his attorney's banking information to make the deposit. I was provided with same & bam my sale agreement was signed & my deposit was in. Next journey was to start the mortgage application process.

ONE STEP FORWARD, TEN STEPS BACK

One of the things I loved about university life was the fact that I got to meet a lot of people who worked in various organisations & this would somehow prove to be beneficial to you at some point. The time had come for me to make use of my NHT links.

My classmate Pam was employed to the National Housing Trust. I remember engaging her in a conversation one evening after class & asking her the process to apply for the mortgage. As luck would have it that was her area of work. She immediately asked me when I would be free to come in & I told her the following day. I had not yet cleared with my supervisor whether I could get some time off but I knew it wouldn't have been an issue as I could work back the time. Pam provided me with a checklist of all the documents I needed to take in with me.

First thing the following morning I was at NHT. I sat with Pam & completed all the forms I needed to & provided all the documents I was asked to take in. Once Pam had done all that she needed to, I was provided with my pre-approval letter to take to my employer to apply for the balance of the loan.

The apartment was being sold for $10.5M & I was required to deposit 10% of the cost which worked out to $1,050,000. NHT would have been financing $4.5M & as such I would need to finance $4,950,000 through the bank.

One thing I've learned throughout my life was the fact that anything major that I was going to try & accomplish, it was never going to come easy. There were going to be a lot of hurdles but in the end I would come out victorious. The first test to this theory came during this mortgage process.

I had submitted my loan application to the bank for the additional $4,950,000. The next correspondence I received I was told that the loan was declined. It was declined on the basis that

I would have exceeded the debt service ratio set by the bank. So how do I fix this? I was told that I had to pay out my existing car loan which had a balance of approximately $360,000 at the time. Where was I going to get this money from now?

I made a call to my brother Junior & explained to him what was happening. He agreed to loan me the money to close the car loan. I was back in business. I closed the car loan & resubmitted my mortgage loan application. Finally, an approval was received but upon closer examination I realised that the approved amount was only $4,725,000, $225,000 less than what I had applied for. When I called to query the shortfall I was advised that NHT had registered their mortgage for $4,725,000 to include their legal fees. So now I had a shortfall of $255,000 that I would need to cover because whilst NHT would have registered a lien for $4,725,000, I would still only be getting the $4.5M.

I remember putting up a status on BB messenger at the time which said " One step forward & ten steps back." My brother Nikkolai saw the post & sent me a message asking what was the problem. I explained to him about the shortfall & he agreed to give me the funds to cover it.

The hurdles were coming fast & furious but I was going over them one by one. The final hurdle came in the form of property insurance. I surely didn't know about the intricacies involved in purchasing a property but I was learning fast.

Mrs.Robinson had called me to check in to see how everything was going. Since the attack, everyone just wanted to see me out of Christopher's space & in my own. So as soon as I mentioned to her that I needed to find some additional funds to pay property insurance, she said don't worry I am to get a partner draw, I will lend you the funds. I really didn't know when I would be able to repay these debts or how, but I knew I would figure it out when the time came.

I had already secured the closing cost from the monies I got from Christopher, so at least I had that covered. So the process was finally over & the wait now was for the transfers to be completed, funds disbursed & then to finally get my keys in my hand.

What did Christopher say again? I can't buy a house on my own?! Well it sure looks like I did.

GUESS WHO IS BACK?

If you guessed Christopher, you are correct. It was December 2011 & once again he was on the rock but this time he was staying at Prudence's house. I don't know whether he had come to get married like he had previously said but whatever the reason behind his visit, it wasn't my business.

I had since changed the padlock on the gate to secure myself. So should Christopher decide to visit, he wouldn't be able to just walk in on us. I was contacted by Trevor who informed me that Christopher had indicated to him that he would have only been providing money for snacks & juice for our son & that he would be giving it to him to take to me. Snacks & juice? So what he has stopped eating food? Trevor went on to say that he didn't know what was happening but he was just relaying the message he got.

I made a promise to myself not to get involved in any more arguments with Christopher. I just wanted him to do what he was supposed to for our son. But as soon as I made this promise I was contacted by the landlord to say that 3 months rent was outstanding. I could not believe what I was hearing as the original agreement made by Christopher when we parted ways over a year ago was for him to pay the rent & for me to cover everything else.

After trying to muster up the patience I would need to have a civil conversation with Christopher, my son came complaining to me that his father kept talking to him about the lady. This was how he referred to Prudence. I asked him what was his father talking about & he said getting married to the lady. My son went on to say that he kept telling him that he didn't want to talk about those things but he wouldn't stop.

More & more I was convinced that there was something mentally wrong with this man. Why would you see it necessary to have such a conversation with a 9 year old child? What interest do you think he would have in your love life?

Once I had given it some thought, I decided against contacting Christopher. I instead gave a message to his friend Trevor & asked him to speak with him in regards to the outstanding rent.

Honestly I was just counting down to get out of his space. I remember visiting 34 & having a conversation about getting furniture made for myself. Everything that was presently in the house belonged to Christopher. I didn't plan on taking anything when I was leaving as I didn't want him hunting me for his belongings.

Annmarie told me that she had a very good furniture man. She called him right away & told him to come by 34 with his catalogue. When I heard catalogue I thought to myself that I probably wouldn't be able to afford him. Anyway, he would arrive shortly after with his catalogue in hand. I was relieved to see that the catalogue was actually just a photo album. I think I might be able to afford him after all.

I looked through his pictures & chose the designs for my dresser & closet & a bunk bed for my son. There was so much more that I would require but for now I was focusing on the necessities to start with as I was running a very tight budget. He gave me a quotation & I paid him a deposit. I had made it clear to him that the items would be needed for March.

I had recently learned that my co-worker's husband operated a pawn shop which sold new & used appliances. I didn't have the money needed to go to Courts or Singer so I found alternatives that were within my budget. I remember visiting the store Good As New & I was able to identify an electric stove, a two door refrigerator & a 42 inch LG television all of which costed me $120,000, might I add that I am still using these appliances to this day. He had agreed to put a payment plan in place seeing that I wouldn't be taking the items now, & would keep the items in store until I was ready to move in.

I had already had my bed base made & now needed to purchase a mattress. I really couldn't afford a mattress & so I went to the foam factory & purchased a queen sized polyurethane foam. It was an affordable substitute.

For the next couple of weeks I was just patiently waiting & counting down. I avoided Christopher as much as was possible as I needed to focus all my energy on getting things in place for the upcoming move. The only contact that was made was to remind him to pick up our son from school during the days. The reminder was necessary because he had forgotten him at school on more than one occasion.

I AM A HOMEOWNER

I was slated to move house on March 10, 2012. Christopher was still in Jamaica & so I decided to give him a heads up to tell him to make some arrangement to move his furniture if it is that he didn't plan on keeping the lease. Sometimes it doesn't pay to be nice & I will elaborate further on why I say this.

I could have just moved out of the property, left his belongings behind & not say anything to him but instead I chose to give him a heads up so he could make the proper arrangements. He asked me the date I was leaving & I advised him accordingly. I don't know why he had bother to ask because the very next day he sent his friends to empty the house.

I remember driving home from school & seeing a Mobile Reserve police truck parked in the driveway. I immediately started wondering if something had happened. As I exited my vehicle I heard a lot of hammering & movement. When I went inside I saw Trevor & another of the gentleman's friend Wayne, they were dismantling the bedroom set. When I asked what was going on they said Christopher told them to come & move out his furniture.

Was this man for real? Is it that he thought I was going to take any of his belongings? I had to quickly gather some garbage bags to remove my clothing from the dresser drawers so they could move it out as well. Christopher told them to take everything with the exception of the bed & television in our son's room & a closet, chest of drawers & a shoe case that I had bought.

I think he thought he was spiting me but I had learned how to quickly adjust to changes in my situation years ago. So that night my mother, my son & I had to sleep on my son's bed but the following day I had my foam delivered to the house. So that night I dropped it on the floor & slept. I knew the situation wasn't forever & so I just needed to tough it out for the next couple of days.

For the next couple of days every night I would make 3 to 4 trips to the apartment moving stuff in my car. Any money that I could save, I had to save it. I was able to move most of the stuff using my car & whatever I couldn't transport via this medium, my friend Levi had agreed to move for me using his van.

I noticed I wasn't hearing anything from the furniture man. I called Annmarie & told her & she also tried calling him & was unsuccessful. We decided to visit his location in Allman Town, I wasn't ready for what I was about to find out.

We arrived at the location & Annmarie walked right in & started asking for him. She quickly said "Nobody nuh bada tell mi seh him nuh deh yah because mi nuh wah fi afi gwan bad in yah & then call the police after. So tell him stop hide & come tell wi wat a gwan fi wi things." I don't know whether I had mentioned before but we had always dubbed Annmarie the rebel & the fighter in the family. So I knew if this man didn't act right he could have possibly gotten his butt whooped.

He eventually emerged from the back of the house & before I could say anything Annmarie said "Weh mi sister things dem deh weh she fi get weekend?" As soon as I heard the umm umm I knew this was not good. He proceeded to show us a frame of something that he said was the dresser & that was about it. He had nothing else to show me out of the three items I was expecting.

I started paying this man from December & sacrificed every month thereafter to make further payments just to ensure that the furniture would be ready when it came time for me to move but guess what, they weren't.

Annmarie behaved very badly. She behaved so badly that before we knew it a crowd of spectators were gathering. She told him that she was giving him another week to deliver the items & if she had to visit him again he better had my money to refund me.

Finally it was moving day & my nephews had come along to assist with some of the lifting & loading of Levi's van. I was finally fully closing the chapter on Christopher & moving forward to the next chapter of my life. As to what awaited me I didn't know for sure but what I knew was that it must be even a little better than what I was leaving behind.

IT IS NEVER ABOUT HOW YOU START

I was in my own home. The moment felt so surreal that I had to constantly remind myself that it was for real. My living room was filled to capacity with garbage bags. I had no living room furniture. The television I had bought from Good As New I placed it on my computer desk for the time being. Yes my computer desk was doubling as a TV stand.

My son was without his bed & so we had to put his foam on the floor in the interim. He however slept in my bed for the most part while my mom slept in his room on the days she was with us.

I had no small appliances so everything had to be done on the stove. I remember the very first electricity bill I got, it was for $14,000, I almost fainted. The fact that we had to be using the electric stove to do everything, wasn't working in our favour.

I remember seeing my mom padding my kitchen counter with sheets. When I asked her what she was doing, she said she was creating an ironing board to be able to iron our uniforms.
I took my time & tried to purchase the appliances little by little. My disposable income was far less, now that I had a $60,000 mortgage payment. Christopher had also stopped assisting financially with our son, he said I was to get my man to help me.

I didn't put much meaning to anything that he was saying. I figured he was just responding emotionally because of the fact that he no longer had the control he did when I was living in his house. He also said that he would have stopped paying my mom to look after our son because my mom might be at my house cooking & washing for my man, so why should he pay her?! My mother quickly said to me that she wouldn't stop taking care of her own grandson because of money. So whether he paid her or not, she would still do what she needed to for him.

I would eventually receive my long overdue furniture. I am so happy that Annmarie didn't have to revisit because I knew it wouldn't have ended well. So the number of items in the partially empty house had increased by three pieces.

I remember reaching out to Christopher & having a discussion with him about furnishing his son's room. I was not about to take no for an answer because I saw the lengths he went to for his eldest son's room while we were in England. He had agreed to have it done & eventually it was.

Now that I had pretty much settled in & things were coming together little by little, it was now time for me to start thinking about repaying all the persons that had loaned me money during the acquisition process. I hadn't ironed out a plan yet but I knew something would work out.

PEOPLE DON'T DOWNGRADE, THEY UPGRADE

I had figured out how to repay all the persons I owed. I was going to sell my car. In 2012 the Mazda Demio became a highly sought after car. It was very similar to the Mazda 2 that I had at the time. Seeing that the car was so popular it was the opportune time to dispose of it.

I remember advertising the car for sale & I received so many queries & interests. I finally settled on one offer & the car was sold for $1.4M which I thought was a good price seeing that the car was now 4 years old & I was only losing $400K off the original purchase price.

Once the sale was completed I repaid the monies loaned to me, tried to get some of the small appliances that I needed for the house & used the difference to try & secure another vehicle. The balance wasn't enough to purchase a car cash & so I paid half cash & borrowed the difference through my credit union. Remember I already had the mortgage payment coming out & so I wanted the car payment to be as small as possible.

After shopping around I ended up with a 2006 Daihatsu Boon. Before now I had no knowledge of this vehicle but it was what was within my budget & so I was ready to work with it. The car was a pre-owned trade in & so the wear & tear to the paintwork was obvious but what was important to me was whether it was going to leave me on the road or not. So once my mechanic gave me the green light I completed the purchase.

The office was buzzing with gossip. Apparently someone saw me coming out of the car & it somehow made the newsflash. Why? I had no idea. The narrative was that people don't downgrade cars, they upgrade & I moved from a fairly new car to an old car.

I remember my supervisor at the time Nicole, had obviously heard the little buzz going around the office & she & I began to hold a little reasoning. I think she thought I was bothered by what was being said seeing that not so long ago Melissa had created another buzz in the office. I remember saying to her "Nicole, these people don't know what my situation is & they will never know because I am not going to tell them but I am choosing now to tell you. I downgraded my car because I have just bought a house. So yes their cars might be fancier than mine but the major difference is theirs are being parked at peoples rented houses while my likkle betsy is being parked at a property I own." When I said all this to her I saw the look on her face & it was somewhere between being proud & not believing that as a young person I was thinking this way.

I don't know why but from the buzz started about my car, Melissa immediately came to mind as the culprit. I mean I could be wrong but I remembered that she told Christopher how my music was always loud in the Mazda whenever I was driving in to work & sometimes I was driving fast as if to say I was showing off on someone. The music was going to be loud in the Boon as well, I made sure to install a good pioneer radio when I was making the purchase. So if she thought the music was loud because I was in a "Kris" car & wanted to be seen, her theory would be proven wrong.

But you see how people can just see you trying to thrive & survive & immediately have a problem with everything that you do? And everytime I think about all the things that girl had to say about me & all the things she did to me, I'm in awe because this was someone who I had known from the 4th grade in primary school.

She knew me from I was bathing in a bath pan because I lived in what could have been considered as a tenament yard & the bathroom facilities were shared & my parents didn't want me using them & so the bath pan was my go to until my dad built another bathroom just for us. I remember another friend from the 4th grade going back to school & telling everyone that I didn't have a bathroom at my house & that I would bathe in a bath pan.

You know what was funny about that particular situation, that girl came to my house all because her mom & my mom knew each other from they were learning trade & her mom had asked my mom to get me to help her with her school work because she wasn't doing so good. So had she not come to my house for the assistance, then she wouldn't have seen me setting up my bath pan to go have my shower. So I was willing to help her to try & bring her up but all she saw was the opportunity to try & bring me down.

I say all this to say that people will know your humble beginnings & all the things that you endured to try to get to where you are & still harbor feelings of envy, jealousy & bad mind towards you instead of just being happy for you & the fact that you aren't where you use to be & you are continually trying to elevate yourself.

CO-PARENTING WOES

I'm sure you all know that Christopher was not going to make co-parenting easy. He was going to try & make things as difficult as possible & my life as miserable as possible all in a bid to somehow get back at me.

After moving house, Trevor would still pick up my son from school & take him home. I made it clear to him not to disclose my current location to Christopher. I knew I couldn't hide forever but until I had figured out how I wanted to deal with Christopher, hiding it was.

They say to give to Caesar what was due to them. Despite everything that had happened, Christopher continued paying our son's prep school fee & provided his lunch money. He didn't really keep in touch with our son often but my son didn't complain because whenever he did make contact all he did was to question my son about me. He was always interested in whether I had a man & if the man was coming to the house. My son didn't appreciate the questioning & so he was happy to not get the calls.

We were able to have a civil conversation & from that conversation we came to the agreement that he would send 200 pounds monthly for my son.

Whenever he was in Jamaica & would ask to see my son, I had to put my fears & feelings aside & try to make it happen. My son refused to go anywhere with him without me present, so as uncomfortable as it was to be there, I made the sacrifice. What I noticed though was that after I would leave, the messages would start coming in about loving & missing me & what we had.

My son's birthday was in August & so most times Christopher would have been here in Jamaica. Once he was here we would come together & try to have a birthday get together for our son.

So for the most part one could say that the co-parenting was going good.

The exceptions to this would be whenever Christopher didn't get his way & he felt as though his ego had been bruised. Should this happen then he would see it necessary to prove a point I guess to say that his assistance was needed & how would he prove this point you might ask? He would stop sending the monthly 200 pounds.

I could never sit here & say his money wasn't needed, IT WAS! I had a lot on my plate & I was struggling to stay afloat. I had pretty much assumed responsibility for my father. Some of my other siblings would assist him if & when they could but I was his go to person for almost everything. So it was a challenge trying to balance my responsibilities & his.

One thing I can tell y'all though is that I was the master of finding a way out. Sometimes finding a way out meant I had to pawn some items; laptop, portable AC, jewellery but if that's what needed to be done to get the extra cash, I was going to do it or better yet what I should say is I did it.

Christopher knew the things to do to try & get under my skin. I remember how he flaunted a business he had opened for Prudence in my face. While all this was being done for her, my child's monthly maintenance had stopped. When he was furnishing her house, he made sure to use the card that he knew I would be able to see all the transactions for.

When I reached out to him & started cursing about the lack of assistance, he made it seem as though my problem was with him spending his money on Prudence. No sir my problem was with you not seeing the need to provide for your son.

What I eventually realised was that if he made advances & little comments about pictures on my whatsapp display, If I wanted him to do right by my child, I couldn't shot it down right away & tell him exactly how I felt. I had to pretend to be okay with this man still telling me that he loved me & a host of other things. So in other words I had to stroke his ego.

I remember being offered one year's worth of mortgage payments which equated to $720,000 at the time & all I had to do was to have sex with him & hang out with him at his request when he comes to Jamaica. I felt so disappointed by the offer. Some people would laugh & say "Yuh pumpum good!" but honestly I didn't find anything about the offer funny. Like I said I felt disappointed. Why? Because in that moment he showed me exactly what was more important to him & what mattered & it wasn't his child.

When this offer was made I was chasing this man every month to get the 200 pounds for my son. Sometimes the abuse & disrespect that I had to subject myself to just to get that money, brought me to tears. I remember on one occasion he had Mary answer his phone & basically told me off about calling Christopher for money. She said all I did was to call for money. I was very puzzled because I wasn't sure what else I should have been calling for.

Once she had said it though I knew that it was based on what he had said to her because I remember calling him one month & I don't know if it is that he was having a bad day but I got cursed out & one of the things he said was that I only called for money & never to check if the person providing the money was okay. I had to remind him that we weren't friends but rather just parents. I don't think this was what I should have said because once again the monthly money stopped.

It was a constant roller-coaster because Christopher was not able to take his feelings & ego out of the situation & just focus on being the best father that he could be to our son. His response to everything was based on feelings & emotions & the fact that I had left him. Why would he still be hanging on to that when he had clearly moved on with his life was something I never understood.

Thankfully I had good people in my corner so wherever he fell short, somebody was always there to back me up. Sometimes it was so unexpected, I would just get a message from my friends in England or America to say that they had sent me a change & I was truly appreciative because they also had their own struggles dealing with.

My back being against the wall helped me to clearly identify the persons who had me & were in my corner & sometimes it is important for us to know because oftentimes the people who we expect to show up for us, they never do.

VISITATION

Christopher's birthday was in March & as such he would usually be in Jamaica around this time. He would usually stay for Easter as well.

Despite us no longer being in a relationship, I honestly tried my best to not let our separation affect the relationship between him & our son. I remember while visiting he complained to me bitterly about not being able to see our son because he refused to take him up on any of his invitations.

I knew for a fact that my son was a homebody, & rarely had any interest in leaving home to go anywhere other than school. With this is mind I told Christopher that I would arrange for him to visit with our son during the Easter break. There was only one condition; he was to visit while I was at work & leave before I got home.

The first day he showed up at approximately 6:30pm. When he called to say he was outside, I asked him why was he only just showing up & he replied with the excuse that he was conducting business & didn't realise that it was so late. He added that he just wanted to drop something off for our son & spend five minutes with him.

Five minutes quickly became three hours. At approximately 9:30pm, I had to go to my son's room & ask him to leave. I expressed to him that it was way past our bedtime. He pretended not to know that it was so late before proceeding to leave.

The next two times he visited, he once again visited in the evening & not during the daytime as was agreed. The third time he showed up in the evening, I told him the arrangement was not working as he was not honouring my request & as such he was not welcome to return the following day.

The visit clearly wasn't about our son, it was obviously about me because had he genuinely wanted to see his son & spend time with him, he would not have allowed anything to jeopardize his ability to visit. The more I thought about it the more I realised that it was probably me that he wanted to see & him deciding to overstay his welcome is to probably be able to watch & see whether a man was actually living with me like he believed.

Despite the visitation not working out, I was still trying to think of ways for him to spend time with our son. It was at this point it was agreed that he would pick my son up after school during the days so they would be able to spend a little time together. This arrangement worked for the most part.

One day while he was dropping off our son, he asked if I could come downstairs as he wanted to say something to me. I was hesitant about granting the request based on the fact that I no longer trusted him. He heard the hesitation & so he quickly declared that it was someone that he wanted to introduce to me.

Introduce? Why? Anyway I went downstairs & yes there was this white British girl in the vehicle. Her name has somehow eluded me. He began to introduce her as his fiancee. When he said fiancee honestly I just wanted to burst out into laughter but I tried to maintain my composure.

Once he had left I couldn't stop laughing. I remember going back inside the house & telling my mom what had just happened & we started laughing again. He clearly thought that he was "popping" style on me, pity he didn't know that that style definitely did spoil.

WE HAVE A NEW ASSIGNMENT FOR YOU

On November 3, 2012 at approximately 3pm I was informed by manager that I would be sent on a special assignment to the Duke Street branch in downtown Kingston. I was told that I would have started as at Monday the 5th. As she broke the news I was at a loss for words. Duke Street? Dung a town? These were the thoughts going through my head. She clearly saw the distraught look on my face & so she said "They asked us to send the best & you are the best. If there is anyone that we believe can get this job done, it's you." Thanks for the vote of confidence I guess.

On Sunday November 4, 2012 my son & I had left home to visit a car wash that was in the vicinity of the Mega Mart supermarket. Monday would have been my first day at a new location & so I decided to get the Boon cleaned up. As I stood in a line of traffic waiting on persons who were turning into Mega Mart, I just felt my car being flung forward. I looked & my foot was still on the brake but the car continued to move. I heard my son screaming & when I looked over despite having his seatbelt on, he was still being flung forward & so I quickly stretched over my hand & held him back.

When everything had stopped & I exited my car, the entire trunk area was smashed in. One would expect the vehicle that caused the damage to be behind me but it wasn't. When I started asking where was the person that hit me, I was pointed to a vehicle some distance down the road. After hitting me that was where it ended up stopping.

My son was just crying non-stop & was complaining about a headache & so I called my brother Junior & he came on the scene & took my son away to the hospital.

I started trying to understand what had really just happened. Apparently the gentleman came off the slope & according to him his phone fell & by the time he bent to pick it up & looked back up he saw a line of cars before him & all his efforts to press brake was futile, his brake had apparently failed. So my car was the first point of contact then I in turn hit the car in front of me & that man hit the car in front of him. Now the plot twist in all this was the fact that the man who caused the accident was uninsured.

I spoke with my work neighbour Mario & had informed him of what had happened & the fact that I would now be stranded with no vehicle & I had to report to Duke Street in the morning. You might be wondering why I couldn't just charter a cab to take me to work, the truth is I couldn't afford it. He told me not to worry about it because he knows of another member of staff who lives in close proximity to me that works at the Duke Street location so he would arrange for him to pick me up in the morning. So that was one problem solved.

Based on the time difference between England & Jamaica, Christopher didn't see the messages sent until the following morning. I remember him calling me all panicky asking if we were okay. My son was cleared by the hospital & was said to have a mild case of whiplash & as for me I had lower back pains that started a few days later. He went on to say that he was really shaken up by the fact that he could have woken up to a message that we were dead. I think the accident really shook him up because for the next couple of months I didn't have to quarrel with him about sending the monthly maintenance. He had also offered me the use of his vehicle until I was able to source another. I was however being allowed to use the vehicle on one condition, I wasn't suppose to transport my man in it. I don't know why everything for him was always about a man. I was actually very single but I was not going to tell him that. Anyway, I accepted the terms & condition of the vehicle loan.

While I waited on the insurance company to pay my claim for the BOON, I started shopping around for cars & once again I settled on a 2009 Daihatsu Boon. I didn't care what anyone had to say about these vehicles, they were very economical & fuel efficient & so had fit very well in my low budget life.

A WAH KINDA CAR THAT

The year was 2013 & Christopher was back in Jamaica for a visit. He had contacted me & informed me of the fact that he had brought a suitcase for my son & wanted to arrange for me to pick it up. We arranged to meet at Usain Bolt's Tracks & Records. I showed up with my son & we all sat together & had a meal.

Once we were done we all walked to the parking lot. When I unlocked my car for my son & I to enter, all I heard was "A wah kinda car that?" Followed by hysterical laughter. "Mi neva hear bout this yah car yah yet!" Followed by more laughter. So I quickly said to him "Well it's taking me from point A to point B & that's all that matters." He took pleasure in trying to put me down & to make it seem that how I was living was less than or below standard.

I was slated to graduate university this year but I didn't foresee it happening as I was finding it very difficult to pay for my final course. Caring for my dad & covering my own monthly expenses, depleted my salary monthly. There was no "wiggle room" for any one off expenses or emergencies. I was living pay check to pay check.

It became necessary to hire a caregiver for my dad after he was found passed out at home on his floor. Thankfully he was very popular in his community & as such when he wasn't sighted all day at his regular spot, the bridge, persons went in search of him & made the discovery. This was now an additional expense.

Some months when I couldn't cover all my bills because I really just didn't have the funds to do so, I had to raffle to see which bill I could opt out of paying & I wouldn't get disconnected. My work neighbour Mario had previously warned me that these days would come, apparently they were the side effects from trying to elevate yourself & not being rich. I will never forget

Mario's words to me "Some days yuh fridge a go jus full a bare ice water because you cah find money fi even buy juice, but on those days just look up at the roof that is over your head & know that it was all worth it." These words encouraged me more than he probably realised.

I remember my friend Levi checking up on me & asking how school was going. He went on to ask if I wasn't supposed to have been graduating this year & I hesitated to respond. Based on my hesitation he said "Stacey what is wrong?" I began telling him about the fact that despite my best efforts I have not been able to put the funds together to pay for my final course & as such I wouldn't be able to graduate. Once I had said this he instructed me to register for the course for the next semester that it was being offered & he would pay for it.

I did as I was instructed & Levi paid for the course, I passed & with that had completed my degree program. Later on he asked me about graduation & I told him that I didn't plan on attending as I didn't have the resources required to rent my gown & to cover all the other costs attached to the graduation exercise. Levi quickly said to me that there was no way I could have studied for that long, completed the course of study & not walk the stage. He saw graduation as being mandatory & so it came as no surprise when he decided to pay all the requisite fees to allow me to participate in the graduation exercise.

Looking back I can clearly see how as soon as a door was closed & I thought all was lost, a window opened.

LOCKED UP

My son's maintenance had once again ceased. I cannot pinpoint a reason why but you would all know by now that Christopher's sole purpose since I moved out of his house was to try & make my life difficult & the one card that he had that he could always play was the monthly maintenance money, so he continued using it to his advantage.

Based on the fact that he had stopped remitting the funds for my son, I stopped communicating with him as I really didn't see the need to. So you can imagine how surprised I was when his friend Trevor placed a call to me to say that he had gotten in a spot of bother with the authorities & was arrested. I could not believe what I was hearing.

Had Trevor not reached out I wouldn't have had a clue as to what was happening. Once I heard the news one thing I knew for sure was that I was not going to let my son know any of what was happening. Lucky for me Christopher rarely contacted our son & as such the fact that he probably wouldn't be hearing from him now for a little while wouldn't raise any red flags.

I remember eventually receiving a call from Christopher, I was so happy to hear his voice. He told me that he had made arrangement with his niece for her to pay our son's school fee for the upcoming term. I encouraged him to try & speak to our son whenever he could as I would not be telling him anything about what was going on.

I think him finding himself in this situation brought out my soft side & for some weird reason I felt myself starting to get close to him again. I don't know if pity or sympathy was taking over my common sense but before I knew it I was having conversations with Christopher about us getting back together & giving things another go.

I spoke to my friends about the possibility of reuniting with Christopher & not one of them said DON'T DO IT! Instead they gave me some lukewarm responses which basically said to me that they weren't in agreement but was trying to somehow be supportive.

Mary was pregnant once again with Christopher's child. I was only just finding this out. Remember he had constantly denied that her first child was his. When I asked him how could he have gotten Mary pregnant, he tried telling me that it was my fault because after I had left him she was the only one he had to turn to & things just happened.

It was at this point in the conversation I heard a very loud voice in my head, I don't know whose it was, it was definitely not the lord though because he wouldn't address me like this. The voice said "Ediat gal! Weh you a do? Weh you a go back deh suh go do? See Mary a go have baby deh, you plan fi deal wid she fi di rest a yuh life?" And just like that I was out of what must have been a moment of temporary insanity. I quickly told Christopher that I had rethink my position & we should let the relationship remain at parents & nothing else.

Now with him getting himself in trouble with the law there wasn't even the possibility of getting the on & off help anymore. The assistance would have stopped completely until he had sorted out himself.

I remember getting a call from his niece in regards to the school fee she was asked to pay. Her call to me was pretty much to say that I should find another school to send my son to as she wasn't prepared to pay the $54,000 school fee. She went on to say that if I wasn't in a position to cover the cost & would have to rely on someone else, then that person has to be able to afford it & she couldn't. I told her in no uncertain terms that my son would not be changing school. He was in the 5th grade & had less than a year left to complete prep school, so why would I disrupt him by moving him? It would have been better for her to suggest paying the amount that she reckoned she could afford & ask me to cover the difference but changing school?!

Things eventually worked out & Christopher was able to cover the school fee without her assistance.

HIGH SCHOOLER

It was March 2014 & my son would be sitting his GSAT exams to matriculate to high school. Christopher had decided to pay him a surprise visit & would show up at his school on the final day of his exams.

I had taken vacation from work for the days he had exams. I think I was more nervous & worried than he was. I wasn't the only one though as I remember the principal ushering out quite a few parents on the first morning of exam & asking us to leave the school compound.

On the second day of exams, once it was pick up time I walked in to sign him out & as he walked outside to the parking lot, he was greeted by Christopher. He was so happy to see him. We would never get back together but there was nothing stopping us from being the best parents we could be to our child. I had always tried to foster this type of parenting but Christopher lacked the maturity needed to make it work.

When it was time for our son to start high school, as was the norm, Christopher agreed to pay his school fee & purchase his uniforms & I was to do books & anything else. I had no problem with the proposed arrangement. Unfortunately, this assistance was only received for the first year of high school all because a female who Christopher knew that worked at my workplace told him that she had seen his son's name on a scholarship listing that was sent out internally.

I received a phone call from a very irate Christopher who asked me why I hadn't told him about the scholarship. I really couldn't understand why he felt as though he needed to have been told. He went on to say that if I was getting a scholarship then I shouldn't have been asking him for any monies for back to school expenses. I explained to him that the scholarship was a benefit to me as a member of staff, he was still required to take care of his responsibilities.

I cannot forget the day I heard my son refer to him as a waste man. I had to pick my jaw up from the floor after he said it. The remark came after he heard me arguing with Christopher about lunch & maintenance money once again. Whilst my son wasn't talkative, when he does speak he is a straight shooter.

I remember the night he went off on Christopher. Once again Christopher had called him & chose to bash me to my son. He was saying that I wasn't allowing him to see my son, that I was poisoning my son's mind against him & a host of other things. But the punch line of the rant was that I was the problem. When my son had obviously heard enough he went on to ask him whether he had ever stopped to think that he might be the problem & that things would be different had he been a better father. Ouch!

What Christopher failed to admit to himself was the fact that he ruined the relationship with our son. Prior to his attack on me, my son adored him. He adored him so much that everytime he would leave to return to England, it negatively affected my son. He would cry for days & not function at school. All this changed after he attacked me in front of him & it gradually got worst because instead of doing all he could to be the best father to his child after the relationship ended, he chose the route of being spiteful & vindictive.

I have always encouraged my son to try & have a relationship with Christopher, sometimes even forcing him to call him but I would still be considered as the bad guy. Despite how I might feel about Christopher, I have never spoken about him negatively to our son. I allowed my son to form his own opinion, which he did & unfortunately it wasn't a good one.

Sad to say that Christopher was so busy blaming everyone else he failed to recognise that he was actually the problem.

GOODBYE MY LOVE

The more I reflect on my life the more I see how God favoured me. I was still trying to balance my expenses & that of my father's. I remember his caregiver Ivy after seeing my constant struggle to pay her & also provide her with grocery for him monthly, pulled me aside & said to me "Stacey, don't worry about food for Keithie, just pay me, I will ensure he eats. After all I have my kids & they have to eat so whatever I prepare, I will ensure your father eats as well." I don't think she realised the weight that she had lifted off my shoulders.

No one could fully understand the weight I carried on my shoulders & sometimes even when the load got very heavy, I still didn't complain, instead I did what I could & kept believing that one day soon things would get better.

My friend Sally dubbed me the magician. She has always said she just couldn't understand how I did it all & even while struggling to stay afloat would still try to assist her whenever I could.

My father had contracted the Chikungunya virus & we all expected him to overcome but unfortunately he didn't. My father was previously diagnosed with Chronic Obstructive Pulmonary Disease (COPD). My father wasn't a smoker but it is was believed that he developed the condition due to years of exposure from working in the bauxite industry & quite possibly secondhand smoking exposure for the years he spent not just operating a bar but also frequenting them.

The Chikungunya virus was believed to cause death in a lot of persons with underlying conditions based on the fact that it exacerbated the condition, my father was no different. He had lost his appetite & I think it was mainly because of all the phlegm that was being produced by his respiratory system. Whenever he tried having even fluids, in no time he would have brought it back up.

The last couple of days spent with my father will forever be etched in my memory. I wasn't sure if he had somehow used how he felt physically to self-diagnose & conclude that he didn't have much time left with us. I wondered about this because he started bidding me farewell at least five days prior to his death.

On the Saturday I visited him with my eldest brother & he sent me to the shop to purchase Hals menthol sweets for him all because he wanted to get rid of me just to be able to tell my brother to look out for me. It was also during this visit that I had asked him how many children he had & he quickly corrected me & said "Not have Stacey, got. I can't have children." He confirmed that he had fathered eighteen kids & proceeded to say that he preferred his girls. When I asked him how could he have said such a thing in the presence of his son, he just looked up to the ceiling.

On the Sunday while visiting with him again he just randomly told me that he preferred the Pentecostal church. It was funny he said this because I grew up with the understanding that our family was Catholic. After telling me this he asked me whether I knew the song Any Day Now & I told him no. He began educating me that it was sung by a man called Chuck Jackson. I told him that I would have looked it up. When I got home that morning & listened to the song on YouTube, the message was clear & I cried my eyes out.

On that same visit he had also asked me to call two of my sisters as he wanted to speak with them. I was able to get through to my sister Maxine & he spoke with her but despite my best efforts I wasn't getting through to Moy. I saw how disappointed he looked when I told him that I was not getting through to her.

As luck would have it, as soon as I was about drive away from his house, my sister Moy called back & so I ran back inside & gave him the phone to speak to her. I could see the change in his mood once he had gotten the opportunity to have a conversation with her.

The following day he was hospitalised & for the next two days that I had visited, he basically used hand gestures to wave goodbye. His voice was very faint, I had to put my ear to his mouth to hear anything he was saying whenever he tried to speak. He was also on oxygen & so his mask blocked whatever little sound left his mouth. One of the last things he said to me was that he wished all his children could have been at his bedside. I reminded him how impossible of a ask that was for numerous reasons & he said he understood.

On Thursday October 16, 2014 at approximately 8:25am I received the call that he was gone. This was one of the hardest things that I had ever had to deal with in my life. Whilst I was happy that he was out of the discomfort that he was experiencing, I still wasn't ready for him to go.

My father wasn't perfect & neither are you & I & so I opted to look past his imperfections & loved him for who he was, faults & all & some of my siblings will tell you he had a lot but I had learned to love him unconditionally.

I had never lost anyone so close to me & so it took me years to get to the point where I could speak about his memory & not fall apart. Memories might be all I had left but I was grateful for them. They are worth more to me than any material possessions.

If you are blessed enough to still have your parents or a parent around, don't take their presence for granted & think they are going to be around forever. Make the most of everyday you are afforded with them.

Sometimes we might be at odds with them for whatever reason but I do encourage you to extend that olive branch & try to make peace. Don't allow pride & ego to result in you missing out on time that cannot be regained.

BLOCK & DELETE

One thing I knew for sure was the fact that my father's death made me less tolerable of certain things & Christopher's games was one such thing.

In the summer of 2016 he visited with Mary & their two children. He had made contact with me to query whether I was at work & I confirmed that I was. He said he would have been passing by shortly to drop off his portion of funds to cover the back to school expenses. I remember seeing 5pm & not hearing back from Christopher & so I decided to return a call to him for him to confirm whether he would still be coming & he confirmed that he was.

It was a Friday & I would usually leave the office at 6pm. When the clock struck six & he was still a no show, I decided to call him back again. All calls to his cellphone went unanswered & so I left the office & went home.

He would return a call the following day to say that he was at Gran Bahia Hotel with Mary & the kids & would have to take the funds to me when he gets back into Kingston.

Long story short, I didn't receive the promised funds. It was as though we were engaged in a constant game of hide & seek. He hid so well that despite being in Jamaica on our son's birthday, he clearly forgot because he made no contact & neither did he even attempt to see him. When he eventually contacted my son two days later, he gave the excuse that he was still out of town, I am not sure how being out of town prevented him from reaching out to his son on his birthday but it somehow did.

When I realised that he had really gone back to England without providing his portion of the back to school funds, this was the last straw for me. It was time to put an end to the constant manipulation all because I needed the assistance. I was also tired of having to constantly chase a grown ass man to play his role as a father & take care of his responsibilities. In that moment I just told myself God will provide.

I proceeded to block & delete Christopher from my whatsapp messenger. He was already deleted from my social media years ago & so whatsapp was the only contact he had with me outside of regular telephone contact.

After he was blocked, I would receive an email saying that if he isn't able to communicate with me via whatsapp then I shouldn't expect any assistance from him as he was not going to chase anyone to give them his money. I pointed out to him that he could always contact me via email like he was doing now his reply to this was he didn't see why he wouldn't be able to contact me via whatsapp but everyone else would be able to. Maybe it was because I didn't have a child with everyone else that wasn't being maintained.

I would also get a few telephone calls from unknown numbers but I ignored them because for the most part, Christopher was the only one who called me unknown & I had made up my mind to not correspond with him any at all going forward. The co-parenting had become too toxic & I didn't want to deal with it anymore.

He had even promised our son to bring him a phone but this was another empty promise. Nevertheless, I purchased a cellphone for my son & provided Christopher with the number & told him he could contact our son directly, he didn't need to go through me. My son seldomly heard from him just the same, nothing changed.

I WILL SEE YOU IN COURT

In March of 2017 I would receive a text message from a strange number that I didn't have saved. It wasn't long before I realised that it belonged to Christopher & he was once again in Jamaica. His issue this time was the fact that I was somehow keeping his son away from him.

Honestly, I didn't see it necessary for him to see my son when he was doing absolutely nothing for him. However, had my son had an interest in seeing him then I would have made it happen but the reality was, he had none.

The first set of text messages started on March 21st at 8:46am. I remember thinking this must be some burning issue. I always wondered why I had saved some of these messages after all these years but look how handy they turned out to be.

The first message I got went like this:

"Well guess what I was going to see him & give him what I have to give him to give you as I honestly don't want to even be in the same space as you. So if I can't give my child what I have because you're a ignorant fool so be it. He will be old enough one day."

Was this man for real? He went on further to make it seem as though he was not in a position financially to do anything for our son & that I was a horrible person for trying to keep his son away from him all because he doesn't have money.

I had to put a few things into perspective for him:

1. People with no money can't fly from England to Jamaica two & three times for the year

2. People with no money can't afford to come to Jamaica & rent a property that they are paying for nightly in USD, & stay there for in excess of a month
3. If you were the doting dad you are making yourself out to be then you would have prioritized your son's wellbeing over a trip to just come to Jamaica & fool around
4. Even 100 pounds out of your plane fare could have done something for your child

I stood my ground & maintained my position, you are not doing anything for my child, so leave him alone. I was told that I was using my son to extort him, he could have even said I was pimping my son & I wouldn't care because he knew what he was saying was far from the truth but once again being the master of manipulation he was trying to see what he could do or say to wear me down & make me change my stance. Not this time.

In one part of the text message exchanges I was being accused of thinking that I was better than him. Like when are you going to realise that this is solely about you taking care of your child? I had to spell it out in no uncertain terms that my actions wasn't because "mi reach" or "mi betta dan him" but it was more because of the fact that I was sick & tired of him being a deadbeat dad & a part time poopa. I was tired of him thinking that he can be in the child's life when he sees fit, feed him when he sees fit & school him when he sees fit.

He proceeded to tell me that I was an ungrateful piece of you know what because had it not been for him I wouldn't have a roof over my head & that my day would come. But just to provide an even clearer picture of what I was really dealing with, after I was called every name under the sun, I was asked whether I wanted to attend a party with him & how he missed my long legs & my body was probably perfect now. Once I redirected the conversation back to the maintenance monies I was owed I received the following message:

"Remember there is a law that governs things like that & I would rather spend that money in court than give it to you nasty piece of shit. I will see you in court idiot."

I have never heard of the parent who is not supporting their child opt to take the one who is to court, but let us see what the judge has to say.

Take me to court.

STAKE OUT

On Thursday April 13, 2017 while at work I received a call from my neighbour to say that there was a gentleman outside the complex asking to either be allowed entry or for my son to be called to come outside to him. Mr.Simmons said he had told the person that he couldn't say whether my son was home or not because he knew I was at work & even if he was home, he would not be able to ask him to come outside to a stranger.

Mr. Simmons said despite telling the person this, they were still parked at the gate. I proceeded to ask the type of vehicle the person was in & once Mr. Simmons said a black Lexus I knew it was Christopher.

I placed a call to my son just to check that everything was okay. While speaking to him I could hear my door buzzer going off in the background. I asked my son whether it was really the buzzer & he confirmed that it was. He said that it had been going off non-stop like somebody had the button held down. I didn't give him any idea as to what was going on.

I remember calling Trevor & asking him to contact Christopher & ask him to leave my house. Once I had said this Trevor went on to say that he had called him & told him of the plan to visit my house thinking that he would have buzzed my door & my son would have let him in. He said once he had said this he told him "Don't go a di woman yard." He clearly didn't know his son because had he known him then he would have known that he could have buzzed that door until Jesus came, he was not going to get an answer. We have NEVER responded to a buzz. Our guests would call once they are outside & at that point we would let them in.

I once again told Trevor to call Christopher & ask him to leave my gate otherwise the police would be called. As you can imagine I became very uneasy & on edge because after all, this man had previously attacked me & since then I have always had my guard up. I no longer considered anything impossible for him to do.

It was time for me to leave work & I was definitely trying to avoid any run ins with Christopher & so I called back Mr. Simmons & asked him to confirm whether the car was still outside & he confirmed that it was. Once I had gotten that confirmation I decided to wait at the office until I had been given the all clear.

I remember sharing the day's events with my work crew (the tenament) & nobody felt comfortable about the idea that Christopher had seen it fit to camp outside my gate. They all agreed that I should remain at the office until I was told that he had left.

Before I could call back Mr. Simmons, he returned a call to me & confirmed that Christopher had left. Even after being told this, I remained at the office a little longer as I wasn't sure whether he had moved from the gate but was still lurking in the community.

While making my way home I would receive a text message from Christopher which read:
"You want to see what I can do? Take it easy you will see." Once I had gotten the message, I forwarded same to my friends who instructed me to make my way to the police station to make a report. Everyone was of the view that I shouldn't take anything Christopher was communicating lightly.

I made my way to the police station & made a report outlining the fact that Christopher was camped out all day outside my house & after leaving proceeded to send me a text message that could possibly be considered a threat.

I was asked to provide Christopher's contact information after which he was contacted by an officer. He was informed of the fact that I had filed a report against him & was instructed not to make any further contact with me & neither was he to visit my home. He was told that any breach of these conditions would result in him being arrested. I remember the DSP with whom I dealt saying to Christopher & I quote "All the time unuh gwan like unuh haunted or obsessed wid the people dem gal pickney & go harm dem tru dem lef unuh."

Before leaving the police station the DSP directed two officers to escort me home. He also provided me with his contact information & told me that should I get any more calls or visits from Christopher, I was to call him immediately. He explained that the matter wasn't to be taken lightly based on the fact that Christopher had previously physically assaulted me.

I finally got home with the flashing blue lights very closely behind. What a day!

DOMESTIC DISPUTE

It was the Saturday after the stake out. I was at the hairdresser & had just finished washing my hair. I heard my phone ring & saw that it was my downstairs neighbour. Once I had answered he proceeded to ask whether I was home my reply to which was no. He went on to say that the police was there with a gentleman & they said they needed to speak with me. I proceeded to ask whether the gentleman was in a black car & once he said yes, I knew it was Christopher.

I remember asking him to put the police men on the phone. Once they came on I queried the reason behind them needing to speak with me. They went on to say that they were there to investigate a domestic dispute. I proceeded to ask them how could I have a domestic dispute with a man that I didn't share a home with?

The officers went on to say that they were also investigating a report that I was keeping my child from his father, my reply to which was that Christopher had informed me that he was taking me to court on the matter, so how did this now become a police matter? O I know how, the policemen were Christopher's friends.

They went on to ask me to report to the Constant Spring Police station for a meeting. I remember calling DSP Bennett & updating him on what had just happened. He was fuming! He could not believe what he was hearing. He queried whether I had gotten the name of the officers & I provided same. I remember hearing him call the officers & telling them to leave my property immediately. They were told to ensure that they took Christopher with them as well. I heard when he said to them "Imagine the lady come report the man earlier this week & I gave the man strict instructions not to go to the lady's house & unuh tek him up & gawn escort him there?! Leave now!"

DSP Bennett went on to ask whether I would consider visiting the police station so that he could have a meeting with both of us to try & understand what the issue was & see how best it could be resolved. I agreed to the meeting & informed him that I would be at the station momentarily.

My brother Junior was scheduled to arrive in Jamaica during the course of the day. While making my way to the police station he called me to confirm his arrival. Once I had told him what was going on, he got very enraged & instructed me to wait on him at home. He said he wanted to accompany me to the police station. I told him not to worry about it, I was okay & I would update him shortly.

I arrived at the police station & DSP Bennett gave me further directives as to where I was to go. Once I was seated inside, he made a call asking the officers to bring Christopher in. This would be the first time that Christopher would be seeing me in about two years. As he walked in the room & saw me seated on the opposite side of the desk, the "ginal" smirk came across his face.

The first thing he said was "Wow, I haven't seen you in so long I didn't even remember what you looked like." My face was straight before, during & after his little opening comment. DSP Bennett went on to ask him what was his issue & he replied by saying that I was extorting him to see his son. I was then asked what was the reason behind me keeping my son away, my simple answer was "He is not doing anything for him. The support is inconsistent, he doesn't know how his son eats, goes to school or survives on a whole. He visits Jamaica very often & we all know tickets from England are very expensive but he can't find money to even provide lunch money for his son to go to school."

Once I had given my response, I heard when DSP Bennett said to him "So why you not looking after the child?" This was the one time I really believed that God was definitely not like man because if he was, Christopher would have either dropped dead or got struck by lightning. The gentleman reckon that he owns &

operates two cleaning companies & he had to clear up his back taxes as well as to pay his staff & this negatively impacted his finances hence the reason for him not being able to take care of his responsibilities." I had never heard so much crap in my life. DSP Bennett went on to ask whether I was informed of what he was saying. I quickly informed him that I was only given that story five days prior at which time DSP Bennett turned to Christopher & said "But a longer than that you nah do nuttn for the child, so what is the real reason?"

When he got backed in a corner, he went off on ten different tangents. The first tangent was that I borrowed a lot of money from him that I hadn't paid him back, the second was that my brother Junior took money from him & didn't pay him back, the third was that he had asked me to let our son meet his daughter & I declined, the fourth was that I was poisoning his child against him, the fifth to the tenth was pretty much the same tune, he was the victim. The fact that all the tangents had no truth to them should not come as a shock.

I think the biggest shocker was when he said he had made plans with our son for the Easter holidays & I am ruining those plans by keeping his son a way from him. DSP Bennett went on to ask how old was the child & while he sat their clearly trying to maths it out, I replied fourteen going on fifteen. It was at this point DSP Bennett said "But this is a big young man, let us call him & hear what he has to say."

A call was placed to my son. I proceeded to ask him whether he had made any plans with his father, his reply to which was no. I went on further to ask whether he wanted to do something with his father, his reply to which was also no. Once the call had ended, DSP Bennett remarked "That didn't sound like a child that wanted to go anywhere with anyone." Christopher quickly replied that my son was only saying what he thought I wanted him to say, it wasn't how he really felt. He decided to call our son from his phone to once again ask the same questions but unfortunately for him our son didn't take his call.

I was now ready to leave. In my opinion I had wasted enough of my time & nothing had been resolved. I still didn't hear anything being said about the missing maintenance money & when I could expect some assistance with our child but what he did decide to close the show with was a call to Mary.

When he said he was going to call his partner & she could confirm what he was saying, I was very confused. Like where is this going & what exactly was she going to confirm? Anyway, Mary came on the phone. She was always not one to go on speaker because as soon as she answered, she was ready to go off on him. He had to quickly stop her & say "Hold on, answer this first. What was the reason our daughter didn't meet her brother when we were in Jamaica the last time?" Mary went on to say "Well you said Stacey said she wasn't going to let him meet her because you didn't give her any money." I burst into laughter.

I didn't even give him time to think I quickly reminded him that I had no objection to my son meeting his sister BUT him Christopher was too busy hiding from me because he didn't want to cover his portion of the back to school expenses, hence the reason why the meeting didn't happen. I also pointed out that Mary's statement was not credible as she was only repeating what she was told. It doesn't mean she was told the truth & in this case she definitely wasn't told the truth.

At the end of the session DSP Bennett proceeded to warn Christopher to leave me alone, do not call or text my phone & he was reminded not to come to my house. DSP Bennett then instructed him to leave before me because according to him he didn't want us meeting up in the parking lot & anybody getting any ideas.

Once I got home, my son started questioning me about the call I had placed to him earlier & I explained to him the reason for same & he maintained that his father had not reached out & made any plans with him. I told him not to worry about it.

CHILDREN DO GROW UP

Christopher never quite understood the fact that our child matured & became more aware of all that was going on & was able to make decisions for himself. He didn't need anyone to tell him anything. Christopher on the other hand always believed that my son's reaction towards him was influenced by me, but this was far from being true. Let us examine some of the things that in my estimation led to the breakdown of the father son relationship.

At the top of the list was his attack on me which was carried out in the presence of the child. As young as our son was, this was a life changing experience for him. He had lost all trust in his father to the point where he no longer felt comfortable around him. At the tender age of nine years old, his focus had shifted from that of an innocent child to that of a child who felt that it was now his responsibility to protect his mother from his father.

The second incident that I can clearly recall that got my son very upset was when Christopher turned up at his first Manning Cup match at school with his then girlfriend Natalie. My son was very upset & I couldn't understand why. On our way home when I tried to deep dive, his question to me was "Why did he have to bring her? My friends know that he is my father because they see him picking me up from school & now he is here with another woman & he knew you would be here. Now my friends are going to know everything." I had to explain to him that Christopher & I not being together was nothing to feel ashamed about. A lot of parents do part ways when things aren't working between them. So the situation wasn't unique to him.

The third incident was when Christopher sent my son pictures of his daughter & made it known that Mary was her mother. I recall my son coming to me & saying "Of all the people that he could have had a child with, he had a child with Mary?! I have no sister, I only have one brother." Mary was the topic for many of our arguments & so in my son's mind Mary was partly to be blamed for his family no longer being together.

The fourth incident was after Christopher realised that I no longer had the Boon. He was so shocked when I drove pass him in the VW. The next day when he went to pick up our son from school he struck up a conversation with my son the purpose of which was to belittle me. He went on to say that my car couldn't compare to his & my car didn't have the computer screen that was in his. He proceeded to show my son a feature of the car then proceeded to tell him that his mother's car wasn't able to do it. When my son told me what he said to him in response to all this, I laughed until I cried. My son said "Mommy mi just tell him seh at least my mother car have the new car smell, yours don't have that." He always tried to use whatever he could to put me down to our son to make it seem like he was the "superior" or "rich" parent. Some birthdays he would ask me what I was getting our son only so he could ensure that he bought something that in his mind my son would consider to be bigger or better than my gift.

Another defining moment was when Christopher would pick up our son from school with some young girls as passengers. I remember my son complaining to me that he could hardly find space in the car to sit when he was picked up. He also told me that he didn't like how the girls spoke to Christopher & that the conversations in the car was sometimes not for children. When I said to him "What do you mean by how they speak to your father?" He replied by saying "They disrespect him & all he does is laugh like it is funny." Remember this was his father, somebody who he knew he was expected to respect. Hearing other people who didn't look much older than him disrespect his dad, & also seeing his dad's reaction to the disrespect was a trigger for him.

Some of the other things was the fact that Christopher rarely kept in touch with our son once he was in England & when he decided to make contact the conversation was mainly about me. He would question our son & ask him things like who lives at the house, whether I had a man & a host of other things. My son hated it & would complain bitterly. I remember telling my son that whenever he was asked these things, he should tell his father that he is a child & had no business in adult matters. I remember encouraging Christopher to ask about school, subjects he was doing & anything that he was struggling with as topics of discussion. I told him that he should be thinking about even doing a father son talk as our son was getting older. Christopher's response to this suggestion was to ask our son if he had kissed any girls as yet. Once again our son was not amused. It was clear that I was expecting someone who mentally wasn't older than my son to step up & act like an adult.

He also made our son a lot of unfulfilled promises. He would tell him that he would be taking phones & other gadgets for him & when he gets to Jamaica there is nothing. I can't forget the year he said he was taking a school shoes for him. As soon as he arrived in Jamaica I started asking for the shoe because I wanted to ensure that it fits. Christopher strung us out until the Saturday before the Monday that school was scheduled to reopen & then proceeded to tell us that he didn't bring the shoe & we should meet him at Payless so that he could purchase one. My son could look forward to disappointment more than he could look forward to Christopher keeping his word to him.

The icing on the cake was the fact that my son saw how difficult it was for me at times to take care of all the expenses. He saw the constant struggle, he saw when things were getting disconnected & the challenge I had getting them back on. He saw me crying many times while trying to navigate all the things that were happening in my life & as he grew older he saw the constant sacrifices that were made to ensure that he was never at a disadvantage & all his immediate needs were met.

So while Christopher was constantly concerned about what I might be telling our son about him, our son was growing & seeing that I was the only one going all out for his wellbeing. He was getting older & seeing that I was the only one that he could rely on. Christopher was so caught up in what he thought I had to say that he didn't realise that it was his action or better yet inaction that was driving our son's thoughts & perception of him.

My son is now nineteen years old going on twenty & the relationship with his father is still very strained because his father taught him at a very young age how to be without him & he has now mastered that lesson. I do encourage him to try & keep in contact but at this stage of his life I can only encourage, I can't & won't force.

Never forget that children do grow up & as they get older they will be able to decipher who was the problem, just ensure it's not you.

THE FINAL HOORAH

These days peace reigns between Christopher & I based on the fact that the only means of contact still remains at email & I do not make contact unless it is something urgent to do with our son. I have taken back my power in the situation & I refuse to lose it again.

Our son is an adult now & as such I leave him to communicate with his father how he chooses to, I don't get involved in that process.

I would like to take this opportunity to encourage somebody to never to give up no matter what your life might look like presently. Always believe that it will never remain the same, change will come. Be expectant & prepare for your change.

Single parents, I salute you all. I know it's not easy & I know at times you are feeling as though you are failing your child but continue giving of your best & doing what you need to do for them. Believe me your efforts aren't going unnoticed & they will be rewarded in the long run once you see your child/children achieving their goals, excelling in all areas & just becoming well rounded humans.

I encourage y'all to make peace your priority & to not be afraid of leaving situations where there is no peace to be found. Always remember too that it's self before others, if you don't take care of you, you can't effectively take care of anyone else.

Readily accept that people will come & go in your lives. You don't owe anyone your loyalty to remain in a situation that isn't bringing you peace, joy, peace of mind, love & happiness. Some people are stepping stones that will aid on your path & journey to where you are really supposed to be. We must remain aware so we can clearly decipher when we are still collecting stones as opposed to when we have used all our stones & built a bridge to the other side where our life partner resides.

Don't sit in situations in fear of leaving & possibly having a worse experience with someone else. I was held captive for years by this thought. The probability of you leaving & finding better or worse are the same & as such there is nothing to lose.

Know your worth & add tax & if tax isn't enough, add customs duty too. You are unique in your own special way, don't allow anyone to take you for granted & treat you less than. By knowing your worth you will attract more like minded people who not only sees your worth but also wants to add to it.

Never regret anything that has happened in your life. Always believe that everything happened exactly how it was supposed to. It was my England experiences that gave me the strength I needed to overcome when history once again repeated itself & I had little to no assistance from Christopher.

Love yourself! Love for self will save us from a lot of unfavourable situations. Our love for self will result in us always wanting to do what is best for us & not what is best for everyone else around us. A lot of the things we choose to deal with is as of a result of the false belief that we are loved by an individual when in reality we are only being used or manipulated by them. Love doesn't hurt, people who doesn't know how to love us does.

Life is easy, people make it hard. Don't be one of those people who make it hard, there are already too many in the world. Be someone who makes it easy. Be honest & open about your feelings & intentions. Admit when something is working & when it isn't, & once it isn't, start working on the exit. Don't be afraid to wave the white flag & surrender as not every loss is a loss. Sometimes it's only through losing that you are able to see how you have won. I can attest to this.

If you are giving your all & your best & it still doesn't seem to be enough, you are giving it to the wrong person. Rethink your position & the beneficiary. Never settle for less than you deserve just to be able to say that you have someone.

Accept the things you cannot change but change the things you cannot accept. Don't live according to someone's definition of you, define yourself. Know who you are & what you are about & embrace your individuality,at the end of the day you can only be you. Remove yourself from toxic & energy draining situations. Always remember that the longer we stay in situations that aren't for us, the situations that are for us continues to pass us by.

Finally, accept the things that have happened in your life so they can no longer hold you captive & make you a prisoner. Accept that they have happened, burying them & opting not to face them will give them power & control over you. Take back your power, free yourself & focus on becoming MENTALLY FIT.

Love & Light

Made in the USA
Monee, IL
21 February 2022

91562013R00184